A Bibliography of
American Doctoral Dissertations
in Classical Studies and Related Fields

by
LAWRENCE S. THOMPSON

THE SHOE STRING PRESS, INC.
1968

Library of Congress Catalog Card Number: 67-24191
Printed in the United States of America

185812

To Mae, who knows when to stop work

CONTENTS

PREFACE

This bibliography of American doctoral dissertations in the broad area of classical studies and related fields was planned to include titles from the beginning of graduate study in North America to the present time. Actually, due to the tardiness of bibliographies, there are a number of omissions of 1964 titles, and only a few 1965 titles are included. It is the hope of the compiler that at some future time a supplement to this bibliography may be issued, not simply to bring the bibliography up to date, but also to include unavoidable omissions.

There are numerous causes of omissions. For one thing, neither lists in American Doctoral Dissertations nor even institutional lists and abstracts are complete. Further, titles are often deceptive, and the classifications are frequently capricious or are not provided with adequate indices. Thus a work on Roman law was accidentally located with dissertations listed under a political science department, and a study dealing with Ptolemaic Egypt was found under Egyptology. Finally, lists for the older periods are incomplete in many instances, and often they include titles which cannot be found in the institutional libraries. For the period before 1912, when the Library of Congress' List of American Doctoral Dissertations Printed in . . . starts, institutional librarians have been exceptionally helpful. However, this compiler has discovered from sample checks that this list is only about ninety-five to ninety-eight per cent complete within the scope of his definitions for inclusion.

All aspects of the culture of Greece and Rome, from the prehistory of Greece and Italy through the arbitrary terminal date of 500 A.D., are included in the present bibliography: literature, history, art, architecture, archaeology, folklore, religion, law, linguistics, science, philosophy, politics and government, manners and customs, social and economic conditions, indeed, cultural history in general. Two aspects of the policy of inclusion have been difficult to resolve, and some errors of judgement may have been made. The first aspect deals with New Testament and Christian literature. In general, New Testament dissertations have been included only when the subject matter would seem to be useful for linguistic, semantic, or textual studies, or when it seems pertinent to Greek and Roman cultural history.

On the other hand, nearly all Christian literature, Greek and Latin, even when it covers technical subjects, has been included. In both instances (New Testament and Christian literature) dissertations which are strictly exegetical and theological have been excluded, on the assumption that a bibliography on the history of religion similar to the present work will include them. The other aspect of the policy of inclusion which may cause some misunderstanding is the terminal date. In this case the compiler has undoubtedly been arbitrary in many instances, but he will atone for this arbitrariness by going to work at once on a companion bibliography of American doctoral dissertations in mediaeval studies. It is likely that a number of commentaries on ancient authors and studies of their Fortleben and manuscript traditions will turn up in this projected bibliography.

The most important feature of this bibliography is the index. Some colleagues who have glanced at the index in manuscript have suggested that the work is over-indexed, but more than three decades' service as a bibliographer have taught the compiler that no bibliography can be over-indexed. An effort has been made to omit any misleading entries. Some works are inadequately indexed simply because the title is insufficiently descriptive and no abstract or printed version of the dissertation is available. On the other hand, many titles are indexed under entries which might seem to be inapplicable from a mere inspection of the title, but which were generally gleaned from Library of Congress printed cards or, in some instances, from inspection of the original or an abstract. In general, the index includes an average of nearly four subject entries per title and covers all titles. In the latter case, however, some titles which begin with meaningless words (meaningless for the purpose of location) such as "On the . . ." or "Studies in . . ." have been inverted so that the title will begin with the first significant word. In a few instances joint authors of subsequent printed publications have been indexed, although this was not done for the numerous nineteenth-century Johns Hopkins dissertations which were summarized in review-articles in the American Journal of Philology by Gildersleeve. In most cases, the names of ancient authors and titles of their works have been made to conform to the policy of the Oxford Classical Dictionary in its section on abbreviations.

The identification of printed versions and abstracts is far from complete, but there seems to be no practical way to verify this information short of checking the card catalogues of all institutional libraries. In general, this information has been secured from the Library of Congress catalogue and from the

printed files of abstracts available in nearly all research libraries. It should be noted that the full entries of institutional ab-
stracting series have not been given and that it may be assumed
that the publisher of the abstract is the institution. Further,
dates are not given for entries from <u>Dissertation Abstracts</u>.
References to abstracts are not given if the dissertation has
been printed in whole or in part. Finally, it must be pointed out
that dates of original acceptance of dissertations for the degree
are based on guesswork in some cases, particularly in the lists
going back to the turn of the century and published in the early
1900s in the <u>Classical Journal</u>. However, neither are many of
the current bibliographies (even institutional ones) completely
accurate, or, rather, completely unambiguous on this point. If a
date is off by a year or two, the bibliographical source may generally be blamed. In a few instances it has been found that the
title of the printed version was the only one given in the source
but that the title of the original version was different. Some of
these discrepancies may not have been caught in time to make a
change.

The arrangement of the main author list is invariably under
the name of the individual who presented the dissertation, although libraries will generally put the main entry of editions of
ancient authors under the name of that author. In such cases,
the ancient author also appears in the index. Ladies who presented dissertations under their maiden names are generally
entered under maiden names, unless they seem to have been bet-
ter known under their married names.

A strong effort has been made to copy titles exactly as the
source gives them. If the source gives Greek words in transliteration, they have not been transliterated back into Greek. An
exception is the index of Greek words at the end of the index. If
the source transliterates a kappa as C, it remains in this form
both in the main author list and in the title index. Thus the user
of this bibliography will find such discrepancies as Attika and
Attica, Kleisthenes and Cleisthenes, but only for the reason given
above.

The standard library style for recording titles, viz., no capi-
tals and no italicization, has been followed, although a few words
have been capitalized which most libraries would leave in the
lower case. On the other hand, this compiler cites the volumes
of serials by Roman numerals, possibly out of habit, but also
from the conviction that this practice will avoid ambiguity.

The indices of Greek and Latin words at the end are primarily for linguistic, lexicographical, syntactical, and semantic

studies. Some Greek and Latin words in the titles of the dissertations have not been included due to the fact that they do not
seem to be useful in these lists. When dissertations begin with
Greek words in the title index, some arbitrary judgement has
been followed in alphabetizing them. Thus omega goes at the
end of the alphabet rather than before p. A linguistic purist can
criticise the compiler on this point, since, if he searches, he
can find a Scandinavian aa ahead of ab, not after z in this same
bibliography.

Due to the continuing effort — even after the manuscript was
typed — to include every possible title, there have been "a" num-
bers, but it does not appear that this policy is likely to cause
any confusion.

Having reviewed or annotated hundreds of bibliographical
works in many fields during the last three decades, the compiler
knows that nothing is easier than to tear a bibliography to pieces
on the basis of details. The compiler only hopes that this work
will not fall into the hands of a reviewer whose own dissertation
was omitted, and that if such be the fate of this work, the reviewer will patiently bear in mind the impossibility of establishing
and following consistently any immutable policies in the field of
bibliography. Finally, the compiler has observed a tradition
ascribed to the polite Chinese, that the scholar should leave certain errors in the text to permit the reader to feel superior to
the author. Several errors in alphabetizing occur in the author
index, but references have been provided. Deus sit propitius
huic bibliographico!

L. S. T.

Lexington, Kentucky

AUTHOR LIST

A

Abbe, Elizabeth Frances. Entrances in Greek tragedy. Yale, 1903. A1

Abbott, Frank Frost. Colloquial Latin in the letters to Cicero, Yale, 1891. A2

Abbott, Kenneth Morgan. Prolegomena to an edition of the pseudo-Servian commentary on Terence. Illinois, 1934. A3

Abel, David Herbert. The personification of the virtues and vices in early Greek poetry, with special reference to the family-tree. Northwestern, 1941. Abstract: Summaries of doctoral dissertations, IX (1941), 5-9. A4

Adamczyk, Stanley Joseph. Political propaganda in Cicero's essays, 47-44 B.C. Fordham, 1961. Abstract: Dissertation abstracts, XXII, 863. A5

Adamec, Charles Joseph. Character presentation in Tacitus. Yale, 1921. A6

Adams, Louise Elizabeth Whetenhall. A study in the commerce of Latium from the early iron age through the sixth century, B.C. Bryn Mawr, 1920. Printed: Smith College classical studies, XI (1921). 84 p. A7

Adams, Miriam Annunciata, Sister. The Latinity of the letters of Saint Ambrose. Catholic, 1927. Printed: The Catholic University of America, Patristic studies, XII (1927). 140 p. A8

Adelson, Howard Laurence. Roman monetary policy from Diocletian to Heraclius. Princeton, 1952. Abstract: Dissertation abstracts, XIII, 376. A9

Africa, Thomas Wilson. Phylarchus of Athens: a study in tragic history. California, Los Angeles, 1959. A10

Agnew, Malcolm E. Sessions of the Roman senate, 218-201 B.C. Yale, 1936. A11

Akielaszek, Stanislaus A. A preliminary text of the Servian commentary on the Eclogues of Virgil. Fordham, 1951. A12

Albright, Frank P. Funeral customs of the Greeks. Johns Hopkins, 1940. A13

Albritton, Rogers Garland. A study of Plato's Philebus. Princeton, 1957. Abstract: Dissertation abstracts, XVII, 643. A14

Aldrich, Keith Morgan. The Andromache of Euripides. California, Berkeley, 1957. Printed: Nebraska University, Studies, new ser., XXV (1961). 98 p. A15

Aldrich, Maelynette. Repetitions of words in Plautus. Yale, 1916. A16

Alexander, John A. Potidaea. Johns Hopkins, 1939. A17

Alexander, Leigh. The kings of Lydia and a rearrangement of some fragments from Nicolaus of Damascus. Princeton, 1911. Printed: Princeton, Princeton University press, 1914. 61 p. A18

Alexander, William Hardy. Adversaria critica in Suetonii de vita Caesarum librum octavum. California, 1906. Printed: Some textual criticisms on the eighth book of the De vita Caesarum of Suetonius. California University, Publications in classical philology, II, no. 1 (1908). 33 p. A19

Alexander, William John. Participial periphrases in Attic prose. Johns Hopkins, 1883. Printed: American journal of philology, IV (1882), 291–308. A20

Allen, Archibald William. Personal and conventional experience in Propertius. Stanford, 1940. Abstract: Abstracts of dissertations for the degree of doctor of philosophy, XVI (1940/41), 79–81. A21

Allen, Bernard Mary, Sister. Palatinus Latinus 1620: A critical evaluation of its position in the textual tradition of Terence. St. Louis, 1963. Abstract: Dissertation abstracts, XXV, 458. A22

Allen, Carlos Eben. Latin word-order as seen in Caesar's Gallic War. Chicago, 1924. Abstract: Abstracts of theses, Humanistic ser., II (1926), 303–8. A23

Allen, G. H. Centurions as substitute commanders. Michigan, 1905 (?). Printed: University of Michigan studies, Humanistic ser., I (1906), 333–82. A24

Allen, Hamilton Ford. The use of the infinitive in Polybius compared with the use of the infinitive in Biblical Greek. Chicago, 1905. A25

Allen, James Turney. A study of the optative mode in conditional and conditional-relative clauses in Greek. Yale, 1898. Printed: On the so-called iterative optative in Greek. American philological association, Transactions, XXXIII (1902), 101–26. A26

Allen, Katherine. The treatment of nature in the poetry of the
Roman republic (exclusive of comedy). Wisconsin, 1898.
Printed: Wisconsin University, Bulletin, no. 28, Language
and literature ser., I, no. 2 (1899), 89–219. A27

Allen, May Alice. The technical vocabulary of the rhythmic of
Aristoxenos. Yale, 1908. A28

Allen, Reginald Edgar. The status of soul in Plato's philosophy.
Yale, 1958. A29

Allen, Ruth E. The mutilation of the herms: a study in Athenian
politics. Cincinnati, 1951. A30

Allen, Walter, jr. The Yale manuscript of Tacitus (Codex
Budensis Rhenani). Yale, 1936. A31

Allen, William Sims. A study in Latin prognosis. Columbia, 1923.
Printed: Columbia University, Teachers college, Contributions to education, CXXXV (1923). 40 p. A32

Allinson, Francis Greenleaf. On Ionic forms in the second century, A.D., and the obligations of Lucian to Herodotus. Johns
Hopkins, 1880. Printed: Pseudo-Ionism in the second century A.D. American journal of philology, VII (1886), 203–17.
A33

Alston, J. Winifred. The Heraklids. Bryn Mawr, 1941. A34

Aly, Abdellatif Ahmed. The Roman veterans in Egypt. Michigan,
1949. Abstract: Microfilm abstracts, IX, 97–8. A35

Ambrose, John William, jr. Irony in Book IV of Horace's Odes.
Brown, 1962. A36

Ambrose, Zuell Philip. The Homeric and early epic telos.
Princeton, 1963. Abstract: Dissertation abstracts, XXIV,
2022. A37

Ament, Ernest Joseph. The Vatican manuscripts of the Greek
letters of Brutus. St. Louis, 1958. Abstract: Dissertation
abstracts, XIX, 2942. A38

Amory, Anne Reinberg. Dreams and omens in the Odyssey.
Radcliffe, 1957. A39

Amyx, Carrell A. A study of Eretrian black-figure vases. California, 1937. A40

Anderson, Andrew Runni. De Plauti diphthongi ei usu quaestiones.
Harvard, 1903. Printed: American philological association,
Transactions, XXXVIII (1906), 13–86. A41

Anderson, Doris N. The contribution of the mixed manuscripts
to the Tacitus tradition. Yale, 1943. A42

Anderson, Edward P. The eclogues of Virgil and what they owe
to Theocritus. Michigan, 1886. A43

Anderson, James Nesbitt. On the sources of Ovid's Heroides I,
    II, VII, X, XII. Johns Hopkins, 1894.   A44
Anderson, Richard Lloyd. The rise and fall of middle-class
    loyalty to the Roman Empire: a social study of Velleius
    Paterculus and Ammianus Marcellinus. California, Berke-
    ley, 1963.   A45
Anderson, Sara. The Mycenaean pictorial style of vase painting
    in the thirteenth century. Bryn Mawr, 1943.   A46
Anderson, Warren D. Paideia and ethos in Hellenic music, with
    special reference to literary evidence regarding the modes.
    Harvard, 1954.   A47
Anderson, William S. The rhetoric of Juvenal. Yale, 1954.
    A48
Andry, E. Robert. Paul's use of πνευματικός and ψυχικός.
    Southern Baptist, 1942.   A49
Angus, Samuel. The sources of the first ten books of St. Augus-
    tine's De civitate Dei. Princeton, 1906. Printed: Princeton,
    Princeton University press, 1906. 278 p.   A50
Apfel, Henrietta Veit. Literary quotation and allusion in Deme-
    trius Περὶ ἑρμηνείας (De elocutione) and Longinus Περὶ ὕψους
    (De sublimitate). Columbia, 1936. Printed: New York, 1935.
    123 p.   A51
Apostle, Hippocrates George. Aristotle's philosophy of mathe-
    matics. Harvard, 1943.   A52
Applegate, Robert Ashworth, jr. The Alcibiades of Aeschines of
    Sphettus. Princeton, 1949. Abstract: Dissertation abstracts,
    XV, 405.   A53
Aratowsky, Bernard. Ancient Salamis. Johns Hopkins, 1947.
    A54
Arbuthnot, Mabel Florence. The cyclic theory of the Greeks.
    Wisconsin, 1937. Abstract: Summaries of doctoral disser-
    tations, II (1937), 281-3.   A55
Archibald, Herbert Thompson. The fable as a stylistic test in
    classical Greek literature. Johns Hopkins, 1901. Printed:
    Baltimore, J. H. Furst co., 1912. 79 p.   A56
Arkin, Irvin Meinrad. Roman magism at the end of the Republic:
    a re-evaluation in light of the degeneration theory of Wilhelm
    Schmidt. St. Louis, 1964.   A57
Armleder, Paul John. Quotation in Cicero's letters. Cincinnati,
    1957. Abstract: Dissertation abstracts, XVII, 2262.   A58
Armstrong, Charles Johnstone. De epithetis compositis apud
    epicos latinos. Harvard, 1936. Abstract: Summaries of
    theses, 1936, 3-5.   A59
Armstrong, Henry Herbert. The autobiographical element in

Latin inscriptions. Michigan, 1905. Printed: Michigan University, Studies, Humanistic ser., III, pt. 4 (1910), 215–86.
A60

Armstrong, James Franklin. A study of alternative readings in the Hebrew text of the book of Isaiah, and their relation to the old Greek and the Greek recensions. Princeton, 1958. Abstract: Dissertation abstracts, XIX, 2082. A61

Armstrong, James Isbell. The trierarchy and the tribal organization of the Athenian navy. Princeton, 1949. Abstract: Dissertation abstracts, XV, 397. A62

Armstrong, Mary Emma. The significance of certain colors in Roman ritual. Johns Hopkins, 1915. Printed: Menasha, Wis., George Banta publ. co., 1917. 52 p. A63

Arndt, William Frederick. The participle in Polybius and in Saint Paul. Washington, St. Louis, 1935. A64

Arrowsmith, William Ayres. The conversion of Herakles; an essay in Euripidean tragic structure. Princeton, 1955. A65

Ashley, John B. The divinity of Julius Caesar in the writings of Cicero. Fordham, 1960. A66

Ashmead, Ann Harnwell. A study of the style of the cup painter Onesimos. Bryn Mawr, 1959. A67

Askowith, Dora. The toleration and persecution of the Jews in Roman Empire. Columbia, 1915. Printed: New York, 1915. 283 p. A67a

Astour, Michael Czernichow. Helleno-semitica: an ethnic and cultural study in west Semitic impact on Mycenaean Greece. Brandeis, 1962. A68

Atkinson, Alice Minerva. Chronology of Horace's satires and epistles. Pennsylvania, 1895. A69

Atwater, Elizabeth A. A history of classical scholarship in America. Pittsburgh, 1939. A70

Austin, Lucy Estelle. A study of the characters in Cicero's dialogues emphasizing the principles of character selection. North Carolina, 1932. Abstract: Research in progress, 1931–32, p. 18–9. A71

Austin, William M. The prothetic vowel in Greek. Princeton, 1938. Printed: Language, XVII (1941), 83–92. A72

Avery, Harry Costas. Prosopographical studies in the oligarchy of the Four Hundred. Princeton, 1960. A73

Avery, Mary Myrtle. The use of direct speech in Ovid's Metamorphoses. Chicago, 1936. Printed: Chicago, Private edition, distributed by the University of Chicago Libraries, 1937. 99 p. A74

Avery, Maurice Wescott. De numeris lyricis Graecis qui in
carminibus quibusdam nuper repertis audiuntur. Harvard,
1928. Abstract: Summaries of theses, 1928, p. 3-5.   A75
Avery, William T. Julia, daughter of Augustus: a biography.
Western Reserve, 1937.   A76
Axtell, Harold Lucius. The deification of abstract ideas in Roman
literature and inscriptions. Chicago, 1907. Printed: Chicago,
University of Chicago press, 1907. 100 p.   A77
Ayers, Donald Murray. The speeches of Cicero's opponents:
studies in Pro Roscio Amerino, In Verrem, and Pro Murena.
Princeton, 1950. Abstract: Dissertation abstracts, XV, 406.
A78

B

Baade, Eric Crull. Jurisdictions in Roman Egypt. Yale, 1956.
B1
Babbitt, Frank Cole. De Euripidis Antiopa. Harvard, 1895.   B2
Babcock, Alfred R. The position of the copula and of the colorless
ancillary verbs in Greek. Harvard, 1953.   B3
Babcock, Charles L. Erasure of the Antonii names and the dating
of the Capitoline fasti. California, Berkeley, 1954.   B4
Babcock, Clinton Leroy. A study in case rivalry; being an investi-
gation regarding the use of the genitive and accusative in
Latin with verbs of remembering and forgetting. Cornell,
1901 (?). Printed: Cornell studies in classical philology, XIV
(1901). 74 p.   B5
Bacon, Helen H. Barbarians in Greek tragedy. Bryn Mawr, 1955.
Printed: New Haven, Yale University press, 1961. 201 p.
B6
Baden, William Wilson. The principal figures of language and
figures of thought in Isaeus and the guardianship-speeches of
Demosthenes. Johns Hopkins, 1892. Printed: Baltimore,
The Friedenwald co., 1906. 37 p.   B7
Bagan, Philip Vincent. The syntax of the letters of Pope Gelasius I.
Catholic, 1945. Printed: Catholic University of America,
Studies in medieval and renaissance Latin language and litera-
ture, XVIII (1945). 231 p.   B8
Bagby, Alfred. Adverbs in Horace and Juvenal. Johns Hopkins,
1891.   B9
Bailey, John William. Does Hellenism contribute constituent ele-
ments to Paul's Christology? Chicago, 1904. Printed:
Chicago, Press of G. K. Hazlitt & co., 1905. 90 p.   B10
Baker, Charles Aloysius, jr. Montesquieu and Rome: his observa-

tions on the Roman state, 753 B.C. – 476 A.D. Illinois, 1963.
Abstract: Dissertation abstracts, XXIV, 3704.　B11

Baker, Doland Gay. The animals on the coins of the Greek cities.
Harvard, 1932. Abstract: Summaries of theses, 1932, p. 3–4.
B12

Baker, Lawrence Henry. The rhythmical accent of the antibacchiac,
bacchiac, mollossic, paeonic, and spondaic words in Aristóph-
anes, a contribution to the study of the rhythm of prose. Johns
Hopkins, 1920.　B13

Baker, William Wilson. De comicis Graecis litterarum iudicibus.
Harvard, 1901. Printed: Harvard studies in classical philology,
XV (1904), 121–240.　B14

Balcer, Jack Martin. From confederate freedom to imperial tyr-
anny: a study of the restrictions imposed by Athens on the
political self-determination of the member states in the Delian
Confederacy, 473–431 B.C. Michigan, 1964.　B15

Baldwin, Faith P. Gaius Asinius Pollio. Bryn Mawr, 1934.　B16

Baldwin, Florence Theodora. The Bellum civile of Petronius.
Columbia, 1910.　B17

Ball, Allan Perley. The satire of Seneca on the apotheosis of
Seneca. Columbia, 1902.　B18

Ball, Francis Kingsley. De frenis apud antiquos. Harvard, 1894.
Abstract: Classical review, VIII (1898), 197–8.　B19

Ball, Mary Tarcisia, Sister. Nature and the vocabulary of nature
in the works of St. Cyprian. Catholic, 1945. Printed: Catholic
University of America, Patristic studies, LXXV (1946). 303 p.
B20

Ballentine, Floyd George. De nympharum cultu quaestiones
selectae. Harvard, 1903. Printed: Harvard studies in classical philology, XV (1904), 77–119.　B21

Band, Arnold Joseph. Aristophanes: the comedy of issues. Harvard, 1959.　B22

Bandy, Anastasius Constantine. Early Christian inscriptions of
Crete. Pennsylvania, 1961. Abstract: Dissertation abstracts,
XXII, 251.　B23

Baney, Margaret Mary, Sister. Some reflections of life in North
Africa in the works of Tertullian. Catholic, 1948. Printed:
Catholic University of America, Patristic studies, LXXX
(1948), 164 p.　B24

Barbour, Amy Louise. Tryphidorus: His relation to other epics
in form and vocabulary. Yale, 1902.　B25

Barkan, Irving. Capital punishment in ancient Athens. Chicago,
1935. Printed: Chicago, Private edition, distributed by the
University of Chicago Libraries, 1936, p. 41–82.　B26

Barker, Albert Winslow. A classification of the chitons worn by
    Greek women as shown in works of art. Pennsylvania, 1921.
    Printed: Media, Pa., Delaware County institute of science,
    IX, no. 3 (1923). 48 p.   B27
Barker, Glenn Wesley. A critical evaluation of the lexical and
    linguistic data advanced by E. J. Goodspeed and supported
    by C. L. Mitton in a proposed solution to the problem of the
    authorship and date of Ephesians. Harvard, 1962.   B28
Barlow, Jane F. Metrical word-types in the Latin hexameter.
    Johns Hopkins, 1952.   B29
Barnes, Hazel Estella. Katharsis in the Enneades of Plotinus.
    Yale, 1941. Printed: American philological association,
    Transactions, LXXIII (1942), 358–82.   B30
Barnett, Robert John, jr. An anonymous medieval commentary
    on Juvenal. North Carolina, 1964.   B31
Barry, Mary Eileen. The Ecclesiazusae as a political satire.
    Chicago, 1942. Printed: Chicago, 1942. 79 p.   B32
Barry, Mary Finbarr, Sister. The vocabulary of the moral-
    ascetical works of Saint Ambrose; a study in Latin lexicog-
    raphy. Catholic, 1926. Printed: Catholic University of
    America, Patristic studies, X (1926). 287 p.   B33
Bartley, William Tenney. The story of Agamemnon. Yale, 1895.
    B34
Bartling, Walter James. Megalopsychia: an interpretation of
    Aristotle's ethical ideal. Northwestern, 1963. Abstract:
    Dissertation abstracts, XXIV, 3735.   B35
Bartol, Mary. Traces of epic influence in the tragedies of
    Sophocles. Pennsylvania, 1899.   B36
Basiline, Mary, Sister (secular name: Josephine A. Bates).
    The aesthetic motif from Thales to Plato. Colorado, 1921.
    Printed: New York, Schwartz, Kirwin & Fauss, 1921. 99 p.
    B37
Basore, John William. The scholia on hypokrisis in the com-
    mentary of Donatus. Johns Hopkins, 1899. Printed: Balti-
    more, J. H. Furst co., 1908. 85 p.   B38
Bassett, Edward Lewis. De metaphonia Latina. Harvard, 1942.
    Abstract: Summaries of theses, 1942, 3–6.   B39
Bassett, Henry Jewell. Macrinus and Diadumenianus. Michigan,
    1920. Printed: Menasha, Wis., George Banta publ. co.,
    1920. 94 p.   B40
Bassett, Samuel Eliot. The bucolic diaeresis in Homer. Yale,
    1905. Printed: American philological association, Trans-
    actions, XXXVI (1905), 111–24.   B41
Bassett, Thomas J. The causes of Roman national and literary

decline. Syracuse, 1888. (cf. also dissertation by E. H.
Lewis, Syracuse, 1892, with same title.)   B42

Bateman, John Jay. A study of the arguments in the speeches
of Lysias. Cornell, 1958. Abstracts: Dissertation abstracts, XIX, 2942.   B43

Bates, Fred Orlando. The five post-Kleisthenean tribes.
Cornell, 1898. Printed: Ithaca, N. Y., Press of Andrus and
Church, 1898. 71 p.   B44

Bates, Josephine A., see Basiline, Mary, Sister.

Bates, William Nickerson. Quaestiones Lycophroneae. Harvard,
1893. Abstract: Harvard studies in classical philology, VI
(1895), 75-82.   B45

Battle, William James. De exsecrationibus laminis plumbeis
insculptis. Harvard, 1893. Abstract: American philological
association, Proceedings of special session, December 1894,
p. liv-lviii.   B46

Beadle, John. Auxiliary verbs in Latin. Yale, 1894.   B47

Beamer, Maude. Greek art in Ovid's poems. Missouri, 1936.
Printed: Columbia, Mo., 1936. 42 p.   B48

Beardslee, John Walter. The use of φύσις in fifth-century Greek
literature. Chicago, 1913. Printed: Chicago, University of
Chicago press, 1918. 126 p.   B49

Beardsley, Grace Hadley. The Ethiopian in Greek and Roman
civilization. Johns Hopkins, 1922. Printed: Baltimore, The
Johns Hopkins press, 1929. 41 p.   B50

Beaty, Mary Davis. Foreshadowing and suspense in Punicá of
Silius Italicus. North Carolina, 1960. Abstract: Dissertation abstracts, XXI, 1943.   B51

Beaver, Robert P. Roman society in North Africa in the age of
St. Augustine: a study based on the letters of the bishop of
Hippo. Cornell, 1933.   B51a

Bechtel, Edward Ambrose. Sanctae Silviae peregrinatio; the
text and a study of the Latinity. Chicago, 1900. Printed:
Chicago, University of Chicago press, 1902. 160 p.   B52

Beckmann, William Carl. The political use of moral terms in
Herodotus. Wisconsin, 1952. Abstract: Summaries of doctoral dissertations, XIV (1954), 420-1.   B53

Beckwith, Isbon Thaddeus. The Greek sophists. Yale, 1872.
B54

Bedrick, Theodore. The prose adaptations of Avianus. Illinois,
1940. Abstract: Urbana, 1940. 4 p.   B55

Beede, Grace Lucile. Vergil and Aratus: a study in the art of
translation. Chicago, 1936. Printed: Chicago, Private edition, distributed by the University of Chicago Libraries, 1936.
90 p.   B56

Beeler, Madison S. The phonology of Venetic. Harvard, 1936.
B57

Beers, Ethel Ella. Euripides and later Greek thought. Chicago,
1912. Printed: Menasha, Wis., George Banta publ. co.,
1914. 113 p.   B58

Beggs, Gertrude Harper. The adnominal genitive in Lysias.
Yale, 1904.   B59

Behr, Charles Allison. Old comedy and the free state. Harvard,
1960.   B60

Bell, Mary Rebecca. Roman society from Commodus to Alexander Severus. Chicago, 1937. Printed: Chicago, Private
edition, distributed by the University of Chicago Libraries,
1937. 35, 186–7 p.   B61

Bellinger, Alfred Raymond. The dramatic technique of Lucian's
Dialogues. Yale, 1925. Printed: Lucian's dramatic technique.
New Haven, 1928. 40 p.   B62

Belmont, David Eugene. Early Greek guest-friendship and its
role in Homer's Odyssey. Princeton, 1962.   B63

Benardete, Seth. Achilles and Hector: the Homeric hero. Chicago, 1956.   B64

Benario, Herbert W. The sources of Pseudo-Asconius. Johns
Hopkins, 1951.   B65

Bender, F. Boniface, brother. Historical commentary on Cassius
Dio 54. Pennsylvania, 1961. Abstract: Dissertation abstracts, XXII, 1165.   B66

Benedict, Coleman Hamilton. A history of Narbo. Princeton, 1939.
Printed: Princeton, 1941. 93 p.   B67

Benjamin, Anna Shaw. An historical commentary on the second
book of Macrobius' Saturnalia. Pennsylvania, 1955. Abstract:
Dissertation abstracts, XV, 818.   B68

Bennett, Charles Edwin. The use of connecting negatives with
subjunctives, optatives, and imperatives in Latin. Cornell,
1911.   B69

Bennett, Emmett Leslie, jr. The Minoan linear script from Pylos.
Cincinnati, 1947.   B70

Bennett, Harold. Cinna and his times; a critical and interpreta-
tive study of Roman history during the period 87–84 B.C.
Chicago, 1921. Printed: Menasha, Wis., George Banta publ.
co., 1923. 72 p.   B71

Bennett, Howard C., jr. The chronology of Pindar's Persian war
and Sicilian odes. Harvard, 1954.   B72

Bentas, Christos John. An annotated translation of Plutarch's On
music. Tufts, 1964.   B73

Berelson, Louis Julius. Old age in ancient Rome. Virginia, 1934. Abstract: Abstracts of dissertations, 1934, p. 28.   B74

Berg, George Olaf. Metaphor and comparison in the dialogues of Plato. Johns Hopkins, 1903. Printed: Berlin, Mayer and Müller, 1904. 59 p.   B75

Berkowitz, Lucile B. Index Arnobiana. Ohio State, 1965.   B75a

Berlincourt, Marjorie A.: Entered after Bernlohr.

Berman, Albert Anatole. The transmigration of form: recurrent patterns of imagination in Odyssey and the Aeneid. Harvard, 1960.   B76

Bernlohr, Fred Adam. A study of the sixty less common verbs of "saying" in Plautus. Ohio State, 1940.   B77

Berlincourt, Marjorie A. The commentary on Valerius Maximus by Dionysius de Burgo Sancti Sepulchri. Yale, 1954.   B78

Berry, Edmund Grindlay. The history and development of the concept of Θεία Μοίρα and Θεία Τύχη down to and including Plato. Chicago, 1940. Printed: Chicago, Private edition, distributed by the University of Chicago Libraries, 1940. 80 p.   B79

Berry, Kenneth Kelita. The problem of logical unity, as reflected in the logic of Aristotle. Virginia, 1939. Abstract: Abstracts of dissertations, 1939, p. 49–53.   B80

Berry, Marvin Bryan. Virgil's use of synonyms. North Carolina, 1960. Abstract: Dissertation abstracts, XXI, 1943.   B81

Berry, William Eugene. Studies in Greek word-order based upon the Laws of Plato. Chicago, 1923. Abstract: Abstract of theses, Humanistic ser., I (1925), 275–82.   B82

Bertermann, Eugene Rudolf. The theology of Euripides. Washington, St. Louis, 1940.   B83

Bertling, Hugh Martin. The political theory of St. Augustine. Loyola, 1941.   B84

Bevier, Louis. On the genuineness of the first Antiphontean oration. Johns Hopkins, 1881. Abstract: Johns Hopkins University circular, X (1881).   B85

Beyenka, Mary Melchior, Sister. Consolation in Saint Augustine. Catholic, 1950. Printed: Catholic University of America, Patristic studies, LXXXIII (1950). 119 p.   B86

Bickford, John Dean. Soliloquy in ancient comedy. Princeton, The author, 1922. 65 p.   B87

Bill, Clarence Powers. De graecorum theoris et theoriis. Harvard, 1898. Abstract: Notes on the Greek Θεωρός and Θεωρία. American philological association, Transactions, XXXII (1901), 196–204.   B88

Billheimer, Albert. Naturalization in Athenian law and practice.
    Princeton, 1917. Printed: Gettysburg, Pa., Gettysburg
    compiler print, 1922. 128 p.   B89
Billings, Grace Elvina Hadley. The art of transition in Plato.
    Chicago, 1915. Printed: Chicago, Private edition, distrib-
    uted by the University of Chicago Libraries, 1920. 103 p.
    B90
Billings, Thomas Henry. The platonism of Philo Judaeus. Chi-
    cago, University of Chicago press, 1919. 105 p.   B91
Birch, Cordelia Margaret. Traditions of the life of Aesop.
    Washington, St. Louis, 1956. Abstract: Dissertation ab-
    stracts, XVI, 748.   B92
Bisbee, Eleanor. Instrumentalism in Plato's philosophy; a
    functional theory of ideas and of God. Cincinnati, 1929. B93
Bisbee, Harold Leslie. De Tyrrhenis et de Minyis Pisam
    Triphliamque invadentibus. Harvard, 1935. Abstract:
    Summaries of theses, 1935, p. 3-4.   B94
Bishop, J. R. Prolepsis in the Attic orators. Cincinnati, 1903.
    B95
Bishop, John David. The choral odes of Seneca: theme and
    development. Pennsylvania, 1964.   B96
Blackburn, Imri L. Cyrene and the Cyrenaica in the Roman pe-
    riod. Indiana, 1933.   B96a
Blackman, Edward B. The religious views of the early Attic
    orators. Harvard, 1947.   B97
Blackwelder, Boyce W. The casual use of prepositions in the
    Greek New Testament. Northern Baptist, 1953.   B98
Blair, George Alfred. Ἐντελέχεια and Ἐνέργεια in Aristotle.
    Fordham, 1964.   B99
Blake, Robert P. Studies in the religious policy of Constantine
    and his successors. Harvard, 1916.   B99a
Bland, Laura Elizabeth. Aulularia; sive, Querolus; a translation
    with introduction and notes. North Carolina, 1950. Ab-
    stract: Research in progress, 1950, p. 35.   B100
Blanké, Wilton Wallace. The dramatic values in Plautus. Penn-
    sylvania, 1916. Printed: Geneva, N.Y., Press of W. F.
    Humphrey, 1918. 69 p.   B101
Blegen, Carl William. Studies in the history of ancient Corinth.
    Yale, 1920. Printed: Korakou; a prehistoric settlement
    near Corinth. Boston and New York, American school of
    classical studies at Athens, 1921. 139 p.   B102
Blincoe, Mary Nerinckx, Sister. The use of the exemplum in
    Cicero's philosophical works. St. Louis, 1941.   B103

Bliss, Francis R. Valerius Maximus and his sources, a stylistic
approach to the problem. North Carolina, 1952. B104

Blote, Harold Carl. The concepts of nature and matter in early
Greek philosophy. Chicago, 1927. Abstract: Abstracts of
theses, Humanistic ser., V (1928), 5-9. B105

Boak, Arthur Edward Romilly. The Roman magistri: a study in
constitutional history. Harvard, 1914. B105a

Bock, Carolyn Elizabeth. Adequacy of the Latin work lists of the
college entrance examination board as a means for teaching
words of Latin derivation occurring in the general vocabulary of the English language. Michigan, 1948. Abstract:
Microfilm abstracts, VIII, 87-9. B106

Bodle, Alice Johnson. Legal terminology in New Testament
Greek. Ohio State, 1958. Abstract: Dissertation abstracts,
XIX, 801. B107

Bodnar, Edward William. Cyriacus of Ancona and Athens.
Princeton, 1958. Abstract: Dissertation abstracts, XIX,
2341. B108

Boecklin, Rolando. The Syrian Decapolis and the Hauran under
Roman administration to Diocletian. Yale, 1935. B109

Boegehold, Alan Lindley. Aristotle and the Dikasteria. Harvard,
1958. B110

Bogan, Mary Inez, Sister. The vocabulary and style of the so-
liloquies and dialogues of St. Augustine. Catholic, 1935.
Printed: Catholic University of America, Patristic studies,
XLII (1935). 224 p. B111

Bolling, George Melville. The participle in Hesiod. Johns
Hopkins, 1896. Printed: Catholic University of America,
Bulletin, III (1897), 421-71. B112

Bondurant, Bernard Camillus. Decimus Brutus. Printed:
Decimus Junius Brutus Albinus; an historical study. Chicago, University of Chicago press, 1907. 113 p. B113

Bone, Robert Gehlmann. Roman persecution of the non-Chris-
tian religions before 200 A.D. Illinois, 1937. Abstract:
Urbana, 1937. 10 p. B114

Bongiorno, Andrew. Castelvetro's commentary on Aristotle's
Poetics 1447^{a}8-1459^{b}31; an annotated translation. Cornell,
1935. Abstract: Ithaca, N.Y., 1935. 4 p. B115

Bonner, Campbell. De Danaidibus commentatio. Harvard, 1900.
Printed: Harvard studies in classical philology, XIII (1902),
129-73. B116

Bonner, Robert Johnson. Evidence in Athenian courts. Chicago,
1905. Printed: Chicago, University of Chicago press, 1905.
98 p. B117

Boose, Helen A. The psychological and ethical fragments of
    Posidonius. Yale, 1934. B118
Boren, Henry Charles. The reform program of the Livii Drusi,
    tribunes 122 B.C. and 91 B.C. Illinois, 1952. B118a
Born, Lester Kruger. The integumenta on the Metamorphoses
    of Ovid by John of Garland, first edited with introduction
    and translation. Chicago, 1929. Abstract: Abstracts of
    theses, Humanistic ser., VII (1930), 429–32. B119
Borza, Eugene N. The Bacaudae: a study in revolution in late
    Roman Gaul. Chicago, 1963. B120
Bos, Jacob. Josephus' Presentation of first-century Judaism.
    Chicago, 1922. B121
Bosche, Carol Marian. Plato's doctrine of quality: a meta-
    physical interpretation of Philebus 11A–16A. Yale, 1960.
    B122
Bostroem, E. De graecis verbis apud Plautum inventis. New
    York, 1902. Printed: De vocabulis graecis apud Plautum.
    New York, G. E. Stechert, agent, 1902. 87 p. B123
Bothmer, Dietrich Felix von. Amazons in Greek art. Califor-
    nia, Berkeley, 1944. B124
Botsford, George Willis. The development of the Athenian
    constitution. Cornell, 1891. Printed: Cornell studies in
    classical philology, IV (1893). 249 p. B125
Boulter, Cedric G. The Providence painter: a study of Attic
    red-figured pottery. Cincinnati, 1939. B126
Boulter, Elizabeth Patricia Neils. The Heraclidae of Euripides:
    an introduction and commentary. Bryn Mawr, 1953. Ab-
    stract: Dissertation abstracts, XIV, 352. B127
Bourne, Ella. A study of Tibur, historical, literary and epi-
    graphical from the earliest times to the close of the Roman
    Empire. Johns Hopkins, 1914. Printed: Menasha, Wis.,
    George Banta publ. co., 1916. 74 p. B128
Bourne, Frank Card. The public works of the Julio-Claudians
    and Flavians. Princeton, 1941. Printed: Princeton, 1946.
    76 p. B129
Bovie, Smith Palmer. Dominant themes in Virgil's Georgics.
    Columbia, 1955. Abstract: Dissertation abstracts, XV, 352.
    B130
Bowerman, Helen Cox. Roman sacrificial altars; an archaeolog-
    ical study of monuments in Rome. Bryn Mawr, 1912.
    Printed: Lancaster, Pa., The New era printing co., 1913.
    103 p. B131
Bowman, Johnston Alexander. Studies in Ctesias. North-

western, 1938. Abstract: Summaries of doctoral disserta-
tions, VI (1938), 5-8.   B132
Boyd, Clarence E. The library in ancient Rome. Wisconsin,
1909. Printed: Public libraries and literary culture in
ancient Rome. Chicago, University of Chicago press, 1916.
77 p.   B133
Boyer, Blanche Beatrice. On the lost codex Veronensis of
Catullus. Chicago, 1926. Abstract: Abstracts of theses,
Humanistic ser., IV (1928), 255-8.   B134
Brackett, Haven Darling. De enuntiatorum temporalium apud
Herodotum usu atque ratione commentatio. Harvard, 1904.
Printed: American academy of arts and sciences, Proceed-
ings, XLI (1905), 171-232.   B135
Bradeen, Donald W. A history of Chalkis to 388 B.C. Cincinnati,
1947.   B136
Bradley, Barclay White. Use of the chorus in the dialogue por-
tions of Sophocles. Pennsylvania, 1900.   B137
Bradshaw, Mary E. The Illyrian provinces. Wisconsin, 1932.
B137a
Brady, James F. A study of stoicism in Senecan tragedy.
Columbia, 1958.   B138
Brady, Thomas Allan. The reception of the Egyptian cults by
Greeks during the last three centuries before Christ. Har-
vard, 1931. Printed: Missouri University, Studies, X,
no. 1 (1935), 88 p.   B138a
Bräunlich, Alice Freda. The indicative indirect question in Latin.
Chicago, 1913. Printed: Chicago, 1920. 211 p.   B139
Braginton, Mary Victoria. The supernatural in Seneca's trag-
edies. Yale, 1923. Printed: Menasha, Wis., George Banta
publ. co., 1933. 98 p.   B140
Brandt, Joseph G. A contribution to the history of the third
Augustan legion, with special reference to religion. Wis-
consin, 1911.   B141
Brandt, Lida Roberts. Social aspects of Greek life in the sixth
century B.C. Columbia, 1921. Printed: Philadelphia, T. C.
Davis & sons, 1921. 109 p.   B142
Brann, Eva Toni Helene. Protoattic and Corinthian pottery.
Yale, 1956.   B143
Bregolato, Anthony B. Virgilian glosses in the Liber glossarium.
Fordham, 1940.   B144
Brennan, Josephine, Sister. A study of the clausulae in the ser-
mons of St. Augustine. Catholic, 1947. Printed: Catholic
University of America, Patristic studies, LXXVII (1947).
126 p.   B145

Brentlinger, John Allen. The theory of forms in Plato's later
dialogues. Yale, 1962. B146

Bresnahan, John E. Liber II Dracontii De laudibus Dei: translation and text with introduction and commentary. Pennsylvania, 1949. B147

Brewster, Ethel Hampson. Roman craftsmen and tradesmen of
the early empire. Pennsylvania, 1915. Printed: Menasha,
Wis., George Banta publ. co., 1917. 101 p. B148

Bridge, Josiah. Num Lucianus et Cynicum et Fugitives scrip-
serit. Harvard, 1888. Abstract: American philological
association, Transactions, XIX (1888), 33–9. B149

Brilliant, Richard. The use of gestures to denote status in Roman
sculpture and numismatics. Yale, 1960. B150

Brinkerhoff, Dericksen Morgan. Hellenistic statues of Aphrodite:
studies in the history of their stylistic development. Harvard,
1958. B151

Brister, Zeb L. An investigation of the grammatical construction
in the book of Revelation. Southwestern Baptist, 1953. B152

Brockmann, Robert F. The Romanization of North Africa; its
character and extent during the first and second centuries of
the empire. Indiana, 1951. B153

Bromberg, Anne Ruggles. Concordia: studies in Roman marriage
under the empire. Radcliffe, 1961. B154

Brooks, Robert A. Ennius and Roman tragedy. Harvard, 1949.
B155

Brooks, Samuel Stewart. The delineation of character in the
Argonautica of Gaius Valerius Flaccus. Princeton, 1951.
Abstract: Dissertation abstracts, XIII, 550. B156

Brotherton, Blanche Elisabeth Mae. The vocabulary of intrigue
in Roman comedy. Chicago, 1921. Printed: Menasha, Wis.,
George Banta publ. co., 1926. 124 p. B157

Broussard, Joseph Daphis. Eternity in Greek and scholastic
philosophy. Catholic, 1963. Abstract: Dissertation abstracts, XXIV, 3784. B158

Browder, Jonathan Bailey. On the duration of the action in the
Oresteia. Wisconsin, 1897. B159

Brown, Carroll Neidé. De ratione quae inter scholia Euripidis et
Hesychium intercedat. Harvard, 1900. B160

Brown, David Walter. Constitutional history of the early Roman
republic. Yale, 1878. B161

Brown, Edwin Louis. Studies in the Eclogues and Georgics of
Vergil. Princeton, 1961. Abstract: Dissertation abstracts,
XXII, 3191. B162

Brown, Frank E. Pagan religious architecture of Dura Europus.
Yale, 1938. B163

Brown, Hazel Louise. The written and spoken speech controver-
sy. Chicago, 1911. Printed: Extemporary speech in antiquity. Menasha, Wis., George Banta publ. co., 1914. 184 p.
B164

Brown, Helen A. Philosophorum Pythagoreorum collectionis
specimen. Chicago, 1941. Printed: Chicago, 1941. xxviii,
99 p. B165

Brown, James R. D. The conception of measure in early Pythag-
oreanism and Plato. Yale, 1934. B166

Brown, Leighton B. A study in the evolution of the fiscal administrative institutions under the early Roman empire.
Washington, St. Louis, 1937. B167

Brown, Lester Dorman. A study of the case construction of
words of time. Yale, 1903. Printed: New Haven, The Tuttle,
Morehouse & Taylor co., 1904. B168

Brown, Mary Vincentia, Sister. The syntax of the prepositions
in the works of St. Hilary. Catholic, 1935. Printed: Catholic University of America, Patristic studies, XLI (1934).
219 p. B169

Brown, Norman Oliver. Hermes the "thief": with special reference to the Homeric hymn to Hermes. Wisconsin, 1942.
Abstract: Summaries of doctoral dissertations, VII (1942),
281-3. B170

Brown, Robert T. A study of the five sermons of St. Augustine
on St. Cyprian the martyr including introduction, text, translation, and commentary. Southern California, 1948. Abstract: Abstracts of dissertations, 1948, p. 35-7. B171

Brown, Ruth Allison. St. Aureli Augustini De beata vita; a trans-
lation with an introduction and commentary. Catholic, 1944.
Printed: Catholic University of America, Patristic studies,
LXXII (1944). 193 p. B172

Brown, Ruth Martin. A study of the Scipionic circle. Iowa, 1934.
Printed: Iowa Studies in classical philology, I (1934). 95 p.
B173

Brown, Ruth Wentworth. A study of the Maecenas elegies in the
Appendix Vergiliana. Stanford, 1927. Abstract: Abstracts
of dissertations for the degree of doctor of philosophy, III
(1927-28), 99-103. B174

Brown, Truesdell Sparhawk. Onesicritus; a study in Hellenistic
historiography. Columbia, 1949. Printed: California University, Publications in history, XXXIX (1949). 196 p. B175

Brown, William E. Oriental auxiliaries of the imperial Roman
   army. Yale, 1941.   B176
Brownson, Carleton Lewis. Plato's studies and criticisms of
   the poets. Yale, 1897. Printed: Plato's studies in Greek
   literature, American philological association, Proceedings,
   XXVII (1896), 38–40, and Reasons for Plato's hostility to
   the poets, American philological association, Transactions,
   XXVIII (1897), 5–41.   B177
Brubacher, Abraham Royer. Parataxis in Herodotus. Yale,
   1902.   B178
Bruère, Richard Treat. De Ovidii Metamorphoseon aliquot
   codicibus. Harvard, 1936. Abstract: Summaries of theses,
   1936, p. 5–8.   B179
Brumbaugh, Robert Sherrick. The role of mathematics in Plato's
   dialectic. Chicago, 1942. Printed: Chicago, 1942. 85 p.
   B180
Bryan, Stephen J. The corruption of the judiciary in Cicero's
   time. Pittsburgh, 1936.   B181
Bryant, Arthur Alexis. De Atheniensium vita privata titulorum
   ope Atticorum inlustrata. Harvard, 1905.   B182
Bryson, Elizabeth Agnes Emily. Contributions to the study of
   the Thoman recension of Aeschylus. Illinois, 1956. Abstract: Dissertation abstracts, XVI, 1677.   B183
Buchanan, James Junkin. Theorika: a study of monetary
   distributions to the Athenian citizenry during the fifth and
   fourth centuries B.C. Princeton, 1954. Abstract: Disserta-
   tion abstracts, XV, 2173–4.   B184
Buck, Carl Darling. The choregia in Athens and at Ikaria. Yale,
   1889. Printed: American journal of archaeology, V (1899),
   18–33, and American school of classical studies at Athens,
   Papers V (1892), 77–92.   B185
Buck, Charles Henry. A chronology of the plays of Plautus.
   Johns Hopkins, 1938. Printed: Baltimore, 1940. 112 p.
   B186
Buck, Robert John. Middle Helladic matt-painted pottery.
   Cincinnati, 1956. Abstract: Dissertation abstracts, XVI,
   1668.   B187
Buenger, Theodore Arthur. Crete in the Greek tradition.
   Pennsylvania, 1914. Printed: Philadelphia, 1915. 74 p.
   B188
Buetzler, Clemens W. P. The stoic Zeno in the Greek and Latin
   church fathers. St. Louis, 1945.   B189

Buff, Elizabeth Neola. Phronesis in the works of Plato's last
period. Cornell, 1962. Abstracts: Dissertation abstracts,
XXIII, 2906.   B190
Bundy, Elroy L. Hesychia in Pindar. California, Berkeley, 1954.
B191
Bunnell, Frank Scott. Notes on the vocabulary of Apollonius
Rhodius as compared with that of Homer. Yale, 1903.   B192
Burns, Alfred. The life and political career of Lucius Domitius
Ahenobarbus. Washington, 1964.   B193
Burchard, Herbert Morse. Homeric influence on the Palatine
anthology. Chicago, 1900.   B194
Burdick, Lawrence W. Still unsettled voice-usage in Thucydides.
Wisconsin [before 1908].   B195
Burgess, Theodore Chalon. Epideictic literature. Chicago, 1898.
Printed: Chicago University, Studies in classical philology,
III (1902), 89–261.   B196
Burke, John Bruce. Philo and Alexandrian Judaism. Syracuse,
1963.   B197
Burnam, John Miller. Romance forms in Latin. Yale, 1886.
B198
Burnham, William Henry. An historical sketch of the conceptions
of memory among the ancients. Johns Hopkins, 1888.   B199
Burns, Alfred: Entered after Bunnell.
Burns, Earl Thomas. The scholia and fragments of the Pax of
Aristophanes as found in Suidas. Pennsylvania, 1940.   B200
Burns, Mary Ann Theresa. An historical commentary on the
reign of Augustus based on the evidence of Pliny the elder,
Naturalis historia. Pennsylvania, 1960. Abstract: Disserta-
tion abstracts, XXI, 880.   B201
Burrage, Dwight Grafton. Educational progress in Greece during
the Minoan, Mycenaean, and lyric periods. Nebraska, 1920.
Printed: Lincoln, Neb., 1920. 68 p.   B202
Burrage, William Sargent. Quam accurate Sophoclis verba in
Graecis litteris prolata sint quaeritur. Harvard, 1898. B203
Burriss, Eli Edward. Seneca in Corsica. New York, 1922.
Printed: New York, New York University, 1922. 36 p. B204
Burrows, Reynold Lawrence. Prolegomena to Herodian; transla-
tion and textual commentary to Book II, 9, I–III, 15, 8.
Princeton, 1956. Abstract: Dissertation abstracts, XVII,
624.   B205
Burton, Harry Edwin. De rebus sacris apud Aristophanem
repertis. Harvard, 1895.   B206

Bushala, Eugene Waldo. Recent critical work in the fragments of Euripides. Ohio State, 1954. Abstract: Dissertation abstracts, XX, 664. B207

Bushnell, Curtis Clark. Three translations of Æschylus. Yale, 1895. B208

Bushnell, George Ensign. The conditional sentences of Æschylus. Yale, 1878. B209

Butler, Anne Browning. Etiquette and good manners in classical Greek. Cornell, 1909. B210

Butler, Roy Francis. Index verborum comicorum romanorum fragmentorum. Ohio State, 1942. B211

Buttell, Mary Frances, Sister. The rhetoric of St. Hilary of Poitiers. Catholic, 1934. Printed: Catholic University of America, Patristic studies, XXXVIII (1933). 175 p. B212

Buttenwieser, Hilda. The distribution of the Latin classical authors in the middle ages. Chicago, 1930. Abstract: Abstracts of theses, Humanistic ser., VIII (1932), 345-8. B213

Buttrey, Theodore Vern, jr. Studies in the coinage of Marc Antony. Princeton, 1953. Abstract: Dissertation abstracts, XIV, 92. B214

Butts, Herman Robert. The glorification of Athens in Greek drama. Iowa, 1942. Printed: Iowa studies in classical philology, XI (1947). 247 p. B215

Byers, Earl Alexander. St. Augustine: the exponent and synthesizer of fourth century thought. Nebraska, 1920. B216

Byrne, Alice Hill. Titus Pomponius Atticus, chapters of a biography. Bryn Mawr, 1918. Printed: Bryn Mawr, Pa., 1920. 103 p. B217

Byrne, Lee. Seneca's philosophy of life: his tragedies compared with his prose. Pennsylvania, 1901. B218

Byrne, Marie José, Sister. Prolegomena to an edition of the works of Decimus Magnus Ausonius. Columbia, 1915. Printed: New York, Columbia University press, 1916. 101 p. B219

C

Calder, William Musgrave, III. Further researches on the dramatic technique of Sophocles. Chicago, 1958. C1

Caldwell, Robert Wallace. The Chimaera. Johns Hopkins, 1943. C2

Caldwell, Wallace Everett. Hellenic conceptions of peace.
    Columbia, 1919. Printed: Columbia University, Faculty of
    political science, Studies in history, economics and public
    law, LXXXIV (1919; whole ser., no. 195). 141 p.   C3
Calhoun, George Miller. Athenian clubs in politics and litigation.
    Chicago, 1911. Printed: Texas University, Bulletin, 1913.
    172 p.   C4
Callaghan, Honora, Sister. Moral values in Caesar and Cicero.
    Boston College, 1938.   C5
Callahan, John F. The problem of time in ancient philosophy.
    Chicago, 1941.   C6
Cameron, Alister. The Pythagorean background of the theory of
    recollection. Columbia, 1938. Printed: Menasha, Wis.,
    George Banta publ. co., 1938. 101 p.   C7
Cameron, Donald. Quae in Festi sententiis et oratione a Paulo
    mutata sint quaeritur. Harvard, 1902.   C8
Cameron, Howard Don. Studies on the Seven against Thebes of
    Aeschylus. Princeton, 1962. Abstract: Dissertation ab-
    stracts, XXIV, 290.   C9
Campbell, Ernest R. Word studies in the Greek papyri. Northern
    Baptist, 1953.   C10
Campbell, James Marshall. The influence of the second sophistic
    on the style of the sermons of St. Basil the Great. Catholic,
    1922. Printed: Catholic University of America, Patristic
    studies, II (1922). 155 p.   C11
Campbell, LeRoy A. The development of the Mithraic cult pic-
    ture. Yale, 1938.   C12
Canavan, John Joseph. Saint John Chrysostom, Quod nemo
    laeditur nisi a seipso, a new critical edition. Cornell, 1956.
    Abstract: Dissertation abstracts, XVI, 1444.   C13
Canfield, Leon Hardy. A study in the history of the early
    persecutors. Columbia, 1913. Printed: Columbia Uni-
    versity, Faculty of political science, Studies in history,
    economics and public law, LV, no. 2 (1913). 215 p.   C13a
Canter, Howard Vernon. The infinitive construction in Livy.
    Johns Hopkins, 1904. Printed: Columbia, Mo., Press of
    E. W. Stephens publ. co., 1906. 94 p.   C14
Caples, Cornelius M. A new study of the genitive of description
    and the ablative of description. Toronto, 1938.   C15
Cappon, Cormac Gerard. The Gospels as epic. Yale, 1953.
    Abstract: Dissertation abstracts, XIV, 1403.   C16

Capps, Edward. The stage in the Greek theatre. Yale, 1891.
     Printed: The Greek stage according to the extant dramas,
     American philological association, Transactions, XXII (1891),
     5–80.   C17

Capps, Edward, III. The compound words in Pindar. Yale, 1964.
     C18

Carlson, Arthur Ferdinand. The orthography and phonology of
     the Latin papyri. Michigan, 1950. Abstract: Microfilm ab-
     stracts, XI, 335–6.   C19

Carlson, Mary Louise. Roman examples in the Latin Christian
     apologists. Cornell, 1942.   C20

Carpenter, Paul C. The meaning and use of $\beta\acute{\alpha}\pi\tau\iota\sigma\mu\alpha$ in the
     New Testament. Southern Baptist, 1946.   C21

Carpenter, Rhys. The ethics of Euripides. Columbia, 1916.
     Printed: Archives of philosophy, VII (1916). 48 p.   C22

Carpenter, Stanley Sherman. The appropriate name in the Bucol-
     ics of Vergil. Illinois, 1943. Abstract: Urbana, 1943. 5 p. C23

Carroll, Alexander Mitchell. Aristotle's Poetics, C. xxv, in the
     light of the Homeric scholia. Johns Hopkins, 1893. Printed:
     Baltimore, J. Murphy and co., 1895. 66 p.   C24

Carroll, Harry J., jr. Bouletai: an epigraphical and prosopo-
     graphical study of the lists of Athenian councillors which
     survive from the fifth and fourth centuries B.C. with special
     emphasis on deme representation and the social and economic
     status of the councillors. Harvard, 1955.   C25

Carroll, Mary Borromeo, Sister. The clausulae in the Confes-
     sions of St. Augustine. Catholic, 1940. Printed: Catholic
     University of America, Patristic studies, LXII (1940). 89 p.
     C26

Carrubba, Robert William. The arrangement and structure of
     Horace's Epodes. Princeton, 1964.   C27

Carspecken, John F. Apollonius Rhodius and the Homeric epic.
     Harvard, 1950.   C28

Carstensen, Gustav Arnold. The relation of Qoheleth to contem-
     porary Greek philosophy. New York, 1903. Printed: New
     York, Press of Stettiner bros., 1903.   C29

Carter, Harland A. A study of imperial religious policies from
     the accession of Jovian to the death of Theodosius I. Prince-
     ton, 1956. Abstract: Dissertation abstracts, XVIII, 225. C30

Carter, Robert E. Early Attic history in fourth century litera-
     ture. Chicago, 1954.   C31

Cary, Earnest. De Aristophanis Avium apud Suidam reliquiis.
     Harvard, 1903.   C32

Casale, Elizabeth C. A study in Roman ecclesiastical legisla-
    tion: an annotated translation of the sixteenth book of the
    Theodosian Code. Vanderbilt, 1948.   C33
Caskey, Elizabeth G. Democritus and Plato: a comparison of
    the function of the forms in their philosophies. Cincinnati,
    1939.   C34
Caskey, John L. House VI F, a building of the sixth settlement
    of Troy. Cincinnati, 1939.   C35
Caskey, Lacey Davis. The building-inscriptions of the Erech-
    theum. Yale, 1913. Printed: Die Baurechnung des Erech-
    theion für das Jahr 409/8 v. Chr., Deutsches archäologisches
    Institut, Mitteilungen, XXX (1911), 317–43.   C36
Casson, Lionel I. Nine papyrus texts in the New York University
    collection. New York, 1939. Printed: American philological
    association, Transactions, LXVIII (1937), 274–91 and LXIX,
    343–56.   C37
Castle, Clarence Fassett. The use of the aorist participle in
    Homer. Yale, 1888.   C38
Castle, Warren James. The Platonic epigrams. Wisconsin,
    1952. Abstract: Summaries of doctoral dissertations, XIII
    (1953), 372.   C39
Caterall, John Leslie. Livy's use of the period, considered as
    an element in his style and composition. Stanford, 1936.
    Abstract: Abstracts of dissertations for the degree of doctor
    of philosophy, XI (1935/36), 41–4.   C40
Cavarnos, John P. The psychology of Gregory of Nyssa. Har-
    vard, 1947.   C41
Chabot, Marie-Emmanuel, Sister. Le concept de nature chez
    Cicéron. Laval, 1959.   C42
Chacon, Roger José. Plato's theory of punishment. Harvard,
    1958.   C43
Chadwick, Stillman Percy Roberts. The condition of Roman
    colonization from Gaius Gracchus to the death of Augustus.
    Harvard, 1922.   C43a
Chambers, Mortimer H., jr. Studies in the veracity of
    Thucydides. Harvard, 1954.   C44
Chapman, Emmanuel. St. Augustine's philosophy of beauty.
    Toronto, 1934.   C45
Charanis, Peter. The religious policy of Anastasius I, emperor
    of the later Roman Empire, 491–512. Wisconsin, 1935. C46
Charles, John Fredrick. Statutes of limitations at Athens. Chi-
    cago, 1938. Printed: Chicago, Private edition, distributed
    by the University of Chicago Libraries, 1938. 78 p.   C47

Charlton, Daniel J. The portrayal of youthful character in
    Homer. Harvard, 1951.   C48

Charney, Ben L. Brachylogy in the Epistulae morales of Seneca.
    California, 1940.   C49

Chase, George Davis. The origin of Roman praenomina. Har-
    vard, 1897. Printed: Harvard studies in classical philology,
    VIII (1897), 103–84.   C50

Chase, George Henry. De insignibus in clipeis Graecis descriptis.
    Harvard, 1900. Printed: Harvard studies in classical philol-
    ogy, XIII (1902), 61–127.   C51

Chase, Reginald Melville. The use of attributive prepositional
    phrases in colloquial Latin. Chicago, 1926. Abstract: Ab-
    stracts of theses, Humanistic ser., IV (1928). 259–67. C52

Cheek, Philip Macon. Vergil's treatment of the Templum in the
    Aeneid. North Carolina, 1931. Abstract: Research in
    progress, 1930–31, p. 20–1.   C53

Chickering, Edward Conner. An introduction to Octavia praetexta.
    Columbia, 1910. Printed: Jamaica, N.Y., The Marion press,
    1910. 90 p.   C54

Chowen, Richard Henry. The Emperor Hadrian's contributions to
    the general welfare of the eastern provinces. Northwestern,
    1949. Abstract: Summaries of doctoral dissertations, XVII
    (1949), 193–5.   C55

Christiansen, Peder George, jr. The use of images by Claudius
    Claudianus. Wisconsin, 1963. Abstract: Dissertation ab-
    stracts, XXIV, 2468.   C56

Claflin, Edith Frances. The syntax of the Boeotian dialect in-
    scriptions. Bryn Mawr, 1905. Printed: Bryn Mawr college
    monographs, Monograph ser., III (1905). 93 p.   C57

Claghorn, George Stuart. Aristotle's criticism of Plato's
    Timaeus. Pennsylvania, 1953. Printed: The Hague, Nijhoff,
    1954. 149 p.   C58

Clapp, Edward Bull. Conditional sentences in Aischylos. Yale,
    1886. Printed: American philological association, Trans-
    actions, XVIII (1887), 43–58.   C59

Clark, Charles Upson. The text tradition of Ammianus Marcel-
    linus . . . with five manuscript facsimiles. Yale, 1903.
    Printed: New Haven, The author, 1904. 67 p., 5 facsim.
    C60

Clark, Clifford Pease. Numerical phraseology in Vergil.
    Princeton, 1910. Printed: Princeton, The Falcon press,
    1913. 89 p.   C61

Clark, Emily Loring. De Aricotum patria. Boston, 1889. C62

Clark, Frank Lowry. Qua ratione Platonis laudandi usus sit
    Clemens Alexandrinus quaeritur. Harvard, 1902. Abstract:
    American philological association, Proceedings, 1900 (1901),
    p. 17-20.   C63
Clark, Frederick William. The influence of sea-power on the
    history of the Roman republic. Chicago, 1913. Printed:
    Menasha, Wis., George Banta publ. co., 1915. 112 p.   C64
Clark, Robert H. The suppression of intellectual opinion in
    classical Greece. Pittsburgh, 1946.   C65
Clark, Sereno Burton. Utrum Ovidius Epistulas Heroidum XVI-
    XXI scripserit et quo tempore quaeritur. Harvard, 1907.
    Printed: Harvard studies in classical philology, XIX (1908),
    121-55.   C66
Clark, Walter Eugene. Quae de rebus indicis scirent Graeci
    prisci quaeritur. Harvard, 1906.   C67
Clark, Wesley Plummer. Benefactions and endowments in Greek
    antiquity. Chicago, 1928. Abstract: Abstracts of theses,
    Humanistic ser., VI (1929), 299-303.   C68
Clarke, George. Primary and secondary education among the
    Romans. Colorado, 1895.   C69
Clarke, Herbert Morison. Quaestiones de synizesi Homerica.
    Harvard, 1884.   C70
Clarke, Howard William. Myth, rite, and symbol in the Odyssey.
    Harvard, 1960.   C71
Clay, Dorothy Madsen. A formal analysis of the vocabularies of
    Aeschylus, Sophocles and Euripides. Minnesota, 1957. Ab-
    stract: Dissertation abstracts, XVII, 2004.   C72
Cleasby, Harold Loomis. De Seneca tragico Ovidi imitatore.
    Harvard, 1904. Printed: The Medea of Seneca, Harvard
    studies in classical philology, XVIII (1907), 39-71.   C73
Clem, Orlie Martin. Detailed factors in Latin prognosis.
    Columbia, 1924. Printed: Columbia University, Teachers
    College, Contributions to education, CXL (1924). 52 p.   C74
Clement, Willard K. The use of enim in Plautus and Terence.
    Michigan, 1897.   C75
Clifford, Frederick Burr. The Latin manuscript tradition rep-
    resented by the Greek version of Caesar's Bellum Gallicum
    ascribed to Maximus Planudes. Michigan, 1943.   C76
Clift, Evelyn H. Studies in pseudepigrapha of the republic. Johns
    Hopkins, 1937.   C77
Cloud, Frank Levis. Use of the perfect tense in Attic orators.
    Pennsylvania, 1907. Printed: Norristown, Pa., Press of the
    Herald publ. co., 1910. 15 p.   C78

Cohen, Edward E. The Dikai Emporikai: A study of the com-
    mercial maritime courts at Athens in the fourth century
    B.C. Princeton, 1963. Abstract: Dissertation abstracts,
    XXIII, 4328.   C79
Cohen, George Harry. Derivative verbs in -to and verbal modi-
    fication in Latin. Yale, 1914.   C80
Cohen, Maurice Herbert. Plato's use of ambiguity and deliber-
    ate fallacy; an interpretation of implicit doctrines of the
    Charmides and Lysis. Columbia, 1963. Abstract: Dis-
    sertation abstracts, XXIV, 3785.   C81
Cohn-Haft, Louis. The public physicians of ancient Greece.
    Columbia, 1955. Printed: Smith College studies in history,
    XLII (1956). 91 p.   C81
Colburn, Guy B. Epitheta deorum et herorum horatiana ex
    fontibus vel graecis vel latinis derivata. Wisconsin [before
    1908].   C82
Cole, Andrew Thomas, jr. The political theory of Polybius and
    its sources. Harvard, 1960.   C83
Cole, Charles Grenville. The poetical elements in the diction
    and syntax of Tacitus. New York, 1909. Printed: New York,
    G. E. Stechert & co., 1910. 63 p.   C84
Cole, Charles Nelson. De Vergilio Catulli imitatore. Harvard,
    1901.   C85
Cole, Erma Eloise. The Samos of Herodotus. Yale, 1910. Print-
    ed: New Haven, Conn., The Tuttle, Morehouse & Taylor co.,
    1912. 39 p.   C86
Coleman, Christopher Bush. Constantine the Great and Christian-
    ity; three phases: the historical, the legendary, and the
    spurious. Columbia, 1914. Printed: Columbia University,
    Faculty of political science, Studies in history, economics,
    and public law, LX, no. 1 (1914; whole ser., no. 146). 259 p.
    C87
Coleman, William M. Refutation of Mommsen's theory of Caesar's
    agrarian policy. George Washington, 1950.   C87a
Colton, Robert Edward. Juvenal and Martial. Columbia, 1959.
    Abstract: Dissertation abstracts, XX, 664.   C88
Colwell, Ernest Cadman. The character of the Greek of the
    fourth Gospel. Chicago, 1929.   C89
Combellack, Frederick M. The technique of dialogue in Greek
    epic. California, 1937.   C90
Comparette, Thomas Louis. The inscriptional hexameters. Chi-
    cago, 1901.   C91

Conacher, Desmond J. Conceptions of pleasure in the pre-
      Socratic philosophers. Chicago, 1951.   C92
Conant, Joseph Michael. The younger Cato: a critical life with
      special reference to Plutarch's biography. Columbia, 1953.
      Abstract: Dissertation abstracts, XIV, 115.   C93
Congdon, Lenore Olive Keene. Greek caryatid mirrors: techni-
      cal, stylistic and historical considerations of an archaic-
      early classical bronze series. Harvard, 1963.   C94
Connor, Helen Margaret. A study of the syntax of the Strate-
      gemata of Frontinus. Cornell, 1921. Printed: Ithaca, N.Y.,
      Cornell publications printing co., 1923. 104 p.   C95
Connor, Walter Robert. Studies in Ephoros and other sources
      for the cause of the Peloponnesian war. Princeton, 1961.
      Abstract: Dissertation abstracts, XXII, 1983.   C96
Conrad, Carl William. From epic to lyric: a study in the
      history of traditional word-order in Greek and Latin poetry.
      Harvard, 1964.   C97
Cook, F. A. Critique on the Choephori of Aeschylus, the Electra
      of Sophocles and the Electra of Euripides. Syracuse, 1885.
      C98
Cook, W. Hoyt. Boxing in Greek art and literature. Johns Hop-
      kins, 1940.   C99
Cooke, John Philip. Studies in epic time-designations. Chicago,
      1935. Printed: Chicago, Private edition, distributed by the
      University of Chicago Libraries, 1938. 60 p.   C100
Cooley, Arthur Stoddard. De natura deorum quid senserint
      antiqui Graeci. Harvard, 1896. Abstract of portion on Zeus
      printed: American philological association, Proceedings,
      XXXII (1901), cxl-xcliii; XXXIII (1902), lxv-lxviii.   C101
Coon, Raymond Huntington. The foreigner in Hellenistic comedy.
      Chicago, 1916. Printed: Chicago, 1920. 87 p.   C102
Cooper, Frederic Taber. Word formation in the Roman sermo
      plebeius. Columbia, 1895. Printed: New York, Trow, 1895.
      329 p.   C103
Cooper, Robert Franklin. The genitive with parts of the body in
      Greek. Johns Hopkins, 1908.   C104
Copley, Franklin Olin. The pathetic fallacy in Greek poetry from
      the close of the fifth century. Stanford, 1935. Abstract: Ab-
      stracts of dissertations for the degree of doctor of philosophy,
      X (1934/35), 37-41.   C105
Corcoran, Thomas Henry. The Roman fishing industry of the late
      republic and early empire. Northwestern, 1957. Abstract:
      Dissertation abstracts, XVIII, 1041.   C106

Cordes, Humphrey Henry, jr. The religious use of oracles in
    Attic tragedy. Chicago, 1961. C107
Cordray, Janice M. The structure of Horace's odes. Johns
    Hopkins, 1952. C108
Corea, Peter Vincent. Freedom in the thought of Plato, Aris-
    totle, Augustine and Kant. Boston, 1961. C109
Costelloe, M. Joseph. Religious crimes and Roman law during
    the republic. Johns Hopkins, 1958. C110
Coughanowr, Euphrosyne Natsi. The verbal categories in the
    Greek of the Synoptic Gospels. Illinois, 1955. Abstract:
    Dissertation abstracts, XV, 2529. C111
Coulter, Cornelia Catlin. Retractatio in the Ambrosian and
    Palatine recensions of Plautus; a study of the Persa,
    Poenulus, Pseudolus, Stichus and Trinummus. Bryn Mawr,
    1911. Printed: Bryn Mawr College monographs, Monograph
    ser., X (1911). 118 p. C112
Coulter, James Albert. Plato and sophistic myth: studies in
    Plato's Apology and Symposium. Harvard, 1962. C113
Courtney, Humphrey James. A study of eighteen manuscripts
    of Dares Phrygius. St. Louis, 1959. C114
Coutant, Victor Carlisle Barr. Alexander of Aphrodisias: Com-
    mentary on book IV of Aristotle's Meteorologica, translated
    into English with introduction and notes. Columbia, 1936.
    Printed: New York, 1936. 99 p. C115
Covey, Delvin L. Psychological vocabulary in Roman poetry.
    Illinois, 1952. Abstract: Dissertation abstracts, XIII, 87.
    C116
Cowles, Frank Hewitt. Gaius Verres; an historical study.
    Cornell, 1916. Printed: Cornell studies in classical philol-
    ogy, XX (1917). 207 p. C117
Craft, John Richard. The civic water supply of ancient Greece.
    Johns Hopkins, 1940. C118
Craig, Virginia Judith. Martial's wit and humor. Pennsylvania,
    1906. Printed: Lancaster, Pa., Steinman & Foltz, 1912.
    53 p. C119
Crake, John E. A. Archival material in Livy 218-167 B.C. Johns
    Hopkins, 1939. C120
Cramer, Richard W. The legal language of the Pauline epistles.
    Dallas Theological, 1952. C121
Craven, Lucile. Anthony's oriental policy until the defeat of the
    Parthian expedition. Missouri, 1918. Printed: Missouri
    University, Studies, Social science ser., III, no. 2 (1920).
    87 p. C122

Crawford, Cecil C. The Pythagorean philosophy of number.
Washington, St. Louis, 1950. C123

Crawford, Frederick Stuart, jr. Quo modo Graeci vocales e et
o designaverint. Harvard, 1938. Abstract: Summaries of
theses, 1938, p. 3–6. C124

Crawford, Grace A. Mithraic architecture. Yale, 1937. C125

Crawford, Mary Sinclair. Life of St. Nicholas. Pennsylvania,
1923. Printed: Philadelphia, 1923. 115 p. C126

Creaghan, John Sylvester. Violatio sepvlcri: an epigraphical
study. Princeton, 1951. Abstract: Dissertation abstracts,
XV, 1050. C127

Cressman, Edmund Dresser. The semantics of -mentum,
-bulum, and -culum. Yale, 1913. Printed: Kansas University, Humanistic studies, I, no. 4 (1915). 56 p. C128

Crittenden, Albert Robinson. Sentence structure in Virgil.
Michigan, 1908. Printed: Ann Arbor, Mich., 1911. 72 p.
C129

Cronin, James Farley. The Athenian jury in action. Chicago,
1934. Printed: Chicago, Private edition, distributed by the
University of Chicago Libraries, 1936. 18–54, 129–40 p.
C130

Crosby, Henry Lamar. De comicorum Graecorum temporibus
quaeritur. Harvard, 1905. C131

Crosby, Margaret. Halicarnassus from its foundation to 129 B.C.
Yale, 1934. C132

Cross, Robert Brandt. An analysis of themes and ideas in Greek
elegiac poetry. Southern California, 1948. Abstracts of dissertations, 1948, p. 38–41. C133

Crouch, Owen L. The use of tenses in I John. Southern Baptist,
1948. C134

Crumley, John Jackson. On the social standing of freedman as
indicated in the Latin writers. Preceded by a discussion of
the use and meaning of words libertus and libertinus. Johns
Hopkins, 1904. Printed: Baltimore, J. H. Furst co., 1906.
42 p. C135

Cunningham, Maurice P. The singular and plural of substantives
in Latin poetic diction. California, 1941. C136

Cunningham, Robert L. The Aristotelian notion of nature. Laval,
1951. C137

Curran, Leo Christopher. Studies in the language of Propertius,
I. Yale, 1961. C138

Curry, Victor B. The nature and use of the ἵνα Clause in the New
Testament. Southern Baptist, 1949. C139

Curtis, Charles Newman. The Homeric conception of sin.
Boston, 1885. Not available in Boston University Library.
C140

Cutt, Thomas. Meter and diction in Catullus' hendecasyllabics.
Chicago, 1936. Printed: Chicago, Private edition, distrib-
uted by the University of Chicago Libraries, 1936. 67 p.
C141

D

Dadson, Thomas McCosh. The persistence of paganism in the
western Roman empire from Theodosius to Charlemagne.
Chicago, 1927. Abstract: Abstracts of theses, Humanistic
ser., V (1928), 527–32. D1

Daitz, Stephen G. The De Chersoneso and the Philippica quarta
of Demosthenes: the texts and their relationship. Harvard,
1953. D2

Daly, Emily Joseph, Sister. A paleographical textual and
historical commentary on a ninth century manuscript of
Boethius. Fordham, 1946. D3

Dana, Francis Marion. The ritual significance of yellow among
the Romans. Pennsylvania, 1919. Printed: Philadelphia,
1919. 38 p. D4

Dane, Nathan, II. The D2 recension of the alphabetical corpus of
Greek proverbs. Illinois, 1941. Abstract: Urbana, 1941.
5 p. D5

Daniel, John Franklin. Prolegomena to the Cypro-Minoan script.
Pennsylvania, 1941. Printed: American journal of archaeology, 2d ser., XLV (1941), 249–82. D6

Daniel, W. B. A comparative study of quin and quominus in the
Latin language. Johns Hopkins, 1901. D7

Daniels, Ernest Darwin. A study of P. Papinius Statius' Thebais
and his imitation of Vergil's Aeneid. New York, 1905.
Printed: Berlin, Druck von G. Bernstein, 1906. 45 p. D8

Danker, Frederick William. Threnetic penetration in Aeschylus
and Sophocles. Chicago, 1964. D9

Darkow, Angela Charlotte. The spurious speeches in the Lysianic
corpus. Bryn Mawr, 1914. Printed: Bryn Mawr, Pa., 1917.
95 p. D10

D'Arms, Edward F. Chapters on the style of Roman elegy: the
verb. Princeton, 1936. D11

Darrow, Frederick Sage. The history of Corinth from Mummius
to Herodes Atticus. Harvard, 1906. D12

Daube, Doris Fulda. Senecas moralische Schriften im Spiegel
    der deutschen Literatur des 18. Jahrhunderts. Texas, 1964.
    D13
Daugman, Joseph. Long vowel augments in Sanskrit and Greek
    aorists. Wisconsin, 1952.   D14
Davidson, George Forester. Quo modo et qua ratione poetae
    scaenici Euripides Menanderque personas in scaenam
    introduxerint. Harvard University, 1932. Abstract: Sum-
    maries of theses, 1932, p. 6-9.   D15
Davidson, Gladys R. Miscellaneous finds from Corinth, 1896-
    1933. Johns Hopkins, 1935.   D16
Davidson, Theresa S. A study in Roman administrative law.
    Vanderbilt, 1944.   D17
Davis, Benson Willis. The administration of the Roman province
    of Crete and Cyrenaica. North Carolina, 1938. Abstract:
    Research in progress, 1937/38, p. 23.   D18
Davis, Eugene W. Severus Alexander. North Carolina, 1948.
    D18a
Davis, George Tobey. A study in Latin prosody: short final
    vowel before initial consonant groups composed of stop and
    liquid. Pennsylvania, 1959. Abstract: Dissertation abstracts,
    XX, 1773.   D19
Davis, Hugh H. The twin invectives of Pseudo-Cicero, Non est
    amplius tempus ocii and of Pseudo-Catiline, Si subtiliter a
    circumstantibus: edited with introduction, apparatus criticus,
    literary parallels, and commentary. Cincinnati, 1950.   D20
Davis, Thurston N., jr. Autarkeia; historical development of a
    concept from Homer to Aristotle. Harvard, 1948.   D21
Davison, Jean Margaret. A study of Attic geometric workshops.
    Yale, 1957. Printed: Yale classical studies, XVI (1961),
    161 p., 142 figs.   D22
Dawson, Christopher M. Landscape painting in Pompeii. Yale,
    1941.   D23
Day, James Hoffman. Historical method in Aristotle's Athenaion
    politeia. Chicago, 1960.   D24
Day, John. Chapters in the history of Piraeus. Johns Hopkins,
    1925.   D25
Deagon, Ann Fleming. The influence of hellenistic and contempo-
    rary Greek historical theory on Tacitus. North Carolina,
    1954. Abstract: Research in progress, 1954, p. 42.   D26
Deane, Sidney Norton. The frieze of the temple at Bassai. Yale,
    1914.   D27

Debevoise, Neilson Carel. Parthian problems. Illinois, 1930.
    Printed: American journal of Semitic languages and litera-
    tures, XLVII (1931), 73-82.   D27a
Deckman, Alice Anna. A study of the impersonal passive of the
    ventum est type. Pennsylvania, 1920. Printed: Philadelphia,
    Pa., 1920. 62 p.   D28
Deems, Mervin Monroe. Social aspects of early Christian ascet-
    icism. Chicago, 1928. Abstract: Abstracts of theses, Hu-
    manistic ser., VI (1929), 427-30.   D29
DeForest, Frederick Marcy. The Greek names of Roman priests,
    military officers, legislative bodies, and magistrates. Yale,
    1898.   D30
DeLacy, M. Rosella, Sister. A study of the clausulae in the works
    of St. Ambrose. Catholic, 1934. Printed: Washington, D.C.,
    The Catholic University of America, 1934. 148 p.   D31
DeLacy, Phillip H. The problem of causation in Plato's philosophy.
    Princeton, 1939. Printed: Classical philology, XXXIV (1939),
    97-115.   D32
Delamarre, Louis. Tacite et la littérature française. New York,
    1905. Printed: Paris, Bonvalot-Jouve, 1907. 223 p.   D33
Delaney, Howard Raymond. The doctrine of four term analogy in
    Aristotle. St. Louis, 1959.   D34
Delano, Charles Cudworth, jr. The private economy of the
    Athenians of the fourth and fifth centuries. New York, 1908.
    D35
Delauney, John-Baptiste Etienne. The evolution of the style of
    Tertullian. Catholic, 1906.   D36
Delcamp, Ernest Woodruff. The motivation of entrances in Roman
    comedy. Chicago, 1924. Abstract: Abstracts of theses, Hu-
    manistic ser., II (1926), 309-17.   D37
Dell, Harry James. The Illyrian frontier to 229 B.C. Wisconsin,
    1964.   D38
Demarary, Coral Edison. Studies in the language of Hermas.
    Michigan, 1941.   D39
Dennis, Charles Edward. Charity among the Romans. Brown,
    1895.   D40
Dennison, Walter. The epigraphic sources of the writings of
    Gaius Suetonius Tranquillus. Michigan, 1896. Printed:
    American journal of archaeology, ser. 2, II (1898), 25-70.
    D41
Derham, M. G. Signa and less usual cognomina in Latin inscrip-
    tions. Colorado, 1904.   D42

Deutsch, Monroe Emanuel. Notes on the text of the Corpus Tibullianum. California, 1911. Printed: California University, Publications in classical philology, II (1912), 173–226.   D43

Deutsch, Rosamund E. The pattern of sound in Lucretius. Bryn Mawr, 1937. Printed: Philadelphia, 1939. 188 p.   D44

Devine, Isabel Clare. A study of the Laudes Dei of Blossius Aemilius Dracontius. Columbia, 1945. Printed: New York, 1945. 109 p.   D45

De Vries, William Levering. Ethopoiia. A rhetorical study of the types of character in the orations of Lysias. Johns Hopkins, 1892. Printed: Baltimore, J. Murphy & co., 1892. 48 p.   D46

DeWitt, Norman Johnston. The Romanization of Gaul. Johns Hopkins, 1938. Printed: Urbanization and the franchise in Roman Gaul. Lancaster, Pa., 1940. 72 p.   D47

DeWitt, Norman Wentworth. The Dido episode in the Aeneid of Virgil. Chicago, 1907. Printed: Toronto, Wm. Briggs, 1907. 78 p.   D48

Dial, S. T. Mythical element in Roman literature. Causes of Rome's national and literary decline. A review of American literature. Syracuse, 1894. (Cf. also dissertation by Henry Orren Sibley, Syracuse, 1893.)   D49

Diamadopoulos, Peter. Aristotle on accountability and responsibility: Ethica nicomachea, book I, i–v. Harvard, 1957.   D50

Dick, Bernard Francis. The role of manticism in Lucan's epic technique. Fordham, 1962. Abstract: Dissertation abstracts, XXIII, 1356.   D51

Dickinson, Frederick Walter Augustine. The use of the optative mood in the works of St. John Chrysostom. Catholic, 1926. Printed: Catholic University of America, Patristic studies, XI (1926), 1–179.   D52

Dickson, Thomas Wyatt. Compound words in the tragic poets, Attic orators and Plato. Johns Hopkins, 1913.   D53

Diggs, Mary. Roman literary men in the Noctes atticae of Aulus Gellius. North Carolina, 1936. Abstract: Research in progress, 1935–36, p. 20.   D54

Dignan, Frank Winans. The idle actor in Aeschylus. Chicago, 1905. Printed: Chicago, University of Chicago press, 1905. 43 p.   D55

Dillon, John J. Cicero as a trial lawyer. Pittsburgh, 1939. Abstract: The Graduate school abstracts of theses, 1940, p. 60–8.   D56

Dimitrou, Penelope. The polychromy of Greek sculpture; to the
    beginning of the Hellenistic period. Columbia, 1951.   D57

Dimock, George E., jr. The use of the particles in Lysias.
    Yale, 1949.   D58

Dimock, George Edward. Parallel scenes in Plautus. Yale,
    1916.   D59

Dinwiddie, Albert Bledsoe. On indirect discourse in Thucydides.
    Virginia, 1892.   D60

Di Raimondo, Dino Salciccia. Word and deed in Greek tragedy.
    Chicago, 1958.   D61

Dittmer, William Anthony. The fragments of Athenian comic
    didascaliae found in Rome (IG xiv, 1097, 1098 a). Princeton,
    1916. Printed: Leiden, E. J. Brill, 1923. 54 p.   D62

Diver, William G. The relation of Latin to Oscan-Umbrian.
    Columbia, 1953.   D63

Dodge, Arthur. A study of the rhetorical question in the Attic
    orators with special reference to the tone of the style as
    affected by the figure. Johns Hopkins, 1906.   D64

Dodge, Louise Preston. Posse and its synonyms in Cicero's
    letters. Yale, 1960.   D65

Doenges, Norman Arthur. The letters of Themistocles: a survey.
    Princeton, 1954. Abstract: Dissertation abstracts, XIV,
    817.   D66

Donohue, James John. The theory of literary kinds: ancient
    classifications of poetry. Iowa, 1941.   D67

Donovan, William Patrick. A study of early Helladic pottery
    with painted decoration. Cincinnati, 1961.   D68

Dooley, Alban. Lactantius and Minucius Felix. Fordham, 1939.
    D69

Doran, John Joseph. The doctrine of measure as an element in
    Plato's conception of personal justice. Stanford, 1924. D70

Dorjahn, Alfred Paul. The Athenian political amnesty of 403 B.C.
    Chicago, 1924. Abstract: Abstracts of theses, Humanistic
    ser., II (1926), 273-6.   D71

Doudna, John C. The Greek of the Gospel of Mark. Yale, 1939.
    D72

Douglas, Claude Cicero. The use of hyperbole in the New Testa-
    ment. Chicago, 1925.   D73

Dow, Sterling. Athenian inscriptions in the official lettering of
    230-200 B.C. Harvard, 1936.   D74

Downer, J. W. Figurative language in the satires of Petronius.
    Pennsylvania, 1905.   D75

Downes, William Ephraim Daniel. De saltatione apud antiquos.
    Boston, 1899. Not available in Boston University Library.
    D76

Downey, Robert E. G. A study of the Comites orientis and the
    Consulares Syriae. Princeton, 1934.   D77

Downing, Joseph K. The treatise of Gregory of Nyssa In illud:
    tunc et ipse filius. Harvard, 1947.   D78

Doyle, C. Joseph, Brother. The syntax of the prepositions ab,
    de, and ex in the commentary on Virgil attributed to Servius.
    Fordham, 1940.   D79

Doyle, Edwin Joseph. Histiaia in antiquity. Harvard, 1959. D80

Doyle, St. Ignatius, Sister. The religious thought in Horace.
    Boston College, 1942.   D81

Drabkin, Norma Loewenstein. The Medea exul of Ennius.
    Columbia, 1937. Printed: Geneva, N. Y., W. F. Humphrey
    press, 1937. 94 p.   D82

Drake, J. H. The principales of the early empire. Michigan,
    1904 (?). Printed: Michigan University, Studies, Human-
    istic ser., I (1904), 261–332.   D83

Dressler, Hermigild. The usage of $\overset{\text{\textquotesingle}}{\alpha}\sigma\kappa\acute{\epsilon}\omega$ and its cognates in
    Greek documents to 100 A.D. Washington, 1947. Catholic,
    1948. Printed: Catholic University of America, Patristic
    studies, LXXVIII (1948). 86 p.   D84

Drews, Robert Herman. Historiographical objectives and
    procedures of Diodorus Siculus. Johns Hopkins, 1960. D85

Drummond, Richard Henry. The Roman republic in the early
    Latin Christian writers. Wisconsin, 1942. Abstract: Sum-
    maries of doctoral dissertations, VII (1942), 283–5.   D86

Du Bois, Elizabeth Hickman. The influence of the stress accent
    in Latin poetry. Columbia, 1906. Printed: Columbia
    studies in classical philology, II (1906). 96 p.   D87

Duckett, Eleanor Shipley. Studies in Ennius. Bryn Mawr, 1915.
    Printed: Bryn Mawr college monographs, Monograph ser.,
    XVIII (1915). 78 p.   D88

Duda, Helen R. R. Animal nature in the Aesopic fables. Illinois,
    1948. Abstract: Urbana, 1948. 5 p.   D89

Duffy, James. A comparative study of religion in the Iliad and
    Odyssey. Chicago, 1934. Printed: Chicago, Private edition,
    distributed by the University of Chicago Libraries, 1937.
    15–68 p.   D90

Du Four, Mary Johnstone. Suetonius, Tiberius, chapters I–XXIII,
    with parallel passages and a historical commentary. Pennsyl-
    vania, 1940.   D91

Duncan, Thomas Shearer. The influence of art on description
     in the poetry of P. Papinius Statius. Johns Hopkins, 1913.
     Printed: Baltimore, J. H. Furst co., 1914. 103 p.   D92
Dunkel, Harold Baker. Panhellenism in Greek tragedy. Chica-
     go, 1937. Printed: Chicago, Private edition, distributed by
     the University of Chicago Libraries, 1937. 58 p.   D93
Dunkin, Paul Shaner. Studies in the social outlook of the middle
     and new comedy. Illinois, 1937. Abstract: Urbana, 1936.
     6 p.   D94
Dunmore, Charles William. The meaning of polis. New York,
     1961. Abstract: Dissertation abstracts, XXII, 4008.   D95
Durham, Charles Love. The subjunctive substantive clauses in
     Plautus, not including indirect questions. Cornell, 1899.
     Printed: Cornell studies in classical philology, XIII (1901).
     120 p.   D96
Durham, Donald Blythe. The vocabulary of Menander considered
     in its relation to the koine. Princeton, 1911. Printed:
     Princeton University press, 1913. 103 p.   D97
Duval, Richard Paul. The currency decree and Athenian imperial
     policy 478–421 B.C. Yale, 1960.   D98

E

Eagle, Edwin Douglas. Aristocratic bias in the writings of
     Plato. Wisconsin, 1937. Abstract: Summaries of doctoral
     dissertations, II (1938), 284–6.   E1
Eakin, Frank. Οὖν in the New Testament. Chicago, 1922.   E2
Earle, Mortimer Lamson. Quaestiones Sicyoniae. Columbia,
     1889. Printed: A Sikyonian statue, American journal of
     archaeology, V (1889), 292–303.   E3
Earp, Cronje Burnford. A study of the fragments of three related
     plays of Accius. Columbia, 1939. Printed: Scottdale, Pa.,
     Mennonite publ. house, 1939. 104 p.   E4
Eaton, Annette Hawkins. The influence of Ovid on Claudian. Cath-
     olic, 1943. Printed: Catholic University of America, Patris-
     tic studies, LXIX (1943). 167 p.   E5
Ebeling, Herman Louis. A study in the sources of the Messeniaca
     of Pausanias. Johns Hopkins, 1891. Printed: Baltimore,
     J. Murphy & co., 1892. 77 p.   E6
Ebert, Edgar P. The philosophy of Posidonius on philosophy.
     Ohio State, 1946.   E7
Eckels, Richard P. Greek wolf-lore. Pennsylvania, 1937. Print-
     ed: Philadelphia, 1937. 88 p.   E8

Eckels, William Alexander. Ὥστε as an index of style in the
    orators. Johns Hopkins, 1901. Printed: Baltimore, J.
    Murphy & co., 1901. 83 p.   E9
Eckman, George Peck. Controversial elements in Lucretius.
    New York, 1897. Printed: New York, C. B. Jackson, 1899.
    121 p.   E10
Eddy, Samuel Kennedy. Oriental religious resistance to Hel-
    lenism. Michigan, 1958. Abstract: Dissertation abstracts,
    XIX (1959), 2070-1.   E10a
Edinger, Harry Glenn. Vocabulary and imagery in Aeschylus'
    Persians. Princeton, 1961. Abstract: Dissertation ab-
    stracts, XXII, 1983.   E11
Edmiston, Homer. Aristotelis poeticam quibus modis scriptores
    aetate inferiores prave interpretati sint quaeritur. Harvard,
    1901.   E12
Edson, Charles Farwell, jr. Five studies in Macedonian history.
    Harvard, 1939. Abstract: Summaries of theses, 1939, p.
    105-6.   E13
Edson, George C. Columella: an ancient viticulturist. Pitts-
    burgh, 1939.   E14
Edwards, George R. Attic black-glazed pottery. Johns Hopkins,
    1939.   E15
Edwards, George Vail. The ablative of quality and the genitive
    of quality. Johns Hopkins, 1899. Printed: New York, The
    Evening post job printing house, 1900. 89 p.   E16
Edwards, John Bowen. The demesman in Attic life. Johns Hop-
    kins, 1914. Printed: Menasha, Wis., George Banta publ. co.,
    1916. 63 p.   E17
Edwards, Martha Elizabeth. Decius. A study of the Roman em-
    pire in the middle of the third century. North Carolina,
    1936. Abstract: Research in progress, 1935/36, p. 61-2.
    E18
Edwards, Philip Howard. The poetic element in the Satires and
    Epistles of Horace. Johns Hopkins, 1905. Printed: Balti-
    more, J. H. Furst co., 1905. 47 p. (Part I only.)   E19
Edwards, Philip K. Problems of the quota-lists. Johns Hopkins,
    1935.   E20
Eenigenburg, Elton M. The experience of divine anger in Greek
    tragedy. Columbia, 1950. New York, 1949. 128 p.   E21
Einarson, Benedict. Studies in Nemesius. Chicago, 1932. Ab-
    stract: Abstracts of theses, Humanistic ser., IX (1934),
    363-6.   E22

Elden, Wallace Stedman. The conditional period in the writings
of Quintus Horatius Flaccus. Michigan, 1900. Printed:
Waterville, Me., Mail publ. co., 1900. 128 p.   E23

Elder, John Petersen. De Servii Commentariis Danielinis, ut
aiunt, in Aeneidos libros primum et secundum confectis.
Harvard, 1940. Abstract: Summaries of theses, 1940,
p. 3-6.   E24

Elderkin, George Wicker. Aspects of the speech in the later
Greek epic. Johns Hopkins, 1906. Printed: Baltimore, J. H.
Furst co., 1906. 49 p.   E25

Elford, Alva Doris. Architectural terracottas in the Greek
archaic period. Bryn Mawr, 1942.   E26

Eliot, Charles William John. The coastal demes of Attika from
Aixone to Athens. Toronto, 1961. Printed: Coastal demes
of Attika; a study of the policy of Kleisthenes. The Phoenix
(Toronto), Supplementary volume, V (1962). 181 p.   E27

Eller, Henry Matrau. Studies in ἀπὸ κοινοῦ in Ovid. Chicago,
1939. Printed: Chicago, Private edition, distributed by the
University of Chicago Libraries, 1938. 106 p.   E28

Elliott, Kathleen Overmyer. Text, authorship and use of the
first Vatican mythographer. Radcliffe, 1942.   E29

Elliott, Van Courtlandt. Roman senators in the time of Hadrian
and Antoninus Pius. North Carolina, 1933. Abstract: Research in progress, 1932/33, p. 15.   E30

Ellis, Alice W. Reliefs from a sarcophagus decorated with an
amazonomachy in the Fogg Museum. Radcliffe, 1936.   E31

Ellspermann, Gerard L. The attitude of the early Christian Latin writers toward pagan literature and pagan culture. Catholic, 1949. Printed: Catholic University of America, Patristic studies, LXXXII (1949). 267 p.   E32

Elmer, Herbert Charles. Que, et, atque in the inscriptions of the
republic, in Terence, and in Cato. Johns Hopkins, 1888.
Printed: American journal of philology, VIII (1887), 292-
328.   E33

Elmore, Jefferson. The syntax of certain Latin verbs of desire
in the literature of the republic. Stanford, 1901. Printed:
Berlin, L. Simon, 1901. 75 p.   E34

Else, Gerald Frank. Quo modo Plato ideas expresserit. Harvard, 1934. Abstract: Summaries of theses, 1934, p. 3-6.
E35

Emery, Annie Crosby. The historical present in early Latin.
Bryn Mawr, 1896. Printed: Ellsworth, Me., Hancock county
publ. co., 1897.   E36

English, Basil R. The problem of freedom from Homer to
    Pindar. Toronto, 1937.   E37
English, Robert Byrns. The right hand in classical art and lit-
    erature. Michigan, 1906.   E38
Enlow, Eugene I. The meaning of κρίσις in the New Testament.
    Southern Baptist, 1953.   E39
Epps, Preston Herschel. The place of Sparta in Greek history
    and civilization. Chicago, 1929. Abstract: Abstracts of
    theses, Humanistic ser., VII (1930), 419–22.   E40
Erim, Kenan Terfik. The "Hispanorum" coins—problems in
    Sicilian numismatics and history. Princeton, 1958.   E41
Eskridge, James Burnette. The influence of Cicero upon Augus-
    tine in the development of his oratorical theory for the
    training of the ecclesiastical orator. Chicago, 1912.
    Printed: Menasha, Wis., George Banta publ. co., 1912. 58 p.
    E42
Etheridge, Sanford Grant. Plutarch's De virtute morali: a study
    in extraperipatetic Aristotelianism. Harvard, 1961.   E43
Evans, Alvin Eleazar. Studies in Roman law in Livy. Michigan,
    1908.   E44
Evans, Vivian I. The personality and religious life of Augustine.
    Yale, 1935.   E45
Ewald, Marie Liguori, Sister. Ovid in Contra orationem Sym-
    machi of Prudentius. Catholic, 1941. Printed: Catholic Uni-
    versity of America, Patristic studies, LXVI (1942). 220 p.
    E46
Exler, Francis Xavier. The form of the ancient Greek letter; a
    study in Greek epistolography. Catholic, 1923. Printed:
    Washington, D.C., Catholic University of America, 1923.
    140 p.   E47

F

Fackenheim, Emil Ludwig. "Substance" and "perseity" in medi-
    aeval Arabic philosophy, with introductory chapters on Aris-
    totle, Plotinus and Proclus. Toronto, 1945.   F1
Fagles, Robert. The conquest of the mind: a study of the Au-
    gustan Odyssey. Yale, 1959.   F2
Fairchild, William DeForest, jr. Demosthenes and his use of
    the argument from probability. Northwestern, 1951. Ab-
    stract: Summaries of doctoral dissertations, XIX (1951),
    5–8.   F3

Fairclough, Henry Rushton. The attitude of the Greek tragedians
    toward nature. Johns Hopkins, 1896. Printed: Toronto,
    Rowsell and Hutchison, 1897. 82 p.   F4
Fales, De Coursey, jr. The arena-bath area at Curium in Cyprus:
    a study of Roman and early Christian architecture. Harvard,
    1957.   F5
Falk, Kenneth Sawyer. Lucretius as an Epicurean poet. Harvard,
    1961.   F6
Farber, Jay Joel. Xenophon's theory of kingship. Yale, 1959.
    F7
Feemster, Wilhelmina Mary. The origins and early history of the
    proconsular and the propraetorian imperium. Chicago, 1943.
    F8
Feldman, Louis H. Cicero's conception of historiography. Har-
    vard, 1951.   F9
Fenik, Bernard Carl. The influence of Euripides on Vergil's
    Aeneid. Princeton, 1960.   F10
Fenton, Daniel Higgins. Repetition of thought in Plautus. Yale,
    1916. Printed: New Haven, Yale University press, 1921.
    56 p.   F11
Fenwick, Rose B. A contribution to the Fortleben of Cicero's
    De amicitia. Fordham, 1943.   F12
Ferguson, Alice Catherine. The manuscripts of Propertius.
    Chicago, 1934. Printed: Chicago, Private edition, distrib-
    uted by the University of Chicago Libraries, 1934. 68 p.
    F13
Ferguson, James Fulton. The Edict of Diocletian, edited with an
    introduction and with a commentary on chapters 1-5. Yale,
    1912.   F14
Ferguson, Wilbert Perry. Theism in Greek and Roman religions.
    Syracuse, 1896.   F15
Ferguson, William Duncan. The legal and governmental terms
    common to the Macedonian Greek inscriptions and the New
    Testament, with a complete index of the Macedonian in-
    scriptions. Chicago, 1906. Printed: Chicago University,
    Department of Biblical and patristic Greek, Historical and
    linguistic studies in literature related to the New Testament,
    2d ser., Linguistic and exegetical studies, I, II, pt. 3 (1913).
    109 p.   F16
Ferguson, William Scott. The Athenian archons of the third and
    second centuries before Christ. Cornell, 1899. Printed:
    Cornell studies in classical philology, X (1899). 98 p.   F17

Ferrill, Arther L. A political biography of Seneca. Illinois, 1964. F17a

Feyer, Anthony. Exposition of the Adversus haereses of Irenaeus: the argument for cultural continuity. Pittsburgh, 1935. Abstract: The Graduate school abstracts of theses, 1936, p. 89–96. F18

Fields, Donald Eugene. The technique of exposition in Roman comedy. Chicago, 1935. Printed: Chicago, Private edition, distributed by the University of Chicago Libraries, 1938. 200 p. F19

Filbey, Edward Joseph. The supplementary participle in Herodotus. Wisconsin, 1908. Printed: Urbana, 1917. 71 p. F20

Finch, Chauncey Edgar. The Urbana manuscript of Apuleius. Illinois, 1937. Abstract: Urbana, 1937. 5 p. F21

Finch, Henry LeRoy, jr. The Greek idea of limitation; an interpretation of Greek ethos and of Plato's philosophy in relation to it. Columbia, 1953. Abstract: Dissertation abstracts, XII, 77. F22

Fink, Robert O. Roman military accounts and records. Yale, 1934. F23

Finley, John Huston, jr. Quo modo poetae epici Graeci heroas sententias fabulas moribus publicis accommodaverint. Harvard, 1933. Abstract: Summaries of theses, 1933, p. 3–8. F24

Finley, Moses I. Studies in land and credit in ancient Athens. Columbia, 1950. Printed: New Brunswick, N.J., Rutgers University press, 1952. 332 p. F24a

Finn, Margaret R. A history of Latin paleography (from its inception up to 1681). Fordham, 1950. F25

Fisher, W. W. A comparison of the leading God-Ideas of Aeschylus and Sophocles. New York, 1900. F26

Fiske, George Converse. Quas sententias gens Claudia habuerit de re publica administranda quaeritur. Harvard, 1900. Printed: The politics of the patrician Claudii, Harvard studies in classical philology, XIII (1902). 59 p. F27

Fitzgerald, Thomas R. Limitations on freedom of speech in the Athenian assembly. Chicago, 1957. F28

Fitzgerald, William H. The word-group honos-honestus-inhonestus in the Latin literature of the early republic. Fordham, 1957. F29

Fives, Daniel Christopher. The use of the optative mood in the
    works of Theodoret, Bishop of Cyrus. Catholic, 1937.
    Printed: Catholic University of America, Patristic studies,
    L (1937). 106 p.   F30
Fletcher, William G. Urbanization in the Roman provinces.
    Johns Hopkins, 1938.   F31
Flickinger, Minnie Keys. The ἁμαρτία of Sophocles' Antigone.
    Iowa, 1935. Printed: Scottdale, Pa., Mennonite press, 1935.
    82 p.   F32
Flickinger, Roy Caston. Plutarch as a source of information on
    the Greek theater. Chicago, 1904. Printed: Chicago, Uni-
    versity of Chicago press, 1904. 64 p.   F33
Flint, William Willard. The use of myths to create suspense in
    extant Greek tragedy. Princeton, 1921. Printed: Concord,
    N. H., Rumford press, 1922. 87 p.   F34
Fluck, Edward J. A study of the Greek love-names. Johns Hop-
    kins, 1934.   F35
Fobes, Francis Howard. De libris aliquot Suetonianis. Harvard,
    1912. Abstract: Harvard studies in classical philology,
    XXIII (1912), 167.   F36
Folkemer, Lawrence D. S. Aurelii Augustini De fide et operibus.
    Hartford Seminary, 1946.   F37
Folliot, Frederick John William. De principiis cultus impera-
    torum Romanorum quaestio, quid indigenum quidve ex-
    traneum videatur. Harvard, 1927. Abstract: Summaries of
    theses, 1927, p. 3-6.   F38
Folse, Mary Elizabeth. Greek art in the Latin epics. Missouri,
    1934. Printed: Missouri University, Studies, X, no. 3 (1936),
    52-74.   F39
Fontenrose, Joseph E. The cults of the Milesian Didyma. Cali-
    fornia, 1934.   F40
Forman, Lewis. The difference between the genitive and dative
    used with ἐπί to denote superposition. Johns Hopkins, 1894.
    Printed: Baltimore, Press of the Friedenwald co., 1894.
    67 p.   F41
Fornara, Charles William. Strategia of Athens, 501/0-405/4.
    California, Los Angeles, 1961.   F41a
Forte, Bettie Lucille. Greek sentiment toward Rome and the
    Romans: a study in Greco-Roman relations. Bryn Mawr,
    1962. Abstract: Dissertation abstracts, XXIV, 1166.   F42
Fossom, Andrew. The ἅπαξ λεγόμενα of Plato. Johns Hopkins,
    1887.   F43

Foster, Benjamin Oliver. De quartae declinationis apud priscos
    Latinos usu. Harvard, 1899.   F44
Foster, Frederick Montague. The divisions in the plays of
    Plautus, with a chapter on the divisions in the plays of Ter-
    ence. Michigan, 1912. Printed: The divisions in the plays
    of Plautus and Terence. Iowa University, Studies in lan-
    guage and literature, new ser., LXI (1913). 22 p.   F45
Foster, Herbert Baldwin. On the significance of the deus ex
    machina in the extant dramas of Euripides. Johns Hopkins,
    1900.   F46
Foster, Joseph A. The Cena Trimalchionis of Petronius in the
    Codex traguriensis. Pittsburgh, 1938.   F47
Foster, Walter Eugene. Studies in archaism in Aulus Gellius.
    Columbia, 1912. Printed: New York, Princeton University
    press, 1912. 67 p.   F48
Foushee, William Linwood. The relation of Plato to animate
    nature. Johns Hopkins, 1900.   F49
Fox, Margaret Mary, Sister. The life and times of St. Basil the
    Great as revealed in his works. Catholic, 1939. Printed:
    Catholic University of America, Patristic studies, LVII
    (1939). 172 p.   F50
Fox, William Sherwood. The Johns Hopkins tabellae defixionum.
    Johns Hopkins, 1911. Printed: The Lord Baltimore press,
    1912. Published also in a more complete version as Supple-
    ment to the American journal of philology, XXXIII (1911),
    1-32.   F51
Francoeur, M. Petronilla, Sister. The relationship in thought
    and language between Lucius Annaeus Seneca and Martin of
    Braga. Michigan, 1944.   F52
Frank, Elfrieda. The Marian party. Virginia, 1951. Abstract:
    Abstracts of dissertations, 1951, p. 3-7.   F53
Frank, Tenney. Attraction of mood in early Latin. Chicago,
    1903. Printed: Lancaster, Pa., Press of the New era print-
    ing co., 1904. 59 p.   F54
Franklin, Alberta Mildred. The Lupercalia. Columbia, 1921.
    Printed: New York, 1921. 102 p.   F55
Franklin, Susan Braley. Traces of epic influence in the tragedies
    of Aeschylus. Bryn Mawr, 1893. Printed: Baltimore, The
    Friedenwald co., 1895.   F56
Fraser, William Ritchie. Metaphors in Aeschines the orator.
    Johns Hopkins, 1897. Printed: Baltimore, 1897. 73 p. F57
Frazer, Richard McIlwaine, jr. The Agricola manuscripts of
    Pliny's Letters. North Carolina, 1959. Abstract: Disserta-
    tion abstracts, XX, 2787.   F58

Fredricksmeyer, Ernest Adolph. The religion of Alexander the
    Great. Wisconsin, 1958. Abstract: Dissertation abstracts,
    XIX, 1747.   F59
Freeman, Sarah E. The excavation of a Roman temple at
    Corinth. Johns Hopkins, 1934.   F60
Freeman, Walter Houghton. De textus Ovidi carminum ama-
    toriorum historia. Harvard, 1912. Abstract: Harvard
    studies in classical philology, XXIII (1912), 168–70.   F61
French, Ruth Calista. The Greek versions of Jerome's Vita
    sancti Hilarionis. Illinois, 1935. Abstract: Urbana, 1935.
    9 p.   F62
Friberg, Hans Daniel. Love and justice in political theory: a
    study of Augustine's definition of the commonwealth. Chica-
    go, 1944. Printed: Chicago, 1944. 70 p.   F63
Frogen, George H. The change from the Attic to the Ionic alpha-
    bet in Athenian decrees (circa 570 to 317 B.C.). Minnesota,
    1956. Abstract: Dissertation abstracts, XV, 2529.   F64
Frost, Frank Jasper. The scholarship of Plutarch: the biog-
    rapher's contribution to the study of Athenian history, 480–
    429 B.C. California, Los Angeles, 1961.   F64a
Fulmer, Dorothy J. The Tornaesius edition of Petronius. Pitts-
    burgh, 1937.   F65
Funk, Robert W. The syntax of the Greek article: its importance
    for critical Pauline problems. Vanderbilt, 1954.   F66

G

Gallaway, William Francis. On the use of μή with the participle
    in classical Greek. Johns Hopkins, 1896. Printed: Balti-
    more, J. Murphy & co., 1897. 79 p.   G1
Gallery, Leo Norbert. The Latinity of the Dacian inscriptions.
    Harvard, 1940. Abstract: Harvard University, Summaries
    of theses, 1940, p. 6–8.   G2
Gambet, Daniel G. Cicero's reputation from 43 B.C. to A.D. 79.
    Pennsylvania, 1963. Abstract: Dissertation abstracts, XXV,
    459.   G3
Game, Josiah Bethea. An introduction to the Philippics of Cicero
    and to the study of his invective. Yale, 1909.   G4
Gannon, M. Ann I., Sister. The active theory of sensation in
    Plotinus and St. Augustine. St. Louis, 1952.   G5
Ganns, George Edward. Parataxis by means of καί in the Gospel
    of St. Luke. St. Louis, 1934.   G6

Gapp, Kenneth S. A history of Roman famines to time of Trajan.
    Princeton, 1934.   G7

Gard, Donald Hugh. The exegetical method of the Greek transla-
    tor of the book of Job. Princeton, 1950. Abstract: Disserta-
    tion abstracts, XV, 578.   G8

Garvey, Mary Patricia, Sister. Saint Augustine: Christian or
    neo-Platonist? From his retreat at Cassisiacum until his
    ordination at Hippo. Marquette, 1939. Printed: Milwaukee,
    Marquette University press, 1939. 267 p.   G9

Gates, Arthur Matthews. The form and use of the proper name
    in Latin literature. Johns Hopkins, 1910.   G10

Gay, Frank Roy. Studies in the Sophoclean tradition. Chicago,
    1927. Abstract: Abstracts of theses, Humanistic ser., V
    (1928), 383–7.   G11

Gebhard, Elizabeth Repogle. The theater at Isthmia. Chicago,
    1964.   G12

Gefficken, Katherine Allston. A dominant structural pattern in
    the poems of Catullus: its use and its relation to other struc-
    tural devices. Bryn Mawr, 1962. Abstract: Dissertation ab-
    stracts, XXIII, 4346.   G13

Gehman, Henry Snyder. The interpreters of foreign languages
    among the ancients; a study based on Greek and Latin sources.
    Pennsylvania, 1913. Printed: Lancaster, Pa., Intelligencer
    printing co., 1914. 67 p.   G14

Gehrke, Ralph D. A study of the prayers in Euripidean drama.
    Chicago, 1960.   G15

Gelsinger, Michael George Howard. De Codice Vergiliano
    Bernensi 165. Harvard, 1929. Abstract: Summaries of
    theses, 1929, p. 3–4.   G16

Gephart, Rodger F. C. Suetonii Tranquilli vita Domitiani;
    Suetonius' life of Domitian, with notes and parallel passages.
    Pennsylvania, 1915. Printed: Philadelphia, 1922. 120 p.
    G17

Gerber, Douglas Earl. The idea of fate in the poetry of Pindar.
    Toronto, 1960.   G18

Gershenson, Daniel Enoch. Studies in Theocritus' pastoral
    idylls. Columbia, 1961. Abstract: Dissertation abstracts,
    XXII, 1165.   G19

Gerwig, Anna Mary. Scholarship on Caesar in the twentieth
    century. Pittsburgh, 1945.   G20

Giangrande, Lawrence. The use of spoudaiogeloion in Greek and
    Roman literature. St. Louis, 1961. Abstract: Dissertation
    abstracts, XXII, 3193.   G21

Gienapp, Norman Frank. Paired expressions in Homer. Illinois, 1958.   G22

Giles, A. H. The similes of Homer. Syracuse, 1882.   G23

Gill, David Henry. The classical Greek cult table. Harvard,
1964.   G24

Gilleland, Brady B. The reworking and development of material
in Cicero's Rhetorica. North Carolina, 1955. Abstract:
Research in progress, 1954/55, p. 42-3.   G25

Gillespie, Walter Hamilton. De libertinorum statu apud Romanos antiquos. Harvard, 1900.   G26

Gillespie, William Ernest. The development of the weather sign
as a literary subject. Princeton, 1937. Printed: Vergil,
Aratus and others; the weather-sign as a literary subject.
Princeton, 1938. 72 p.   G27

Gilliam, James Frank. The Roman garrison of Dura. Yale,
1940.   G28

Gillingham, Allan G. The prooemia in Cicero's works on philosophy, politics, and rhetoric. Harvard, 1950.   G29

Gillis, Carroll O. Greek participles in the doctrinal Epistles of
Paul. Southwestern Baptist, 1937.   G30

Gillis, Daniel John. Argumentation in Isocrates. Cornell, 1963.
Abstract: Dissertation abstracts, XXIV, 3736.   G31

Gillis, John Hugh. The coordinating particles in Saints Hilary,
Jerome, Ambrose and Augustine; a study in Latin syntax and
style. Catholic, 1939. Printed: Catholic University of
America, Patristic studies, LVI (1938). 237 p.   G32

Gimborn, Didacus Thomas, Brother. The syntax of the simple
cases in St. Hilary of Poiters. Catholic, 1938. Printed:
Catholic University of America, Patristic studies, LIV (1939).
190 p.   G33

Giocarinis, Kimon Theodore. An analysis of an unpublished late
thirteenth century extreme Aristotelian commentary on the
Nicomachean Ethics of Aristotle. Wisconsin, 1953. Abstract:
Summaries of doctoral dissertations, XV (1955), 304-5. G34

Gioscia, Victor Joseph. Plato's image of time (an essay in philosophical sociology). Fordham, 1963. Abstract: Dissertation abstracts, XXIV, 775.   G35

Glass, Meta. The fusion of stylistic elements in Vergil's
Georgics. Columbia, 1913. Printed: New York, 1913. 93 p.
G36

Goethals, Thomas R. The Aethiopica of Heliodorus: a critical
study. Columbia, 1959. Abstract: Dissertation abstracts,
XXII, 1984.   G37

Glava, Zoë Athena. A study of Heliodorus and his romance, the
    Aethiopica, with a critical evaluation of his work as a seri-
    ous source of information on ancient Aethiopia. New York,
    1937. Printed: New York, Published under the auspices of
    the Graduate school of New York University, 1937. 20 p.
    G38
Glick, Mary Kathryn. Studies in colloquial exaggeration in Ro-
    man comedy. Chicago, 1938. Printed: Chicago, Private
    edition, distributed by the University of Chicago Libraries,
    1941. 140 p.   G39
Goddard, Farley Brewer. Studiorum Cyrenensium capita
    antiquaria historica. Harvard, 1883. Printed: Researches
    in the Cyrenaica. American journal of philology, V (1884),
    31–53.   G40
Godolphin, Francis R. B. The chronology of Greek middle come-
    dy. Princeton, 1938. Abstract: Microfilm abstracts, I, 9.
    G41
Goetchius, Eugene Van Ness. Some completive constructions in
    the Pauline Epistles. Union Theological, 1963. Abstract:
    Dissertation abstracts, XXIV, 2587.   G42
Goethals, Thomas R.: Entered after Glass.
Goggin, Mary G. Rhythm in the prose of Favorinus. Yale, 1938.
    G43
Goggin, Thomas Aquinas, Sister. The times of Saint Gregory of
    Nyssa as reflected in the letters and the Contra Eunomium.
    Catholic, 1948. Printed: Catholic University of America,
    Patristic studies, LXXVIX (1947). 217 p.   G44
Goheen, Robert Francis. The imagery of Sophocles' Antigone;
    a study of poetic language and structure. Princeton, 1948.
    Printed: Princeton, Princeton University press, 1951.
    171 p.   G45
Golann, Cecil Paige. The life of Apuleius and his connection
    with magic. Columbia, 1952. Abstract: Dissertation ab-
    stracts, XII, 423.   G46
Golden, Leon. Aeschylus and Ares: a study in the use of mili-
    tary imagery by Aeschylus. Chicago, 1958.   G47
Goldstein, Jonathan A. The letters of Demosthenes. Columbia,
    1959. Abstract: Dissertation abstracts, SS, 1018.   G48
Goltz, Eleanor J. The political, economic, and religious rela-
    tions between the Roman republic and Egypt. Cornell, 1949.
    G49
Goode, Gaylia Myrna. The appropriate name in Petronius.
    Illinois, 1939. Abstract: Urbana, 1941. 6 p.   G50

Goodell, Thomas Dwight. The genitive case in Sophokles. Yale,
   1884. Printed: American philological association, Transactions XV (1884), 5-35.   G51
Goodfellow, Charlotte Elizabeth. Roman citizenship; a study of
   its territorial and numerical expansion from the earliest
   times to the death of Augustus. Bryn Mawr, 1935. Printed:
   Lancaster, Pa., Lancaster press, 1935. 124 p.   G52
Goodrich, Grace Gertrude. Dionysos in the satyr-drama. Wisconsin, 1913. Abstract: Wisconsin University, Studies in
   language and literature, XV (1922), 81-6.   G53
Goodrich, Sidney P. The fifteen-year indiction cycle. Princeton, 1937.   G54
Goodwin, Charles Jaques. Appollonius Rhodius; his figures,
   syntax, and vocabulary. Johns Hopkins, 1890.   G55
Gordis, Warren Stone. The estimate of moral values expressed
   in Cicero's letters; a study of the motives professed or ap-
   proved. Chicago, 1905. Printed: Chicago, University of
   Chicago press, 1905. 102 p.   G56
Gordon, Colin D. The subsidization of border peoples as a Ro-
   man policy in imperial defence. Michigan, 1948.   G57
Gorman, Mary Rosaria, Sister. The nurse in Greek life. Cath-
   olic, 1917. Printed: Boston, Foreign languages print. co.,
   1917. 51 p.   G58
Gottlieb, Carla. The restoration of the "Nereid" monument at
   Xanthos. Columbia, 1951. Abstract: Dissertation abstracts,
   XII, 174.   G59
Gottlieb, J. On the problem of Cicero's De inventione and the
   Ars ad Herennium. New York, 1904.   G60
Gould, Josiah Bancroft, jr. The philosophy of Chrysippus. Johns
   Hopkins, 1962.   G61
Gould, Thomas F. Plato and Democritus. Cornell, 1954. G62
Grabosky, Hymen Leo. The philosophical discourse falsely at-
   tributed to Flavius Josephus and the New Testament. Penn-
   sylvania, 1912.   G63
Grace, Frederick Randolph. Archaic sculpture in Boeotia. Har-
   vard, 1938.   G64
Grace, Virginia F. The stamped amphora handles found in the
   Agora excavations 1931-32: a catalogue treated as a chro-
   nological study. Bryn Mawr, 1934.   G65
Gradilone, Thomas J. The text of the Parentalia and Professores
   of Decimus Magnus Ausonius. Fordham, 1962.   G66
Grady, Eleanor Hunsdon. Epigraphic sources of the Delphic
   Amphictyony. Columbia, 1930. Printed: Walton, N. Y., The
   Reporter co., 1931. 107 p.   G67

Graeber, Rowland P. The digressions in the Histories and Annals of Tacitus. Yale, 1949. G68

Graham, Hugh Frederick. The character of Agamemnon as de-
picted in Greek and Latin poetry from Homer to Quintus
Smyrnaeus. Southern California, 1952. Abstract: Abstracts of dissertations, 1952, p. 72–5. G69

Grandjouan, Clairève. Plastic lamps of imperial times from the
Athenian Agora. Bryn Mawr, 1955. G70

Grant, Esther Lucille. An edition of the anonymous Liber de
origine gentis romanae. Ohio State, 1935. Abstract: Abstracts of dissertations, XIII (1935), 85–93. G71

Grant, John R. De decretis atticis quae e memoria scriptorum
veterum tradita sunt. Harvard, 1948. G72

Grant, Lawrence Otto. The history of ἐν τῷ with the infinitive
and its bearing on Luke's writings. Southern Baptist, 1945.
G73

Grant, Mary Amelia. The ancient rhetorical theories of the
laughable; the Greek rhetoricians and Cicero. Wisconsin,
1919. Printed: Wisconsin University, Studies in language
and literature, XXI (1924). 166 p. G74

Grant, William Leonard. The Partitiones oratoriae of M. Tullius
Cicero: an introduction and commentary. Toronto, 1943.
G75

Graser, Elsa Rose. The economic significance of the edict of
Diocletian on maximum prices. Johns Hopkins, 1941. G76

Graves, Frank Pierrepont. The Philoktetes of Sophocles. Boston, 1892. Not available in Boston University Library. G77

Graves, Haydon Thompson. Quo modo mythis Graeci in rebus
publicis gerendis usi sint. Harvard, 1931. Abstract: Summaries of theses, 1931, p. 3–5. G78

Graves, Joseph Alvin. M. Tullii Ciceronis pro A. Cluentio
habito oratio ad judices. Yale, 1878. G79

Gray, William Dodge. An investigation of the laws of rhythm in
the clausulae of books I and II of the De officiis of Cicero.
Cornell, 1907. G80

Green, Corrine Washington. Word studies in the Consolatio attributed to Cicero together with an Index verborum. North
Carolina, 1948. Abstract: Research in progress, 1945/48,
p. 57–8. G81

Green, Edwin Luther. Diodorus and the Peloponnesian war.
Johns Hopkins, 1897. Printed: Baltimore, J. Murphy & co.,
1899. 51 p. G82

Greenberg, Nathan A. The poetic theory of Philodemus. Harvard, 1955. G83

Greenlee, Jacob H. The Gospel text of Cyril of Jerusalem.
    Harvard, 1947.   G84
Greenwood, Sam Lee. Geographical allusion in Attic tragedy.
    Chicago, 1938. Printed: Chicago, Private edition, distrib-
    uted by the University of Chicago Libraries, 1938. 68 p.
    G85
Greer, Russel Mortimer. Quatenus vita Vergiliana Aelio Donato
    attributa re vera Suetonio Tranquillo debeatur quaeritur.
    Harvard, 1926. Abstract: Summaries of theses, 1926,
    p. 3–5.   G86
Gresseth, Gerald K. The politics of Lucan. California, Berke-
    ley, 1951.   G87
Grether, Gertrude E. The divinity of women in the Roman im-
    perial families, 27 B.C.–235 A.D. Cornell, 1939.   G88
Grey, William Richard. The treatment of philosophy and philos-
    ophers by the Greek comic poets. Johns Hopkins, 1893.
    Printed: Baltimore, The Friedenwald co., 1896. 43 p. G89
Grier, Elizabeth. Accounting in the Zenon papyri. Columbia,
    1934. New York, Columbia University press, 1934. 77p. G90
Gries, Konrad. Constancy in Livy's Latinity. Columbia, 1949.
    Printed: New York (?), 1949. 176 p.   G91
Grieve, Lucia Catherine Graeme. Death and burial in Attic
    tragedy. Pt. I. Death and the dead. Columbia, 1898. Print-
    ed: New York, 1898. 83 p.   G92
Griffin, George Russell. Forms and uses of address in Plautus.
    Marquette, 1943.   G93
Griffin, Mack Hall. The administration of the Roman province
    of Cappadocia. North Carolina, 1929. Abstract: Research
    in progress, 1928/29, p. 22–3.   G94
Griffiths, Anna Henwood. Temple treasures: a study based on
    the work of Cicero and the Fasti of Ovid. Pennsylvania,
    1943.   G95
Grimaldi, William. The enthymeme in Aristotle. Princeton,
    1956. Abstract: Dissertation abstracts, XVII, 1330.   G96
Grimes, James Miller, jr. The life of Caracalla. North Caroli-
    na, 1940. Abstract: Research in progress, 1939/40, p. 115–
    6.   G97
Grimm, John Crawford Milton. The construction ἀπὸ κοινοῦ
    in the works of Horace. Pennsylvania, 1916. Printed: Phil-
    adelphia, 1928. 39 p.   G98
Grimm, Richard Eugene. Pindar's second Pythian Ode. Prince-
    ton, 1960.   G99
Grise, Finley Christopher. Content and method in high-school

Latin from the viewpoint of pupils and of teachers. Peabody,
1924. Printed: George Peabody College for Teachers,
Contributions to education, XIX (1925). 92 p.   G100

Grosser, Dorothy E. E. Studies in the influence of Rhetorica ad
Herennium and Cicero's De inventions. Cornell, 1954.   G101

Grossman, Betty Greenfield. The Eleusinian gods and heroes in
Greek art. Washington, St. Louis, 1959.   G102

Groten, Frank J., jr. The tradition of the Helen legend in Greek
literature. Princeton, 1955.   G103

Gruber, Hester Jane. Civitates liberae under the Roman republic. Bryn Mawr, 1942.   G104

Gruen, Erich Stephen. Criminal trials and Roman politics, 149-
78 B.C. Harvard, 1964.   G105

Gruenenfelder, John Bernard. Plato's theory of scientific knowledge in the later dialogues. Notre Dame, 1961.   G106

Grummel, William C. The life and political career of L.
Calpurnius Piso Caesoninus. New York, 1949.   G107

Guernsey, R. The Greek views of the influence of environment
upon men and animals. Johns Hopkins, 1901.   G108

Guillet, E. S. Caius Trabatius Testa, Jurisconsulte correspondant de Cicéron, ami de César et d'Auguste. Montréal, 1941.
G109

Guiriceo, Marie A. The church fathers and the kingly office.
Cornell, 1955.   G110

Gulick, Charles Burton. De scholiis Aristophaneis quaestiones
mythicae. Harvard, 1894. Printed: Harvard studies in
classical philology, V (1894), 83-166.   G111

Gummere, Richard Mott. De variis similitudinum generibus
apud poetas latinos ante aetatem Augusteam. Harvard, 1907.
G112

Gunnerson, William Cyrus. The history of u-stems in Greek.
Chicago, 1905. Printed: Chicago, University of Chicago
press, 1905. 72 p.   G113

Guss, Evelyn Grace. A study of the vocabulary of Aristophanes'
Plutus. Pittsburgh, 1962.   G114

Guthrie, Kenneth Sylvan. Numenius of Apaméa, the father of neo-
Platonism; works, biography, message, sources, and influ-
ence. Columbia, 1914. Printed: London, G. Bell and sons;
Grantwood, N.J., Comparative literature press, 1917. 215 p.
G115

Guthrie, Patrick C. F. The Roman vilicus. Toronto, 1949. G116

Gutwirth, Marc Raphael. Hesiod and his view of man. Harvard,
1964.   G117

H

Haatvedt, Rolfe A. Coins from Karanis. Michigan, 1950.   H1

Hackermann, Louis F. Servius and his sources in the commentary on the Georgics. Columbia, 1941.   H2

Hadas, Moses. Sextus Pompey. Columbia, 1930. Printed: New
York, Columbia University press, 1930. 181 p.   H3

Haddad, George M. Aspects of social life in Antioch in the
Hellenistic-Roman period. Chicago, 1950.   H4

Hadzsits, George Depue. Prolegomena to a study of the ethical
ideal of Plutarch and of the Greeks of the first century A.D.
Michigan, 1902. Printed: Cincinnati University, University
studies, 2d ser., II, no. 2 (1906). 66 p.   H5

Hadzsits, W. D. The apotheosis of the Roman emperors. Michigan, 1902.   H6

Haggett, Arthur S. A comparison of Apollonius Rhodius
with Homer in prepositional usage. Johns Hopkins, 1897.
Printed: Baltimore, J. Murphy & co., 1902. 75 p.   H7

Hahn, E. Adelaide. Coordination of non-coordinate elements in
Vergil. Columbia, 1929. Printed: Geneva, N.Y., W. F.
Humphrey, 1930. 264 p.   H8

Hahn, Stanley R. Βασιλεία and its cognates in the New Testament. Southern Baptist, 1951.   H9

Haight, Elizabeth Hazelton. The sea in Greek poetry. Cornell,
1909.   H10

Haile, Charles Henry. The clown in Greek literature after
Aristophanes. Princeton, 1911. Printed: Princeton, The
Falcon press, 1913. 40 p.   H11

Hale, Clarence Benjamin. The text tradition of the Aesopic
fables belonging to the so-called Augustana recension. Illinois, 1941. Abstract: Urbana, 1941. 5 p.   H12

Hale, William Henry. Comparison of the evolution of the
Prakrit dialects from Sanskrit and Italian from Latin. Yale,
1863.   H13

Haley, Joseph Boyd. Some model uses in the papyri. Wisconsin,
1921. Printed: Wisconsin University, Studies in language
and literature, XV (1922), 29–32.   H14

Hall, Arthur Pinckney. Some verb uses in Pliny's Letters. Yale,
1886.   H15

Hall, Clayton Morris. Nicolaus of Damascus' life of Augustus; a
historical commentary embodying a translation. Johns Hopkins, 1922. Printed: Smith College classical studies, IV
(1923). 96 p.   H16

Hall, Edith H. The decorative art of Crete in the Bronze Age. Bryn Mawr, 1908. Printed: Pennsylvania University, Department of archaeology, Transactions, II, pt. 1 (1906). 47 p. H17

Halle, Lydia. A study in moralization in Livy. Bryn Mawr, 1958. Abstract: Dissertation abstracts, XIX, 2606. H18

Halliwell, William J. The style of Pope St. Leo the Great. Catholic, 1939. Printed: Catholic University of America, Patristic studies, LIX (1939). 98 p. H19

Halton, Thomas Patrick. Studies in the De providentia of Theodoret of Cyrus. Catholic, 1963. Abstract: Dissertation abstracts, XXIV, 4181. H20

Hamblen, Albert Arthur. An investigation to determine the extent to which the effect of the study of Latin upon a knowledge of English derivatives can be increased by conscious adaptation of content and method to the attainment of this objective. Pennsylvania, 1925. Printed: Philadelphia, 1925. 81 p. H21

Hamilton, Hollister Adelbert. The negative compounds in Greek. Johns Hopkins, 1899. Printed: Baltimore, J. Murphy & co., 1899. 62 p. H22

Hammer, Jacob. Prolegomena to an edition of the Panegyricus Messalae. The military and political career of M. Valerius Messala Corvinus. Columbia, 1926. Printed: Albany, N.Y., Boyd printing co., 1925. 101 p. H23

Hammond, Gilbert Romine. Mythical elements in Roman life. Syracuse, 1886. H24

Hanfmann, George M. A. Metal objects from Olynthus. Johns Hopkins, 1935. H25

Hanley, Stella Marie, Sister. Classical sources of Prudentius. Cornell, 1960. H26

Hansen, Hazel Dorothy. Early civilization in Thessaly. Stanford, 1926. Printed: The Johns Hopkins University studies in archaeology, XV (1933). 203 p. H27

Hanson, John A., jr. Roman theatre-temples. Princeton, 1957. H28

Happe, Kenneth Fredric. Sophocles' Philoctetes: a study in structure. Yale, 1964. H29

Harcum, Cornelia Gaskins. Roman cooks. Johns Hopkins, 1913. Printed: Baltimore, J. H. Furst co., 1914. 84 p. H30

Harding, Caleb Richmond. The orator Dinarchus. Johns Hopkins, 1887. H31

Hardy, William George. Greek epigrammatists at Rome in the
    first century B.C. Chicago, 1923. Abstract: Abstracts of
    theses, Humanistic ser., I (1925), 293-6.   H32
Hare, Annie C. Devotees of oriental gods in Italy and the
    western provinces of the Roman empire. Johns Hopkins,
    1934.   H33
Haring, Ellen Stone. Substantial form in Aristotle's Metaphysics.
    Princeton, 1959.   H34
Harkins, Paul William. The text tradition of Chrysostom's com-
    mentary on John. Michigan, 1948. Abstract: Microfilm ab-
    stracts, VIII, 103-4.   H35
Harland, James Penrose. Prehistoric Aigina; a history of the
    island in the bronze age. Princeton, 1920. Printed: Paris,
    H. Champion, 1925. 120 p.   H36
Harmon, Austin Morris. The clausula in Ammianus Marcellinus.
    Yale, 1908. Printed: Connecticut academy of arts and
    sciences, Transactions, XVI (1911), 117-245.   H37
Harper, George McLean. Village administration in the Roman
    province of Syria. Princeton, 1924. Printed: Yale classical
    studies, I (1928). 72 p.   H38
Harper, Hubert Hill, jr. Suetonius in certain mediaeval florilegia.
    North Carolina, 1952. Abstract: Research in progress, 1931/
    52, p. 44-6.   H39
Harper, James Edwin. The cities of Gaul from the third to the
    seventh century. Chicago, 1963.   H40
Harrell, Hansen Carmine. Public administration in Athenian law.
    Chicago, 1934. Printed: Missouri University, Studies, XI
    (1936). 42 p.   H41
Harrer, Gustave Adolphus. Studies in the history of the Roman
    province of Syria. Princeton, 1913. Printed: Princeton, N.J.,
    Princeton University press, 1915. 94 p.   H42
Harrington, Hester. The prototypes of designs on Roman lamps.
    Radcliffe, 1935.   H43
Harris, Cecil T. The moral and social significance of Juvenal's
    sixth satire. Columbia, 1953.   H44
Harris, Clarence Owen. The life and works of Archilochus on
    the basis of the original sources. Cornell, 1906.   H45
Harris, Josephine M. A study of the hexameters in the Carmina
    epigraphica of Bücheler. Washington, St. Louis, 1936.   H46
Harris, Robert Rivers. Allegory in the Cathemerinon of Pruden-
    tius. North Carolina, 1961. Abstract: Research in progress,
    1961/62, p. 33, Dissertation abstracts, XXIII, 627.   H47

Harris, William Asbury. Plato as a narrator. A study in the myths. Johns Hopkins, 1892. Printed: Richmond, Va., Walthall brothers, 1892. 48 p.   H48

Harrison, Evelyn Byrd. Roman portraits from the Athenian Agora. Columbia, 1952. Abstract: Dissertation abstracts, XII, 612.   H49

Harrison, Everett Falconer. The use of doxa in Greek literature with special reference to the New Testament. Pennsylvania, 1950. Abstract: Microfilm abstracts, XI, 1027-9.   H50

Harrison, Robert Rice. An historical catalogue of Greek sculpture in the three dimensional slide collection of the State University of Iowa. Iowa, 1957. Abstract: Dissertation abstracts, XVII, 2969.   H51

Harrod, Samuel Glenn. Latin terms of endearment and of family relationship: a lexicographical study based on v. VI of the Corpus inscriptionum latinarum. Princeton, 1909. Printed: Princeton, N. J., Falcon press, 1909. 92 p.   H52

Harrop, A. H. De Vergilii Theocritum imitandi modo. Boston, 1905.   H53

Harry, Joseph Edward. A rhetorical study of the Leptinian orations. Johns Hopkins, 1889. Printed: Baltimore, Press of Isaac Friedenwald co., 1891. 48 p.   H54

Harsh, Philip Whaley. Studies in dramatic "preparation" in Roman comedy. Chicago, 1933. Printed: Chicago, University of Chicago press, 1935. 103 p.   H55

Harström, Carl Axel. A contribution to the comparative study of the imagery in Catullus and Horace. Yale, 1899. Printed: The use of sense-epithets in poetry. American philological association, Proceedings, 1900 (1901), p. 17-20.   H56

Harter, Nathan Francis Rosebery. A literary history of the legend of the Argonautic expedition through the middle ages. Pittsburgh, 1954. Abstract: Dissertation abstracts, XIV, 2339.   H57

Harvey, John F. Moral theology in the Confessions of St. Augustine. Catholic, 1951.   H58

Harwood, Floyd Clayton. Ancient geography and ethnography as a literary form. Yale, 1917.   H59

Hassel, David John. Method and scientia in St. Augustine: a study of books VIII to XV in his De trinitate. St. Louis, 1963.   H60

Hastings, Carroll B. Παρουσία and related terms in the New Testament. Southern Baptist, 1950.   H61

Hastings, Harold Ripley. On the relations between inscriptions
and sculptured representations upon Attic tombstones.
Wisconsin, 1910. Printed: Wisconsin University, Bulletin,
no. 485, Philology and literature ser., V, no. 2 (1912). 49 p.
H62

Hatch, Aldis Brainard, jr. The origin and development of the
cohors praetoria. Yale, 1942.   H63

Hatch, William Henry Paine. De verborum ἀλιτήριος, ἀλιτρός,
ἀραῖος, ἐναγής, ἐνθύμιος, παλαμναῖος, προστρόπαιος
usu apud scriptores Graecos usque ad annum ccc ante
Christum natum. Harvard, 1904. Printed: Harvard studies
in classical philology, XIX (1908), 157–86.   H64

Hatfield, James Taft. A study of Juvencus. Johns Hopkins, 1890.
H65

Hathorn, Richmond Y. The political implications in the trial of
P. Clodius, 61 B.C. Columbia, 1950. Abstract: Microfilm
abstracts, X, 114–5.   H66

Haviland, Diantha Sibley. The early group of Cretan seals.
Bryn Mawr, 1964.   H67

Hawes, Edward Southworth. Summarium usus Plautini in
enuntiationibus condicionalibus. Harvard, 1884.   H68

Hawthorne, John G. Gorgias of Leontini: a critical appraisal
with translation and commentary of the extant fragments.
Chicago, 1949.   H69

Hayes, Kiffin Rockwell. A study of the clausula in Cicero's philosophical works. North Carolina, 1953.   H70

Hayley, Herman Wadsworth. Quaestiones Petronianae. Harvard,
1890. Printed: Harvard studies in classical philology, II
(1891). 40 p.   H71

Haynes, Laurine. The collation of a manuscript of Cicero's De
officiis in the library of the University of North Carolina.
North Carolina, 1932. Abstract: Research in progress,
1931/32, p. 19–20.   H72

Haynes, Richard Pierce. Plato's theory of forms and the self-
predication assumption. Illinois, 1962.   H73

Hayward, Eitel Almero John. Sheep raising in the western Roman world. Princeton, 1942. Abstract: Dissertation abstracts, XII, 255.   H74

Healey, Robert Fisher. Eleusinian sacrifices in the Athenian
law code. Harvard, 1961.   H75

Heath, Martha Calef. Early Helladic sealings from the house of
the tiles at Lerna. Yale, 1957.   H76

Heaton, John W. Mob violence in the late Roman republic, 133–
49 B.C. Illinois, 1935. Printed: Illinois University, Illinois
studies in the social sciences, XXIII, no. 4 (1939). 107 p.
H77

Heermance, Theodore Woolsey. Material in the Attic orators
for a history of the tradition of the Persian wars. Yale,
1898. H78

Heibges, Ursula Margarete. The religious beliefs of Cicero's
time as reflected in his speeches. Bryn Mawr, 1962. Abstract: Dissertation abstracts, XXIII, 4347. H79

Heidel, William Arthur. Pseudo-Platonica. Chicago, 1895.
Printed: Baltimore, The Friedenwald co., 1896. 78 p. H80

Heider, Andrew Bernard. The blessed Virgin Mary in early
Christian Latin poetry. Catholic, 1918. Printed: Washington, D.C., 1918. 79 p. H81

Hellems, Fred Burton Ranney. Lex de imperio Vespasiani: A
consideration of some of the constitutional aspects of the
principate at Rome. Chicago, 1902. Printed: Chicago,
Scott, Foresman & co., 1902. H82

Heller, John L. The lament for the dead in Roman folk-custom
and literature. Princeton, 1934. H83

Helmbold, William Clark. The epigrams of Theocritus. Yale,
1935. Printed: Classical philology, XXXIII (1938), 37–62.
H84

Hemphill, Wesley Lynn. Codex coxianus of the Homilies of
Chrysostom on Ephesians and his commentary on Galatians.
Pennsylvania, 1915. Printed: Norwood, Mass., Norwood
press, 1916. 74 p. H85

Henderson, Charles, jr. A lexicon of the stylistic terms used in
Roman literary criticism. North Carolina, 1955. Abstract:
Research in progress, 1954/55, p. 43–4. H86

Hennesy, James Emmet. The background, sources, and meaning
of infinity in St. Gregory of Nyssa. Fordham, 1963. H87

Hennion, Robert B. The diobelia. Columbia, 1952. H88

Henry, Collice. The language of the Culex, a poem of the Appendix Vergiliana. Stanford, 1927. Abstract: Abstract of dissertations for the degree of doctor of philosophy, II (1926/27),
99–103. H89

Henry, Margaret Young. The relation of dogmatism and scepti-
cism in the philosophical treatises of Cicero, Columbia, 1925.
Printed: Geneva, N.Y., W. F. Humphrey, printer, 1925.
117 p. H90

Henry, Rose de Lima, Sister. The late Greek optative and its
　　use in Gregory Nazianzen. Catholic, 1943. Printed: Catho-
　　lic University of America, Patristic studies, LXVIII (1943).
　　108 p.　H91
Hentig, Harmut von. Thucydides sophos. Chicago, 1954.　H92
Herkert, Charles H. Historical commentary drawn from the
　　Natural history of Pliny the Elder for the years 54-76 A.D.
　　Pennsylvania, 1956. Abstract: Dissertation abstracts, XVI,
　　1677.　H93
Herman, Beaumont A. Psychological aspects in the style of
　　Tacitus. Boston College, 1937.　H94
Herr, Margaret Whilldin. The additional short syllables in
　　Ovid. Pennsylvania, 1937. Printed: Linguistic society of
　　America, Language dissertation, XXV (1937). 31 p.　H95
Herrick, Frederick Morris. Attic law of status, family relations
　　and succession, in the fourth century, B.C., systematically
　　and comparatively considered. Columbia, 1890. Printed:
　　New York, Middleditch, 1890. 73 p.　H96
Herrling, Walter Gottlieb Louis. The Romanization of Raetia.
　　Chicago, 1940. Printed: Chicago, 1943. 68-162 p.　H97
Herron, Margaret Clare, Sister. A study of the clausulae in the
　　writings of St. Jerome. Catholic, 1937. Printed: Catholic
　　University of America, Patristic studies, LI (1937). 132 p.
　　H98
Hershbell, Jackson Paul. A commentary on the fragments of the
　　poem of Parmenides. Harvard, 1964.　H99
Hersman, Anne Bates. Studies in Greek allegorical interpreta-
　　tion: I. Sketch of allegorical interpretation before Plutarch.
　　II. Plutarch. Chicago, 1906. Printed: Chicago, The Blue
　　sky press, 1906. 64 p.　H100
Hess, William Huie. Studies in the Ecclesiazusae of Aristophanes.
　　Princeton, 1963. Abstract: Dissertation abstracts, XXV,
　　460.　H101
Hetherington, William Perboyre. An aesthetic study of nine
　　plays of Aeschylus and Sophocles. Toronto, 1942.　H102
Hetzler, Florence M. An introduction to the philosophy of
　　nature: the commentary of St. Thomas Aquinas on book one
　　of the Physics of Aristotle. Fordham, 1959.　H103
Hewitt, Joseph William. De rationibus Iovis Graecorum placandi
　　capitula. Harvard, 1902. Printed: Harvard studies in clas-
　　sical philology, XIX (1908), 61-120.　H104
Hiatt, Vergil Emery. Eavesdropping in Roman comedy. Chicago,
　　1946. Printed: Chicago, 1946. 92 p.　H105

Hickman, Ruby Mildred. Ghostly etiquette on the classical stage. Iowa, 1939. Printed: Iowa studies in classical philology, VII (1938). 228 p.   H106

Highbarger, Ernest Leslie. Chapters in the history and civilization of ancient Megara. Johns Hopkins, 1923. Printed: Johns Hopkins University studies in archaeology, II (1927). 65 p. H107

Hildreth, Henry Theodore. De usu plusquamperfecti indicativi Latini usque ad Augusti aetatem commentatio. Harvard, 1895. H108

Hill, Forbes Iverson. The genetic method in recent criticism on the Rhetoric of Aristotle. Cornell, 1963. Abstract: Dissertation abstracts, XXIV, 2187.   H109

Hill, Ida Carleton Thallon. Lycosura and the date of Damophon. Columbia, 1905. Printed: American journal of archaeology, 2d ser., X (1906), 302–29.   H110

Hindman, Jennie L. Theories of acting: Aristotle to Lucian. Louisiana, 1951.   H111

Hinman, Willis S. Literary quotation and allusion in the Rhetoric, Poetics and Nicomachean ethics of Aristotle. Columbia, 1935. Printed: Staten Island, N.Y., 1935. 201 p.   H112

Hirst, Gertrude Mary. The cults of Olbia. Columbia, 1901. Printed: Journal of hellenic studies, XXII (1902), 245–67, and XXIII (1903), 24–53.   H113

Hitt, James Alfred. A study of πρᾶξις in the major works attributed to Aristotle: with an application of the findings to an interpretation of πρᾶξις as used by Aristotle in the Poetics in reference to Greek tragic poetry. Princeton, 1954. Abstract: Dissertation abstracts, XIV, 2339.   H114

Hixson, Ivy May. The nature and extent of the lost prose works of the Roman republic. North Carolina, 1952. Abstract: Research in progress, 1951/52, p. 46–7.   H115

Hoadley, Harwood. On the authenticity and date of the Sophoclean Ajax, verses 1040–1420. Columbia, 1909. Printed: Lancaster, Pa., The New era printing co., 1909. 52 p.   H116

Hobson, Alponzo Augustus. The Diatessaron of Tatian and the synoptic problem; being an investigation of the Diatessaron for the light which it throws upon the solution of the problem of the origin of the synoptic Gospels. Chicago, 1904. Printed: Chicago University, Department of Biblical and patristic Greek, Historical and linguistic studies in literature related to the New Testament, I, iii (1904). 81 p. H117

Hock, F. W. The metrical variants in Plautus. New York, 1907.
H118

Hodgman, Arthur Winfred. De re metrica titulorum Latinorum
praeter saturnios dactylicosque. Harvard, 1896. Printed
in part: Harvard studies in classical philology, IX (1898),
133–68. H119

Hoeing, Charles. The Codex dunelmensis of Terence. Johns
Hopkins, 1898. Printed: American journal of archaeology,
2d ser., IV (1900), 310–38. H120

Hoelie, Charles. Commentary on the Vita Pauli of St. Jerome.
Ohio State, 1953. Abstract: Dissertation abstracts, XX,
2788. H121

Hoerber, Robert George. The theme of Plato's Republic.
Washington, St. Louis, 1944. H122

Hoey, Allan Spencer. The official religion of the Roman impe-
rial army. Yale, 1940. Printed: New Haven, 1940. p. 9–10,
40–49, 26–39, 165–210. (The full publication of the
Feriale duranum [by R. O. Fink, A. S. Hoey, and W. F.
Snyder], from which this dissertation is an extract, is in
Yale classical studies, VII [1940].) H123

Hoffman, Herbert. Attic red-figure rhyta. Harvard, 1959. H124

Hoffsten, Ruth Bertha. Roman women of rank of the early Empire in public life as portrayed by Dio, Paterculus, Suetonius
and Tacitus. Pennsylvania, 1939. Printed: Philadelphia,
1939. 95 p. H125

Holde, Clara. Virgil's Eclogues and the Roman year. Fordham,
1937. H126

Holderman, Elisabeth Sinclair. A study of the Greek priestess.
Michigan, 1911. Printed: Chicago, University of Chicago
press, 1913. 54 p. H127

Holliday, Vivian Loyrea. Poetry in Cicero's Letters and Lucian's
Bellum Civile. North Carolina, 1961. Abstract: Dissertation abstracts, XXII, 2787. H128

Hollingsworth, Inez L. Problems of the later Latin hexameter
from Commodianus to the Carolingians. Washington, St.
Louis, 1939. H129

Hollingsworth, John Emory. Antithesis in the Attic orators from
Antiphon to Isaeus. Chicago, 1913. Printed: Menasha, Wis.,
George Banta publ. co., 1915. 87 p. H130

Holloway, Robert Ross. The elder turtles of Aigina. Princeton,
1960. H131

Holmes, David Hull. Die mit präpositionen zusammengesetzten
Verben bei Thukydides. Johns Hopkins, 1893. Printed:
Berlin, Weidmann, 1895. 47 p. H132

Holsinger, George Robert, jr. Seneca's use of stoic themes,
with an index of ideas to Books I–VII of the Epistulae
morales. Ohio State, 1957. Abstract: Dissertation abstracts, XVII, 3006.   H133

Holstein, Justus Frederick. Rites and ritual acts as prescribed
by the Roman religion according to the commentary of
Servius on Vergil's Aeneid. New York, 1915. Printed: New
York, Voelcker bros., 1916. 37 p.   H134

Holtsmark, Erling Bent. Some aspects of style and theme in the
Persae of Aeschylus. California, Berkeley, 1963. Abstract:
Dissertation abstracts, XXIV, 5393.   H135

Holtzhausser, Clara A. An epigraphic commentary on Suetonius's
life of Tiberius. Pennsylvania, 1918. Printed: Philadelphia,
1918. 47 p.   H136

Holzworth, Elizabeth. The archives of the temple of Socnobrasis
at Bacchias. Yale, 1941.   H137

Holzworth, Jean. An unpublished commentary on Ovid's Fasti by
Arnulfus of Orleans. Bryn Mawr, 1940. Printed: Hugutio's
Derivationes and Arnulfus' commentary on Ovid's Fasti,
American philological association, Transactions, LXXIII
(1942), 259–76.   H138

Hooton, Earnest Albert. The pre-Hellenistic stage in the evolution of the literary art at Rome. Wisconsin, 1911. Abstract:
Abstracts of theses, I (1917), 35–57.   H139

Hope, Edward William. The language of parody; a study in the
diction of Aristophanes. Johns Hopkins, 1905. Printed:
Baltimore, J. H. Furst co., 1906. 62 p.   H140

Hopkins, Herbert Muller. De vocabulis Graecis apud Plautum
repertis. Harvard, 1898.   H141

Hornsby, Roger Allen. Studies in the reign of Valerian and
Gallienus. Princeton, 1952. Abstract: Dissertation abstracts, XV, 562.   H142

Horwood, Richard Batstone. An edition of part (VII 211–X 546)
of the commentary on Lucan's De bello civili by Arnulph of
Orleans (based on MSS. Vindob. no. 130 and no. 212).
Toronto, 1941.   H143

Hostetter, Winifred Hager. A linguistic study of the vulgar
Greek life of Aesop. Illinois, 1955. Abstract: Dissertation
abstracts, XV, 818.   H144

Houghton, Herbert Pierrepont. Moral Significance of animals as
indicated in Greek proverbs. Johns Hopkins, 1907. Printed:
Amherst, Mass., Carpenter and Morehouse, 1915. 65 p.
H145

Householder, Fred Walters, jr. Literary quotation and allusion
in Lucian. Columbia, 1941. Printed: New York, King's
crown press, 1941. 103 p.   H146

Howard, Albert Andrew. De usu quodam infinitivi perfecti Latini
commentatio. Harvard, 1885. Printed: Harvard studies in
classical philology, I (1890), 111–38.   H147

Howard, Hartley. The influence of the Roman farmer's diction
upon the literary language. Chicago, 1937. Printed: Chicago, Private edition, distributed by the University of Chicago Libraries, 1937. p. 5–26, 77–9.   H148

Howard, Joseph Henry. Case usage in Petronius' satires. Stanford, 1900.   H149

Howe, Darwin Blair. Possible influences of Ionian philosophers
upon the educational theory of Plato. Colorado State College,
1962. Abstract: Dissertation abstracts, XXIV, 170.   H150

Howe, Herbert Marshall. The Epicureans of the Roman republic.
Wisconsin, 1949. Abstract: Summaries of doctoral dissertations, X (1950), 610–1.   H151

Howe, Lawrence Lee. The pretorian prefect from Commodus to
Diocletian (A.D. 180–305). Chicago, 1941. Printed: Chicago,
University of Chicago press, 1942. 141 p.   H152

Howe, Thalia Phillies. An interpretation of the Perseus-Gorgon
myth in Greek literature and monuments through the classical period. Columbia, 1952. Abstract: Dissertation abstracts, XII, 613.   H153

Hower, Charles Clare. Studies on the so-called Accursiana
recension of the life and fables of Aesop. Illinois, 1936.
Abstract: Urbana, 1936. 8 p.   H154

Howes, George Edwin. De versibus Homericis apud Platonem
et Aristotelem repertis. Harvard, 1895. Printed: Harvard
studies in classical philology, VI (1895), 153–237.   H155

Hoxie, Edna May. The influence of Latin on English literature.
Boston, 1909.   H156

Hoy, Louise Price. Political influence in Roman prosecutions:
78 B.C. to 60 B.C. with a listing of the trials. Bryn Mawr,
1952. Abstract: Dissertation abstracts, XIV, 1366.   H157

Hritzu, John Nicholas. The style of the letters of St. Jerome.
Catholic, 1939. Printed: Catholic University of America,
Patristic studies, LX (1939). 121 p.   H158

Hubbe, Rolf Oskar. Public service in Miletus and Priene in Hellenistic and Roman imperial times. Princeton, 1950. Abstract: Dissertation abstracts, XIII, 550.   H159

Hubbell, Harry Mortimer. The influence of Isocrates on Cicero,

Dionysius and Aristides, Yale, 1913. Printed: New Haven, Yale University press, 1914. 72 p.   H160

Hughes, Barbara Lenore. The dramatic use of imagery in Aeschylus. Bryn Mawr, 1955. Abstract: Dissertation abstracts, XVI, 117.   H161

Hugill, William Meredith. Panhellenism in Aristophanes. Chicago, 1935. Printed: Chicago, University of Chicago press, 1936. 106 p.   H162

Hulley, Karl Kelchner. Hieronymus quatenus artem criticam noverit. Harvard, 1941. Abstract: Summaries of theses, 1941, p. 3–5.   H163

Hullihen, Walter. Antequam and priusquam; with special reference to the historical development of their subjunctive usage. Johns Hopkins, 1900. Printed: Baltimore, The Lord Baltimore press, 1903. 107 p.   H164

Humphrey, Edward Frank. Politics and religion in the days of Augustine. Columbia, 1912. Printed: New York, 1912. 221 p.   H165

Hunn, Myrta Eleanor. The myths of Plato. Cornell, 1907.   H166

Hunter, Alice Cushman. Cognatio in Aeneide P. Vergilii Maronis cum notis et comparatione tractationis necessitudinis in ceteris scriptis. Nebraska, 1906.   H167

Hurd, Fayette. Blood vengeance among the ancient Hebrews and the Greeks. Michigan, 1891.   H168

Hussey, George Benjamin. The metaphors and similes of Plato. Johns Hopkins, 1887.   H169

Huston, Hollis W. A critical survey and evaluation of the earliest Greek manuscripts of the New Testament. Duke, 1949. H170

Hutchins, Lucy. The position of demonstrative adjectives in Plautus and Terence. Chicago, 1936. Printed: Chicago, Private edition, distributed by the University of Chicago Libraries, 1936. 302 p.   H171

Hutson, Frederick Le Roy. Sparta in Greek opinion. Chicago, 1909.   H172

Hutton, James. The influence of the Greek anthology. Cornell, 1927. Abstract: Ithaca, N.Y., 1927. 7 p.   H173

Hutton, Thomas C. Index verborum of Dictys Cretensis. Vanderbilt, 1938.   H174

Hyde, Edmund Morris. The Delphic Oracle. Yale, 1882.   H175

Hyskell, Ira David. A study of the Latinity of Solinus. Chicago, 1918. Printed: Chicago, Private edition, distributed by the University of Chicago Libraries, 1925. 58 p.   H176

I

Illinworth, Alfred Scott. The text of Luke in the menologion of
the Greek lectionary. Chicago, 1958.   I1
Immerwahr, Heinrich R. Records of entertainers from Dura.
Yale, 1943.   I2
Ingersoll, James W. D. The use of quod in Cicero. Yale, 1894.
I3
Ingham, Charles Samuel. The conjunction quod in St. Augustine's
De civitate Dei. Yale, 1891.   I4
Irwin, James F. Liber I Dracontii De laudibus Dei with introduc-
tion, text, translation, and commentary. Pennsylvania, 1942.
Printed: Philadelphia, 1942. 133 p.   I5
Irwin, Mary Roberta. Republicanism and freedom of speech in
Rome in the first century. Cornell, 1945.   I6
Isaac, James P. The Emperor Marcian. Harvard, 1924.   I7
Isenberg, Meyer William. The order of the discourses in Plato's
Symposium. Chicago, 1940. Printed: Chicago, Private edi-
tion, distributed by the University of Chicago Libraries,
1940. 72 p.   I8

J

Jackson, Carl Newell. Quas partes equi habebant in religionibus
Graecorum. Harvard, 1901.   J1
Jackson, William Taylor. Seneca and Kant; or, An exposition of
stoic and rationalistic ethics with a comparison and criticism
of the two systems. Michigan, 1881. Printed: Dayton, O.,
United brethren publishing house, 1881. 109 p.   J2
Jaffee, Harold Burton. Horace: an essay in poetic therapy. Chi-
cago, 1944. Printed: Chicago, 1944. 101 p.   J3
Jahn, John Nicholas Henry. A critical study of the sources of the
history of the Emperor Nero. New York, 1921. Printed:
New York (?), 1920. 44 p.   J4
James, Fleming. The peace of Philocrates. Pennsylvania, 1899.
J5
Jameson, Harriet Clara. The manuscript tradition of Jerome's
Vita sancti Malchi. Illinois, 1935. Abstract: Urbana, 1935.
9 p.   J6
Jameson, Michael H. The offering at meals: its place in Greek
sacrifice. Chicago, 1950.   J7
Jefferis, J. D. The theology of the Aeneid; its antecedents and
development. Toronto, 1934.   J8

Jeffers, Samuel A. The philosophical vocabulary of Lucretius. Michigan, 1900. J9

Jefferson, Elmore. The syntax of certain Latin verbs of desire. Stanford, 1901. J10

Jeffords, Clyde Ray. The origin and development of the subordinating functions of the particle dum. Cornell, 1904. J11

Jenison, Elsie Safford. The history of the province of Sicily. Columbia, 1919. Printed: Boston, Mass., The Colonial press, C. H. Simonds co., 1919. 125 p. J12

Jenkins, Edgar Bryan. Index of Terence. North Carolina, 1931. Abstract: Research in progress, 1930/31, p. 21. J13

Jensen, Richard Carl. Dawn and dusk in the epics of Lucan. North Carolina, 1961. Abstract: Dissertation abstracts, XXIII, 627. J14

Jepson, John James. The Latinity of the Vulgate Psalter. Catholic, 1915. Printed: Baltimore, John H. Furst co., 1915. 95 p. J15

Jernigan, Charlton Coney. Incongruity in Aristophanes. Duke, 1935. Printed: Menasha, Wis., George Banta publ. co., 1939. 48 p. J16

Johannes, Wilfred Clemens. The people of Menander: a study of nouns designating family, occupation, social and servile class. Michigan, 1963. Abstract: Dissertation abstracts, XXIV, 2896. J17

Johannesen, Rolf T. Timgad: a study of the social and economic history of a Roman provincial town in Africa. Wisconsin, 1923. J18

Johns, Walter Hugh. The technical terms in Cicero's rhetorical works. Cornell, 1935. Abstract: Ithaca, N.Y., 1934. 5 p. J19

Johnson, Allan Chester. A comparative study in selected chapters in the syntax of Isaeus, Isocrates and the Attic psephismata preceding 300 B.C. Johns Hopkins, 1909. Printed: Athens, C. Meisner & N. Kargaduris, 1911. 78 p. J20

Johnson, Charles William Leverett. Musical pitch and the measurement of intervals among the ancient Greeks. Johns Hopkins, 1896. Printed: Baltimore, J. Murphy & co., printers, 1896. 76 p. J21

Johnson, Franklin Plotinus. Foundations for a study of Lysippus. Johns Hopkins, 1921. Printed: Osceola, Mo., 1925. 48 p. J22

Johnson, Harriet Dale. The Roman tribunal. Johns Hopkins, 1926. Printed: Baltimore, 1927. 66 p. J23

Johnson, Isabelle Lavinia. Index criticus verborum Daretis
     Phrygii. Vanderbilt, 1938. Printed: Nashville, Tenn., dis-
     tributed by the Joint university libraries, 1938. 119 p. J24
Johnson, Joe Edgar. Roman portrait art: its source and real-
     ism. Harvard, 1932. Abstract: Summaries of theses, 1932
     (1933), p. 4-6. J25
Johnson, Rozelle Parker. Compositiones variae (an introductory
     study). Illinois, 1933. Printed: Compositiones variae, from
     Codex 490, Biblioteca capitolare, Lucca, Italy, an introduc-
     tory study. Illinois University, Illinois studies in language
     and literature, XXIII, no. 3 (1939). 116 p. J26
Johnson, Van Loran. The factor of inheritance in the Julio-
     Claudian succession. Wisconsin, 1936. Abstract: Summaries
     of doctoral dissertations, I (1937), 265-6. J27
Johnston, George Wesley. The Querolus, a syntactical and sty-
     listic study. Johns Hopkins, 1895. Printed: Toronto, The
     publishers' syndicate, limited, 1900. 73 p. J28
Johnston, John Adelbert. First century Homer: A study of
     Homer and the Homeric epics in Greek and Latin literature
     of the first century A.D. Pittsburgh, 1936. Abstract: The
     graduate school abstracts of theses, 1937, p. 217-24. J29
Johnston, Leslie Dent. Classical origins of Christmas customs.
     Illinois, 1936. Abstract: Urbana, 1936. 7 p. J30
Johnston, Mary. Exits and entrances in Roman comedy (Plautus
     and Terence). Columbia, 1933. Printed: Geneva, N.Y., The
     W. F. Humphrey press, 1933. 152 p. J31
Jolliffe, Harold Richard. The critical methods and influence of
     Bentley's Horace. Chicago, 1936. Printed: Chicago, Pri-
     vate edition, distributed by the University of Chicago li-
     braries, 1939. 152 p. J32
Jolliffe, Richard Orlando. Phases of corruption in Roman ad-
     ministration in the last half-century of the Roman republic.
     Chicago, 1916. Printed: Menasha, Wis., George Banta publ.
     co., 1919. 109 p. J33
Jones, Edith Carrington. Avianus in the middle ages; manu-
     scripts and other evidences of Nachleben. Illinois, 1944.
     Abstract: Urbana, 1944. 11 p. J34
Jones, Elizabeth Hunter. A fifteenth-century manuscript of
     Porphyrio's commentary on Horace. North Carolina, 1959.
     Abstract: Dissertation abstracts, XX, 2789. J35
Jones, Frances F. The pottery. Bryn Mawr, 1952. Printed:
     Chapter VI of vol. I (The Hellenistic and Roman periods) of

Hetty Goldman, ed., Excavations at Gözlü Kule, Tarsus
(Princeton, Princeton University press, 1950).   J36

Jones, Frank Pierce. The ab urbe condita construction in Greek;
a study in the classification of the participle. Wisconsin,
1937. Printed: Linguistic society of America, Language
dissertation, XXVIII (1939). 96 p.   J37

Jones, Frank William Oliver. Structural elements in Odyssey.
Wisconsin, 1941. Abstract: Summaries of doctoral dissertations, VI (1942), 274-6.   J38

Jones, Franklin Weeks. The origin of the Roman delator. Northwestern, 1942. Abstract: Summaries of doctoral dissertations, X (1942), 186-90.   J39

Jones, Horace Leonard. The poetic plural of Greek tragedy in
the light of Homeric usage. Cornell, 1909. Printed: Ithaca,
N.Y., Press of Andrus & Church, 1909. 167 p.   J40

Jones, Julian Ward, jr. An analysis of the allegorical inter-
pretations in the Servian commentary on the Aeneid. North
Carolina, 1959. Abstract: Dissertation abstracts, XX, 2790.
J41

Jones, Leslie Webber. De deis dacicis. Harvard, 1925. Printed:
The cults of Dacia, California University, California publications in classical philology, IX, no. 8 (1929), 245-305.   J42

Jones, Robert E. Cicero's accuracy of characterization in his
dialogues. Johns Hopkins, 1934.   J43

Jones, Roger Miller. The Platonism of Plutarch. Chicago, 1913.
Printed: Menasha, Wis., George Banta publ. co., 1916.
153 p.   J44

Jones, Theodore Tolman. De sermone Celsiano. Harvard, 1929.
Abstract: Summaries of theses, 1929, p. 4-7.   J45

Jones, Thomas Madison. Case construction of similis and its
compounds. Johns Hopkins, 1903. Printed: Baltimore, The
Friedenwald co., 1903. 45 p.   J46

Jones, Tom B. The literary sources for the reign of Diocletian
(Part one). Michigan, 1934.   J47

Jones, William Robert. The text tradition of Avianus. Illinois,
1940. Abstract: Urbana, 1940. 7 p.   J48

Joseph, Arthur, Sister. L'art dans Saint-Augustin. Laval, 1944.
J49

Joseph, Henry Howard. The syntax and style of Petronius. Stanford, 1900.   J50

Jungkuntz, Richard Paul. Epicureanism and the church fathers.
Wisconsin, 1961.   J51

Juniper, Walter H. A study of verbs of saying in Plautus. Ohio
State, 1937.   J52

Juresco, Bettie. A study of the influence of orphism on the dialogues of Plato. Texas, 1941.   J53

K

Kagan, Donald. Politics and policy in Corinth 421–336 B.C.
Ohio State, 1958.   K1

Kahn, Charles E. Anaximander and the origins of Greek cos-
mology. Columbia, 1958.   K2

Kaiser, Leo Max. Contributions toward a critical edition of the
Vita sancti Pauli by Jerome. Illinois, 1943. Abstract:
Urbana, 1943. 6 p.   K3

Kaltenbach, Philip E. The non-citizen troops in the Roman
army (264–201 B.C.). Johns Hopkins, 1948.   K4

Kane, Thomas Franklin. Case forms with and without prepositions, used by Plautus and Terence to express time. Johns
Hopkins, 1895. Printed: Baltimore, Press of F. N. Green,
1895. 94 p.   K5

Kapetanopoulos, Elias Andreou. The early expansion of Roman
citizenship into Attica during the first part of the empire
(200 B.C.–A.D. 70). Yale, 1964.   K6

Kaplan, Arthur. The Senatus consultum ultimum. Virginia,
1944.   K7

Kapsalis, Peter T. Gestures in Greek art and literature. Johns
Hopkins, 1947.   K8

Kardara, Chrysoula P. A study on Rhodian pottery. Chicago,
1952.   K9

Katterhenry, Edwin A. A critique of Aristotle's doctrine of the
mean. Cincinnati, 1939.   K10

Kaufmann, Leo Bernard. Predication and reality in Plato. St.
Louis, 1957.   K11

Kazakevich, Emily G. Studies concerning Agis and Cleomenes.
Yale, 1949.   K12

Keaney, John Joseph. The structure, dating, and publication of
Aristotle's Athenaion politeia. Harvard, 1959.   K13

Kee, Howard C. The paleography of dated Greek New Testament
manuscripts before 1300. Yale, 1951.   K14

Keenan, Mary Emily, Sister. The life and times of St. Augustine
as revealed in his letters. Catholic, 1935. Printed: Catholic University of America, Patristic studies, XLV (1935).
221 p.   K15

Keep, Robert Porter. Quintilian: his life, times, and work.
    Yale, 1869.   K16
Keep, Winthrop Leicester. The separation of the attributive
    adjective from its substantive in Plautus. California, 1911.
    Printed: California University, Publications in classical
    philology, II, no. 7 (1911), 151–64.   K17
Keim, Charles Zane. Lambinus and the Greek in the text of
    Cicero's letters to Atticus. Pittsburgh, 1937. Abstract:
    The Graduate school abstracts of theses, 1938, p. 170–5.
    K18
Keinath, Herman O. A. Pagan domestic religion in Greco-Ro-
    man Egypt. Michigan, 1937.   K19
Keirns, Mary Elizabeth. The use of Greek words in Roman
    satire. Chicago, 1932. Abstract: Abstracts of theses, Hu-
    manistic ser., IX (1934), 383–91.   K20
Keith, Arthur Leslie. Simile and metaphor in Greek poetry from
    Homer to Aeschylus. Chicago, 1910. Printed: Menasha,
    Wis., George Banta publ. co., 1914. 138 p.   K21
Kek, Anna Margaret Dale. Oportere, debere, convenire, decere,
    necesse esse, opus esse, and usus esse in republican Latin.
    Cornell, 1941.   K22
Keller, Ruth M. Neglected uses of iste. Chicago, 1938.   K23
Kellogg, George Dwight. The use of the subjunctive in indepen-
    dent sentences in Cicero's correspondence. Yale, 1898.
    Printed: Complementary and supplementary defining para-
    taxis, American philological association, Proceedings, XXIX
    (1898), 47–52; and Critical notes in Cicero's letters, ibid.,
    XXXII (1900), 4–5.   K24
Kelly, M. Jamesetta, Sister. Life and times as revealed in the
    writings of St. Jerome exclusive of his letters. Catholic,
    1943.   K25
Kelly, Thomas. A history of Argos ca. 1100 to 546 B.C. Illinois,
    1964.   K26
Kelly, Thomas Armond. Sancti Ambrosii Liber de consolatione
    Valentiniani; a text with a translation, introduction and com-
    mentary. Catholic, 1939. Printed: Catholic University of
    America, Patristic studies, LVIII (1940). 324 p.   K27
Kendall, William F. Paul's use of $\dot{\alpha}\nu\tau\iota$ and $\dot{\upsilon}\pi\acute{\epsilon}\rho$. Southern
    Baptist, 1936.   K28
Kennedy, David Andrew. The lyrical parts of the Seven against
    Thebes. Yale, 1878.   K29
Kennedy, George A. Prolegomena and commentary to Quintilian
    VIII (Pr. & 1–3). Harvard, 1954.   K30

Kennedy, Gertrude Grossmann. Minoan-Mycenean elements in early Greek representational art. California, Berkeley, 1956. K31

Kennedy, Mary Jackson. The literary work of Ammianus. Chicago, 1906. Printed: Lancaster, Pa., The New era printing co., 1912. 65 p. K32

Kennedy, Myron Leo. The reign of the Emperor Probus, 276-282 A.D. Minnesota, 1955. Abstract: Dissertation abstracts, XV, 2518. K33

Kent, John Harvey. The temple estates of Delos, Rheneia, and Mykonos. Chicago, 1943. K34

Kent, Roland Grubb. A history of Thessaly from the earliest historical times to the accession of Philip V of Macedonia. Pennsylvania, 1903. Printed: Lancaster, Pa., The New era printing co., 1904. 174 p. K35

Kenyan, Grover Cleveland. Antithesis in the speeches of Greek historians. 130 p. Chicago, 1941. Printed: Chicago, private edition, distributed by the University of Chicago Libraries, 1941. 130 p. K36

Kern, James William. Ana and kata in composition and with case. Johns Hopkins, 1899. Printed: Baltimore, The Lord Baltimore press, 1915. 50 p. K37

Keyes, Austin Herbert. Andokides and the mutilation of the Hermae at Athens in 415 B.C. Brown, 1901. K38

Keyes, Clinton Walker. The rise of the equites in the third century of the Roman empire. Princeton, 1913. Printed: Princeton, Princeton University press, 1915. 54 p. K39

Keyes, Gordon Lincoln. Studies in Roman education. Princeton, 1944. Abstract: Dissertation abstracts, XII, 256. K40

Keyser, R. S. On the position of Demosthenes in Greek literature and history. Syracuse, 1881. K41

Kibre, Adele. Prolegomena to the unpublished text of Smaragdus' Commentary on Donatus, De partibus orationis. Chicago, 1930. Abstract: Abstract of theses, Humanistic ser., VIII (1932), 349-53. K42

Kidder, George Vincent. The description of characters in Vergil's Aeneid. Chicago, 1937. Printed: Chicago, Private edition, distributed by the University of Chicago Libraries, 1937. 105 p. K43

Kieffer, John Spangler. Galen's Institutio Logica: English translation, introduction and commentary. Johns Hopkins, 1962. K44

Kiley, Reginald, Sister. A comparison of pagan and Christian satire. A study of Horace and Langland. Boston College, 1939. K45

Kimball, E. A. The nine muses of Greek lyric poetry. Boston, 1905. K46

King, Donald Bernard. Athenian activity in the Hellespont from 600 to 450 B.C. Princeton, 1940. Abstract: Dissertation abstracts, XII, 256. K47

King, F. A. Ποικιλία in Plato. Cincinnati, 1904. K48

King, Harold Vosburgh. The syntax of nouns in Cato's De agriculture. Michigan, 1950. Abstract: Microfilm abstracts, X, 108-9. K49

Kingsbury, Anne E. The historical scholia to Aristophanes: an evaluation. Cincinnati, 1952. K50

Kingsbury, Samuel Shipman. A rhetorical study of the style of Andocides. Johns Hopkins, 1898. Printed: Baltimore, John Murphy co., 1899. 46 p. K51

Kinnavey, Raymond James. The vocabulary of St. Hilary of Poitiers as contained in Commentarius in Matthaeum liber I ad Constantium and De trinitate; a morphological study. Catholic, 1937. Printed: Catholic University of America, Patristic studies, XLVII (1935). 338 p. K52

Kinsey, Robert Samuel. The bovine elements in Greek art and architecture. Johns Hopkins, 1941. K53

Kirk, William Charles. Fire in the cosmological speculations of Heracleitus. Princeton, 1938. Printed: Minneapolis, Burgess publ. co., 1940. 60 p. K54

Kirk, William Hamilton. Demosthenic style in the private orations. Johns Hopkins, 1895. Printed: Baltimore, The Friedenwald co., 1895. 43 p. K55

Kirkwood, Gordon Macdonald. Sophocles' use of the technique of contrast. Johns Hopkins, 1942. K56

Kirkwood, Patricia. The Greek and Latin epyllion. Johns Hopkins, 1943. K57

Kirkwood, William Alexander. De oraculis ad res Graecas publicas pertinentibus. Harvard, 1909. K58

Kirtland, Lynn. Nicias—his family and the tradition of his great wealth. Princeton, 1938. Abstract: Microfilm abstracts, IV, 3-4. K59

Kissling, R. C. The Platonism of Synesius of Cyrene, critically examined and interpreted in the light of Neo-Platonic thought, with a prefatory study of his life, works, and style. Chicago, 1913. Abstract: Abstracts of theses, Humanistic ser., IX (1934), 367-70. K60

Klinck, Arthur W. The paganism of Julian: its development,
    character and influence on his religious policy. Nebraska,
    1935.   K61

Klotsche, Ernest Heinrich. The supernatural in the tragedies of
    Euripides, as illustrated in prayers, curses, oaths, oracles,
    prophecies, dreams and visions. Nebraska, 1918. Printed:
    Nebraska University, University studies, XVIII, nos. 3–4
    (1918). 107 p.   K62

Knapp, Charles. De usu atque elocutione Auli Gelli. Columbia,
    1890. Printed: New York, 1890. 252 p.   K63

Knight, Thomas Stanley. Beyond Parmenides: the problem of
    non-being; an ontological essay developing some implica-
    tions of Plato's distinction between absolute and relative
    non-being. Syracuse, 1956. Abstract: Dissertation ab-
    stracts, XVI (1956), 1152.   K64

Knox, Bernard M. W. Traditional structure and formula in the
    tragic narrative speech. Yale, 1948.   K65

Knudsen, Ann Konrad. A study of the relation between Phrygian
    metalware and pottery in the eighth and seventh centuries
    B.C. Pennsylvania, 1961.   K66

Knudsen, Johannes Henrik Vitstrup. The treatment of the
    Domitian persecution in the history of modern research.
    Hartford Seminary, 1943.   K67

Kober, Alice Elizabeth. The use of color terms in the Greek
    poets, including all the poets from Homer to 144 B.C. ex-
    cept the epigrammatists. Columbia, 1932. Printed:
    Geneva, N.Y., The W. F. Humphrey press, 1932. 122 p.
    K68

Koch, Edwin Oswald. A linguistic stylistic study of the preamble
    to Diocletian's Edictum de pretiis venalum rerum of 301 A.D.
    Ohio State, 1931. Abstract: Abstract of dissertations, VII
    (1931), 158–69.   K69

Koehler, Mathilda Anna. Catilina in classic tradition. New York,
    1919. Printed: New York (?), 1920. 58 p.   K70

Kohler, Ellen Lucille. A study of the wood and ivory carvings
    from Gordion, Phrygia (c. 750–500 B.C.) Bryn Mawr, 1958.
    K71

Kohn, Lucile. De vestigiis Aeschyli apud Sophoclem Euripidem
    Aristophanem. Columbia, 1909. Printed: New York, 1909.
    57 p.   K72

Kominiak, Benedict. The theophanies of the Old Testament in
    the writings of St. Justin. Catholic, 1948. Printed: Catholic

University of America, Studies in sacred theology, 2d ser.,
XIV (1948). 76 p.   K73

Koonce, Dorothy Marie. Formal lamentation for the dead in
Greek tragedy. Pennsylvania, 1962. Abstract: Dissertation
abstracts, XXIII, 1357.   K74

Kovach, Edith M. A. A study of the manuscripts of the Florilegium of the Letters of Symmachus. Michigan, 1950. Abstract: Microfilm abstracts, X, 124-5.   K75

Kovacs, Ruth Cundiff Doss Stafford. The Aesopic fable in ancient
rhetorical theory and practice. Illinois, 1950. Abstract:
Urbana, 1950. 8 p.   K76

Kramer, Frank R. The second Nekuia. Wisconsin, 1936. Abstract: Summaries of doctoral dissertations, I (1937), 267-
9.   K77

Kramer, Ida Frieda. The economic significance of the archaeological finds of Greece in the Severan period. Minnesota,
1943.   K78

Krentz, Edgar Martin. Sextus Empiricus on language and literature. Washington, St. Louis, 1960. Abstract: Dissertation
abstracts, XXI, 1558.   K79

Kuebler, Clark George. The argument from probability in early
Attic oratory. Chicago, 1941. Printed: Chicago, 1944. 66 p.
K80

Kuntz, Olive. Tiberius Caesar and the Roman constitution.
Washington, Seattle, 1922. Printed: Washington (State) University, University of Washington publications in the social
sciences, v. 2, no. 1 (1924). 77 p.   K81

Kupfer, Lillian. Greek foreshadowings of modern metaphysical
and epistemological thought. New York, 1901. Printed:
Norwood, Mass., J. S. Cushing and co., 1901. 63 p.   K82

L

Lacey, Raymond Henry. The equestrian officials of Trajan and
Hadrian: their careers, with some notes on Hadrian's re-
forms. Princeton, 1915. Printed: Princeton, Princeton
University press, 1917. 87 p.   L1

Laing, Gordon Jennings. The genitive of value in Latin and other
constructions with verbs of rating. Johns Hopkins, 1896.
Printed: Chicago, University of Chicago press, 1920. 48 p.
L2

Lake, Agnes K. Campana Supellex: the pottery deposit at
Minturnae. Bryn Mawr, 1934.   L3

Landon, Charles C. Reality and Plato: a criticism of the ideal-
    istic interpretation of Plato on the nature of the real. Har-
    vard, 1954.   L4

Lang, Mabel. Biographical patterns of folklore and morality in
    Herodotus' history. Bryn Mawr, 1943. Abstract: Micro-
    film abstracts, VI, 86.   L5

Lanman, Charles Rockwell. The nasal verbs in Sanskrit, Greek,
    and Latin. Yale, 1873.   L6

Lantz, C. Development of plot and character in the plays of
    Terence. Minnesota, 1903.   L7

Larsen, Jakob A. O. A study of representative government in
    Greek and Roman history— Part I: Greek history. Harvard,
    1928.   L8

Larson, Margaret Elizabeth. The officials of Karanis (27 B.C.-
    337 A.D.): a contribution to the study of local government in
    Egypt under Roman rule. Michigan, 1954. Abstract: Dis-
    sertation abstracts, XIV, 1064.   L9

Lashbrook, Austin Maurice. Lucius Ampelius, Liber memorialis.
    Pennsylvania, 1960. Abstract: Dissertation abstracts, XXI,
    882.   L10

Lattimore, Richmond Alexander. Themes in Greek and Latin
    epitaphs. Illinois, 1934. Abstract: Urbana, 1934. 8 p. L11

Laughlin, Thomas Cowden. Solecisms of the Apocalypse.
    Princeton, 1902. Printed: Princeton, N.J., Robinson & co.,
    1902. 23 p.   L12

Laurence, Patricia Anne: Entered after Lawler.

Law, Helen Hull. Studies in the songs of Plautine comedy. Chi-
    cago, 1920. Printed: Menasha, Wis., George Banta publ.
    co., 1922. 119 p.   L13

Lawall, Gilbert Westcott. Theocritus and Greek bucolic poetry.
    Yale, 1961.   L14

Lawler, Lillian Beatrice. The potential remediability of errors
    in English spelling through the study of high-school Latin.
    Iowa, 1925. Printed: Classical journal, XXI (1925), 132–
    48.   L15

Laurence, Patricia Anne. Typology of women's headdress in
    Attic red-figure vase-painting. California, Berkeley, 1962.
    L16

Lay, Eleanore B. Terra cottas found at Olynthus in 1934. Johns
    Hopkins, 1936.   L17

Layman, Donald Leigh. A commentary on the first book of
    Metamorphoses of Apuleius. Stanford, 1938. Abstract: Ab-
    stracts of dissertations for the degree of doctor of philoso-
    phy, XIV (1938/39), 43–51.   L18

Lazenby, Francis Dupont. Household pets in the literature and art of ancient Greece and Rome. Virginia, 1941. Abstract: Abstracts of dissertations, 1941, p. 28–31. L19

Leacock, Arthur Gordner. De rebus ad pompas sacras apud Graecos pertinentibus quaestiones selectae. Harvard, 1899. Printed: Harvard studies in classical philology, XI (1900). 45 p. L20

Lease, Emory Bair. A syntactic, stylistic and metrical study of Prudentius. Johns Hopkins, 1894. Printed: Baltimore, The Friedenwald co., 1895. 79 p. L21

Lebeck, Anne. Image and idea in the Agamemnon of Aeschylus. Columbia, 1963. Abstract: Dissertation abstracts, XXIV, 4685. L22

Lee, Charles Marston. Varro's Menippean satires. Pittsburgh, 1936. Abstract: The Graduate school abstracts of theses, 1937, p. 227–35. L23

Lee, David Russell. Child-life, adolescence and marriage in Greek new comedy and in the comedies of Plautus, a study of the relations represented as existing between parents and their children. Wisconsin, 1907. Printed: Madison, Wis., 1919. 76 p. L24

Leeman, Elsie Lewis. Cato the elder: an interpretation. Columbia, 1952. Abstract: Dissertation abstracts, XII, 425. L25

Lees, James Thomas. Δικανικός λόγος in Euripides. Johns Hopkins, 1889. Printed: Nebraska University, Studies, I, no. 4 (1892), 367–408. L26

Leffingwell, Georgia Williams. Social and private life at Rome in the time of Plautus and Terence. Columbia, 1918. Printed: Columbia University, Faculty of political science, Studies in history, economics, and public law, LXXXI, no. 8 (whole no. 388). 141 p. L27

Lefkowitz, Mary Rosenthal. Τῷ καὶ ἐγώ; a study of first personal statements in Pindar. Radcliffe, 1961. L28

Leigh, Alexander Bertal. The early kings of Lydia. Princeton, 1911. L29

Leis, M. DeChantal, Sister. Christian utilization of pagan educational facilities. Pittsburgh, 1935. L30

Lejnieks, Valdis. Mood, tense, and aspect in Homeric Greek. Princeton, 1962. Abstract: Dissertation abstracts, XXIII, 2909. L31

Lenaghan, John O. A commentary on Cicero's oration De haruspicum responso. Princeton, 1962. Abstract: Dissertation abstracts, XXIV, 290. L32

Lenardon, Robert J. Studies in the life of Themistokles. Cincinnati, 1954. L33

Leslie, Robert J. The Epicureanism of Titus Pomponius Atticus. Columbia, 1950. Printed: Philadelphia, 1950. 76 p. L34

Lesousky, Mary Alphonsine, Sister. De dono perseverantiae [Sancti Aurelii Augustini]; a translation with an introduction and commentary. Catholic, 1956. Printed: Catholic University of America, Patristic studies, XCI (1956). 310 p. L35

Leutner, Winfred George. The article in Theocritus. Johns Hopkins, 1905. Printed: Baltimore, J. H. Furst co., 1907. 80 p. L36

Levi, Gerson Baruch. Gnomic literature in Bible and Apocrypha, with special reference to the gnomic fragments and their bearing on the proverb collection. Pennsylvania, 1910. Printed: Philadelphia (?), 1918. 113 p. L37

Levin, Donald Norman. Ethical implications of the $\pi\acute{\epsilon}\rho\alpha\varsigma$- $\ddot{\alpha}\pi\epsilon\iota\rho\sigma\nu$ dichotomy as seen particularly in the works of Aeschylus. Harvard, 1957. L38

Levin, Saul. $\dot{}A\rho\chi\omega$ and $\dot{\alpha}\rho\chi\acute{\eta}$. Chicago, 1950. L39

Levine, Edwin B. Sententiae and commonplaces in Cicero's orations. Chicago, 1954. L40

Levitt, Bella. Supreme political power in Greek literature of the fourth century B.C. Pennsylvania, 1943. Printed: Philadelphia, 1943. 110 p. L41

Levy, Clara Brooks Emmons. The Bari type of Beneventan script: manuscripts from Apulia. Radcliffe, 1961. L42

Levy, Harry Louis. The invective In Rufinum of Claudius Claudianus. Columbia, 1936. Printed: Geneva, N.Y., W. F. Humphrey press, inc., 1936. 102 p. L43

Lewis, David Malcolm. Towards a historian's text of Thucydides. Princeton, 1952. Abstract: Dissertation abstracts, XV, 563. L44

Lewis, E. H. The causes of Rome's national and literary decline. Syracuse, 1892. (cf. also dissertation by Thomas J. Bassett, Syracuse, 1888, with same title.) L45

Lewis, Gordon Russell. Faith and reason in the thought of St. Augustine. Syracuse, 1959. Abstract: Dissertation abstracts, XX, 694–5. L46

Lieberman, Samuel. Contact between Rome and China. Columbia, 1953. Abstract: Dissertation abstracts, XIV, 92. L47

Lindsay, Thomas Bond. Consonant-variation in the Italic dialects.

Boston, 1882. Not available in Boston University Library. L48

Linforth, Ivan Mortimer. Semasiological studies in Virgil. California, 1906. L49

Linn, Henry William. The satirical element in the letters of Saint Jerome. St. Louis, 1933. Abstract: Microfilm abstracts, II, 83−4. L50

Linss, Wilhelm C. The four Gospel texts of Didymus the Blind. Boston, 1955. L51

Lipscomb, Herbert Cannon. Aspects of the speech in the later Roman epic. Johns Hopkins, 1907. Printed: Baltimore, J. H. Furst co., 1909. 48 p. L52

Lisle, Robert. The cults of Corinth. Johns Hopkins, 1955. L53

Litchfield, Henry Wheatland. Quibus virtutum vitiorumque moralium exemplis ex suorum annalibus sumptis scriptores latini antiqui usi sint. Harvard, 1911. Abstract: Harvard studies in classical philology, XXII (1911), 181. L54

Little, Evelyn Steel. Homer and Theocritus in English translation: a critical bibliography designed as a guide for librarians in the choice of editions for the general reader. Michigan, 1936. Abstract: Microfilm abstracts, III, 60−1. L55

Lloyd, Robert B. Servius and the Scholia Danielis on the Latin authors of the Republic. Johns Hopkins, 1952. L56

Loane, Helen Jefferson. Trade and industry of the city of Rome (50 B.C.−200 A.D.). Johns Hopkins, 1937. Printed: Johns Hopkins University, Studies in historical and political science, ser. LVI, no. 2 (1938). 158 p. L57

Lockhart, Philip North. The literary criticism of Servius. Yale, 1959. L58

Lodge, Gonzalez. The participle in Euripides. Johns Hopkins, 1886. Results appear in B. L. Gildersleeve, On the stylistic effect of the Greek participle. American journal of philology, IX (1888), 149−50. L59

Lofberg, John Oscar. Sycophancy in Athens. Chicago, 1914. Printed: Menasha, Wis., The Collegiate press, George Banta publ. co., 1917. 104 p. L60

Lombardo, Gregory. St. Augustine's De fide et operibus. Catholic, 1951. L61

Long, Charles Massie. Indicative apodoses with subjunctive protases in the unreal conditional sentences of Livy and Tacitus. Virginia, 1901. Abstract: University of Virginia abstracts of dissertations, 1935, p. 50. L62

Long, Herbert Strainge. A study of the doctrine of metempsychosis in Greece from Pythagoras to Plato. Princeton,
1943.   L63

Long, Omera Floyd. On the usage of quotiens and quotiens-
cunque in different periods of Latin. Johns Hopkins, 1897.
Printed: Baltimore, J. Murphy co., 1901. 48 p.   L64

Lopez, Robert Sabatino. State colleges, public monopolies, and
regalia in the Roman and Byzantine empires. Wisconsin,
1942. Abstract: Summaries of doctoral dissertations, VII
(1942), 144–6.   L65

Lord, Louis Eleazer. Literary criticism of Euripides in the
earlier scholia and the relation of this criticism to Aristotle's Poetics and to Aristophanes, with a note on the
Thanatos scene in the Alcestis. Yale, 1908. Printed: Göt-
tingen, Dieterichsche Univ.-Buchdr., W. F. Kaestner, 1908.
94 p.   L66

Lougee, Dora Aileen. The status of women as seen in the earlier
Latin patristic writers. Illinois, 1923. Abstract: Urbana,
1926. 9 p.   L67

Loughead, Charles Butler. De usu $\overset{\text{,}}{\alpha}\nu\tau\iota\theta\epsilon\sigma\epsilon\omega\varsigma$ apud Herodotum.
Harvard, 1908.   L68

Louison, Betty R. Greek and Roman embassies, 201–189 B.C.
Boston, 1947.   L69

Lowe, Clarence George. The text-tradition of pseudo-Plutarch's
Vitae decem oratorum. Illinois, 1924. Printed: Illinois
University, Studies in language and literature, IX, no. 4 (1924).
53 p.   L70

Lowther, Hugh Sears. The syntax of Martial. Pennsylvania, 1904.
Printed: Lancaster, Pa., Press of the New era printing co.,
1906. 36 p.   L71

Luce, Stephen Bleecker, jr. Quomodo pictores vasorum Graecorum facta Herculis illustraverint quaeritur. Harvard,
1913. Printed: The origin of the shape of the "Nolan" Amphora, American journal of archaeology, 2d ser., XX (1916),
439–74.   L72

Luce, T. James. Appian's exposition of the Roman republican
constitution. Princeton, 1958. Abstract: Dissertation abstracts, XIX, 2341.   L73

Luch, Myron Jacob. The Homeric Olympus. Tulane, 1925.
Printed: Philadelphia, Westbrook publ. co., 1925. 257 p.
L74

Lucki, Emil. The colonate in Frankish Gaul. Chicago, 1940.

Printed: Chicago, 1943. 153–160 p. L75

Ludlum, Charlotte P. Apuleius as a source for the social history of his time. Cornell, 1939. L76

Ludlum, John Henry, jr. Dual Greek text of Judges in codices A and B. Yale, 1957. L77

Lueker, Erwin Louis John. History and religious thought in Pindar. Washington, St. Louis, 1942. L78

Luibheid, Colm. The religious policies of Theodosius II. Princeton, 1961. L79

Lunceford, William M. The problem of the aorist participle in the New Testament. Southern Baptist, 1952. L80

Lund, Nils Wilhelm. Chiasmus in the New Testament. Chicago, 1941. Printed: Chapel Hill, University of North Carolina press, 1942. 428 p. L81

Luper, John T., jr. Aorist tense in the writings of Luke. Southwestern Baptist, 1934. L82

Lyding, Elizabeth. Homeric enjambement. Bryn Mawr, 1949. L83

Lynch, Charles A. De verbis alienarum basium adiumento suppletis in lingua Graeca. Harvard, 1936. L84

M

Maat, William Anthony. A rhetorical study of St. John Chrysostom's De sacerdotio. Catholic, 1944. Printed: Catholic University of America, Patristic studies, LXXI (1944). 85 p. M1

MacAdoo, Thomas Ozro. The modification of adjectives in Greek by means of prefixes. Illinois, 1952. Abstract: Urbana, 1952. 6 p. M2

McCartney, Eugene Stock. Figurative uses of animal names in Latin and their application to military devices; a study in semantics. Pennsylvania, 1911. Printed: Lancaster, Pa., Press of the New era printing co., 1912. 56 p. M3

McCartney, Thomas Benton, jr. On pronouns in oratio obliqua and kindred constructions. Virginia, 1902. Abstract: University of Virginia abstracts of dissertations, 1935, p. 51. M4

McCauley, Leo Paul. The value of accuracy of Porphyrio. Johns Hopkins, 1941. M5

McClernan, Marie. The periphrases in Thucydides. Wisconsin, 1904. M6

McCormick, John Patrick. A study of the nominal syntax and of
   indirect discourse in Hegesippus. Catholic, 1935. Printed:
   Catholic University of America, Patristic studies, XLIII
   (1935). 240 p.   M7

McCown, Chester Charlton. Testamentum Salomonis. Chicago,
   1915. Printed: The Testament of Solomon, edited from
   manuscripts at Mount Athos, Bologna, Holkham Hall, Jerusalem, London, Milan, Paris and Vienna. Leipzig, J. C.
   Hinrichs, 1922. 136, 166 p.   M8

McCrea, Nelson G. The state, as conceived by Plato and Aristotle. Columbia, 1888. Not available in Columbia University
   Library.   M9

McCredie, James Robert. Fortified military camps in Attica.
   Harvard, 1963.   M10

McCullagh, Paul Fletcher. The meaning of νόμος in Greek literature and thought from Homer to Aristotle. Chicago, 1939.
   Printed: Chicago, Private edition, distributed by the University of Chicago Libraries, 1939. 21–78 p.   M11

McCulloch, James A. A lexicographical study of Apuleius' Cupid
   and Psyche. Pittsburgh, 1951. Abstract: The Graduate
   school abstract of theses, 1952, p. 3–5.   M12

McCulloh, William Ezra. Tautometric repetition in the responsive lyrics of Sophocles. Yale, 1962.   M13

McDaniel, Walton Brooks. De quibusdam Hymnorum Homeri-
   corum locis corruptis coniecturae. Harvard, 1899. Printed
   in part: Harvard studies in classical philology, XI (1900),
   73–91.   M14

McDermott, William C. The ape in classical art and literature.
   Johns Hopkins, 1934.   M15

McDiarmid, John Brodie. Theophrastus and the pre-Socratics.
   A study in Theophrastus' use of Aristotle. Johns Hopkins,
   1940.   M16

Macdonald, Janet Malcolm. The uses of symbolism in Greek art.
   Bryn Mawr, 1918. Printed: Chicago, 1922. 55 p.   M17

McDonald, M. Francis, Sister. Saint Augustine's De fide rerum
   quae non videntur: a critical text and translation with introduction and commentary. Catholic, 1950. Printed: Catholic University of America, Patristic studies, LXXXIV (1950).
   147 p.   M18

McDonald, William A. The political meeting places of the
   Greeks. Johns Hopkins, 1940.   M19

MacDonald, William Allan. A history of Abdera, with a prosopographia and testimonia. Johns Hopkins, 1943.   M20

McDonald, William Francis. Ambitus: a history of electoral
corruption in the Roman Republic. Cornell, 1929. Abstract: Ithaca, N.Y., 1929. 6 p.   M21

McDonough, James A. The treatise of Gregory of Nyssa Contra
fatum: a critical text with prolegomena. Harvard, 1952.
M22

McElwain, Mary B. The imperative in Plautus. Cornell, 1910.
M23

McEnerney, John I. The poetic quotations of Dio Chrysostom.
Pennsylvania, 1950.   M24

McFayden, Donald. The history of the title imperator under the
Roman empire. Chicago, 1916. Printed: Chicago, University of Chicago press, 1920. 67 p.   M25

McGeachy, John Alexander, jr. Quintus Aurelius Symmachus
and the senatorial aristocracy of the west. Chicago, 1942.
Printed: Chicago, Private edition, distributed by the University of Chicago Libraries, 1942. 203 p.   M26

McGrath, Charles. Gregory of Nyssa's doctrine on knowledge
of God. Fordham, 1964.   M27

McGregor, Malcolm F. Kleon and the Athenian calendar. Cincinnati, 1937.   M28

Mach, Edmund Robert Otto von. Quaestiones archaeologicae
duae. I. De signo marmoreo quod vulgo Naucydis discobo-
lus appellatur. II. De praepositionis ἐπί apud Pausaniam
usu. Harvard, 1900.   M29

McIntosh, John Strayer. A study of Augustine's versions of
Genesis. Chicago, 1909. Printed: Chicago, University
of Chicago press, 1912. 130 p.   M30

McKay, Alexander Gordon. Athens and Macedon: a study of
relations from the sixth to the mid-fifth century B.C.
Princeton, 1950. Abstract: Dissertation abstracts, XV,
564.   M31

MacKay, Pierre Antony. Studies in the history of republican
Macedonia, 168–146 B.C. California, Berkeley, 1964. M32

MacKendrick, Paul Lachlan. De gente Attica Eumolpidarum.
Harvard, 1938. Abstract: Summaries of theses, 1938,
p. 6–8.   M33

McKenna, Stephen. Paganism and pagan survivals in Spain up to
the fall of the Visigothic kingdom. Catholic, 1938.   M34

Mackenzie, Donald Campbell. The reign of Caracalla. Princeton, 1949. Abstract: Dissertation abstracts, XV, 564. M35

McKeough, Michael John. The meaning of the rationes seminales
in St. Augustine. Catholic, 1926. Printed: Washington, D.C.,
1926. 114 p.   M36

McKibben, William T. Nonlocal uses of in with the accusative
in Apuleius. Chicago, 1942. M37

McKinlay, Arthur Patch. De operibus Boethii quaestiones variae.
Harvard, 1906. Printed: Stylistic tests and the chronology
of the works of Boethius, Harvard studies in classical philology, XVIII (1907), 123–56. M38

McLaurin, Eugene W. The influence of Hebrew and classical,
Septuagint, and Hellenistic Greek elements in the redemp-
tive terms of the Greek New Testament. Texas, 1952. M39

McLean, Hugh Arnold. Studies in Roman colonization. Wisconsin, 1954. Abstract: Summaries of doctoral dissertations,
XV (1955), 590–1. M40

MacLean, Robert A. Periphrasis in Attic tragedy. Chicago,
1912. Abstract: Abstracts of theses, Humanistic ser., II
(1926), 277–9. M41

McLemore, James Sugars. The tradition of the Latin accent.
Virginia, 1912. Printed: Charlottesville, University of
Virginia, 1917. 96 p. M42

MacLennan, John H. A history of Oxyrhynchus. Princeton,
1935. M43

McMahon, Amos Philip. On the second book of Aristotle's
Poetics and the source of Theophrastus' definition of tragedy. Harvard, 1916. Printed: Harvard studies in classical
philology, XXVIII (1917). 46 p. M44

McMahon, Robert Cecil. The technical history of the white
lecythi. Columbia, 1907. Printed: American journal of
archaeology, 2d ser., XI (1907), 7–35. M45

MacMullen, Ramsay. Manufactures for the state in the later Roman empire. Harvard, 1957. M46

McNeil, Donald Francis. The Arithmetica of Boëthius. Southern
California, 1941. M47

McNeil, Mary Donald, Sister. The manuscript tradition of St.
Jerome's Vita Sancti Hilarionis. Illinois, 1934. M48

Macomber, Herrick Mower. De licentiis metricis quae in canticis Sophocleis reperiuntur. Harvard, 1937. Abstract: Summaries of theses, 1937, p. 3–4. M49

MacQueen, David John. The notion of superbia in the writings of
St. Augustine with special reference to the De civitate Dei.
Toronto, 1959. M50

MacRae, D. A. The life of Sophocles, from the sources. Cornell,
1905. M51

McShane, Roger Burnham. The foreign policy of the Attalids of

Pergamum. Illinois, 1959. Abstract: Dissertation abstracts, XX, 1750.   M52

Macurdy, Grace Harriet. The chronology of the extant plays of Euripides. Columbia, 1903. Printed: Lancaster, Pa., The New era printing co., 1905. 128 p.   M53

McVeigh, Terrence A. The allegory of the poets: a study of classical tradition in medieval interpretation of Virgil. Fordham, 1964.   M54

McWhorter, Ashton Waugh. The effect of person on mood: a study based on the ambiguous form of question of the τί ποιήσω type in Aeschylus, Sophocles, and Euripides. Johns Hopkins, 1905.   M55

Madden, Arthur G. Cicero's political treatises and the principate of Augustus. Fordham, 1947.   M56

Maddox, Brougher Petty. The state policy of Antiochus Epiphanes with reference to religion. Southern Baptist, 1945.   M57

Magill, Helen. The Greek drama. Boston, 1877. Not available in Boston University Library.   M58

Magoffin, Ralph Van Deman. A study of the topography and municipal history of Praeneste. Johns Hopkins, 1908. Printed: Johns Hopkins University, Studies in history and political science, ser. XXVI, nos. 9-10 (1908). 101 p.   M59

Magoon, Wallace Herbert. A study of the literary purposes of etymologizing in the golden age of Latin literature. Michigan, 1940.   M60

Maguire, John Damien. De verborum in Livianis orationibus collocatione. Pennsylvania, 1900.   M61

Maguire, Joseph P. Sources of the pseudo-Aristotelian De mundo. Yale, 1936.   M62

Mahoney, Albertus, Brother. Vergil in the works of Prudentius. Catholic, 1934. Printed: Catholic University of America, Patristic studies, XXXIX (1934). 214 p.   M63

Mahoney, Catherine of Siena, Sister. The rare and late Latin nouns, adjectives, and adverbs in St. Augustine's De civitate Dei: a morphological and semasiological study. Catholic, 1935. Printed: Catholic University of America, Patristic studies, XLIV (1935). 202 p.   M64

Mahoney, Hildegarde Marie, Sister. The blind man in Greek legend and literature. Fordham, 1940.   M65

Main, John Hanson Thomas. Locative expressions in the Attic orators. Johns Hopkins, 1892.   M66

Malte, Eric C. Certain papyrological elements in the letters of St. Paul. Pittsburgh, 1947.   M67

Manahan, Henry R. The rewards of authorship at Rome. Northwestern, 1949. Abstract: Summaries of doctoral dissertations, XVII (1949), 5-8. M68

Manatt, James Irving. The earlier and later edition of Aristophanes' Clouds. Yale, 1873. M69

Mandra, Raymond. The time element in the Aeneid of Vergil. Columbia, 1934. Printed: Williamsport, Pa., The Bayard press, 1934. 256 p. M70

Mann, Jesse A. Essential import and the Aristotelian syllogistic. Catholic, 1958. M71

Mann, Mary Emmanuel, Sister. The clausulae of St. Hilary. Catholic, 1936. Printed: Catholic University of America, Patristic studies, XLVIII (1936). 130 p. M72

Manning, Clarence Augustus. A study of archaism in Euripides. Columbia, 1915. Printed: New York, Columbia University, 1916. 98 p. M73

Manning, Joseph M. The contribution of Dom Jean Mabillon, O. S. B., to the science of paleography. Fordham, 1950. M74

Manning, Richard Clarke. Correptio syllabae longae brevem sequentis quatenus apud scriptores fabulae palliatae in interioribus arsibus versuum iambicorum et trochaicorum admissa sit quaeritur. Harvard, 1896. Abstract: On a supposed limitation of the law of "breves breviantes" in Plautus and Terence, Harvard studies in classical philology, IX (1898), 87-95. M75

Mansur, Melvin White. The treatment of Homeric characters by Quintus of Smyrna. Columbia, 1940. Printed: New York, 1940. 81 p. M76

Marcellino, Ralph E. Some aspects of the metaphors of Propertius. New York, 1952. M77

Mare, William Harold. A study of the Greek βωμός in classical Greek literature. Pennsylvania, 1961. Abstract: Dissertation abstracts, XXIII, 1011. M78

Marique, Joseph Marie-Felix. Syrian immigrants to Rome from 200 B.C. to 230 A.D. Johns Hopkins, 1942. M79

Markman, Sidney David. The horse in Greek art. Columbia, 1943. Printed: Johns Hopkins University, Studies in archaeology, XXXV (1943). 211 p. M80

Markowicz, Walter Alexander. The text tradition of St. John Chrysostom's homilies on Genesis and Mss. Michiganenses 139, 78, and Holkhamicus 61. Michigan, 1953. Abstract: Dissertation abstracts, XIII, 802. M81

Marquand, Allan. The logic of the Epicureans. Johns Hopkins,
    1880. Printed: In C. S. S. Peirce, ed., Studies in logic. By
    members of the Johns Hopkins University. Boston, Little,
    Brown, 1883; p. 1–11.   M82
Marshall, Robert Thomas. Studies in the political and socio-
    religious terminology of De civitate Dei. Catholic, 1952.
    Printed: Catholic University of America, Patristic studies,
    LXXXVI (1952). 96 p.   M83
Marti, Berthe Marie. The adoration of the Roman emperor from
    Augustus to Charlemagne. Bryn Mawr, 1934.   M84
Martin, Alfred. A critical examination of the Wescott-Hort textu-
    al theory. Dallas Theological, 1951.   M85
Martin, Ernest Whitney. The birds of the Latin poets. Stanford,
    1910. Printed: Stanford University, Cal., The University,
    1914. 260 p.   M86
Martin, Gladys. Laus Pisonis. Cornell, 1917. Printed: Ithaca,
    N.Y. (?), 1920. 97 p.   M87
Martin, Henry. The language of Latin inscriptions of Spain.
    Johns Hopkins, 1907. Printed: Notes on the syntax of the
    Latin inscriptions found in Spain. Baltimore, J. H. Furst
    co., 1909. 49 p.   M88
Martin, Hubert Milton, jr. Aspects of statesmanship in Plutarch's
    Lives. Johns Hopkins, 1958.   M89
Mason, Cora Catherine. The ethics of wealth in early Greek
    thought. Radcliffe, 1944.   M90
Mason, Merle H. The Leonine Sacramentary, studied from the
    point of view of its general structure and its textual rela-
    tionship to other early Roman and Ambrosian sacramen-
    taries. Brown, 1945.   M91
Mather, Maurice Whittemore. Quo modo iaciendi verbi composita
    in praesentibus temporibus enuntiaverint et scripserint
    antiqui quaeritur. Harvard, 1894. Printed: Harvard studies
    in classical philology, VI (1895), 83–151.   M92
Matson, Frederick R., jr. A technological study of the unglazed
    pottery and figurines from Seleucia on the Tigris. Michigan,
    1939.   M93
Matthews, Gareth Blane. An interpretation and critique of the
    concept of the inner man in the epistemology of St. Augustine.
    Harvard, 1961.   M94
Matthews, Kenneth David, jr. Cicero and the age of Marius.
    Pennsylvania, 1961.   M95
Maurer, Joseph A. A commentary on C. Suetonii Tranquilli Vita
    C. Caligulae Caesaris, chapters I–XXI. Pennsylvania, 1948.
    M96

May, Edward Charles, jr. A rhetorical commentary on Cicero's
   Pro Cluentio. Princeton, 1942.   M97
Mazziotte, M. Martha, Sister. Julius Pomponius Laetus and his
   sources in the commentary on the Aeneid. Fordham, 1944.
   M98
Meader, Clarence Linton. A semasiological study of the pro-
   nouns hic and iste. Michigan, 1901. Printed: The Latin
   pronouns is, his, iste, ipse. New York, The Macmillan co.,
   1901. 222 p.   M99
Meagher, Luanne, Sister. The Gellius manuscript of Lupus of
   Ferrières. Chicago, 1936. Printed: Chicago, Private edi-
   tion, distributed by the University of Chicago Libraries,
   1936. 96 p.   M100
Meares, Kate deRosset. Literary patronage in the silver age of
   Latin literature. North Carolina, 1930. Abstract: Re-
   search in progress, 1929/30, p. 23.   M101
Medford, Richard Carl. Achilles, a study in ancient painting.
   Johns Hopkins, 1943.   M102
Meeter, Henrietta Josephine. The artists of Pergamum. Penn-
   sylvania, 1904. Printed: Lancaster, Pa., New era printing
   co., 1904. 45 p.   M103
Melville, J. On the Roman laws de ambitu. New York, 1901.
   M104
Mendell, Clarence Whittlesey. Sentence connection in Tacitus.
   Yale, 1910. Printed: New Haven, Yale University press,
   1911. 158 p.   M105
Mendelsohn, Charles Jastrow. Studies in the word-play in
   Plautus. I. The name-play, II. The use of single words in
   a double meaning. Pennsylvania, 1904. Printed: Pennsylvania University, Publications, Series in philosophy and
   literature, XII, no. 2 (1907). 155 p. (Only the first of these
   two chapters was the original thesis, presented under the
   title of The name play in Plautus.)   M106
Mendenhall, Maud H. Mineral resources of the Roman empire,
   sources of information and places of deposit. Wisconsin,
   1920.   M107
Menk, Edgar Allen. The position of the possessive pronoun in
   Cicero's orations. Iowa, 1925. Printed: Grand Forks, N.D.,
   1925. 71 p.   M108
Menke, Sebastian G. Elements of Cicero's concept of the common good in the orations. Iowa, 1949.   M109
Merithew, Doris. A paleographical and textual study of a fif-
   teenth century French manuscript of Cicero's De officiis.

Southern California, 1958. Abstract: Abstracts of dissertations, 1958, p. 40-2.   M110

Merker, Irwin L. Studies in sea-power in the eastern Mediter-
ranean in the century following the death of Alexander.
Princeton, 1959.   M111

Merritt, Robert Gray. Euripides and Yeats: the parallel pro-
gression of their plays. Tulane, 1963. Abstract: Dissertation abstracts, XXIV, 3463.   M112

Messenger, Harry Knowles. De temporum et apud Salvianum
usu. Harvard, 1925. Abstract: Summaries of theses, 1925,
p. 114-6.   M113

Messer, William Stuart. The dream in Homer and Greek tragedy.
Columbia, 1918. Printed: New York, Columbia University
press, 1918. 105 p.   M114

Messing, Gordon Myron. De consonantibus quae laryngophoni
vocantur, praecipue quod ad linguam graecam attinet. Harvard, 1942. Abstract: Summaries of theses, 1942, p. 6-7.
M115

Mierow, Herbert Edward. The Roman provincial governor as he
appears in the Digest and Code of Justinian. Princeton,
1925. Printed: Colorado College publications, Language
ser., III, no. 1 (1926). 54 p.   M116

Milden, Alfred William. The limitations of the predicative position in Greek. Johns Hopkins, 1899. Printed: Baltimore,
J. Murphy co., 1900. 43 p.   M117

Milham, Mary Ella. A glossarial index to De re coquinaria of
Apicius. Wisconsin, 1951. Abstract: Summaries of doctoral dissertations, XII (1952), 434-5.   M118

Miller, Anna Bertha. Roman etiquette of the late republic as
revealed by the correspondence of Cicero. Pennsylvania,
1913. Printed: Lancaster, Pa., Press of the New era printing co., 1914. 85 p.   M119

Miller, Charles William Emil. The participle in Pindar. Johns
Hopkins, 1886. Results appear in B. L. Gildersleeve, On the
stylistic effect of the Greek participle, American journal of
philology, IX (1886), 149-50.   M120

Miller, David LeRoy. Aristophanic comedy: a paradigm for an
inquiry into the possibility of comedy in a time of traditional
mythic and symbolic lack-function, and parabolically, a
paradigm for an inquiry into the adequacy of literary criticism of comedy in a time of methodological uncertainty.
Drew, 1963. Abstract: Dissertation abstracts, XXIV, 2468.
M121

Miller, Eugene Wesley. An index verborum of Pliny the Younger.
    Pittsburgh, 1932. Abstract: Abstracts of theses, VIII (1932),
    182–4.   M121a
Miller, Frank Justus. The Latinity of the younger Pliny. Yale,
    1892.   M122
Miller, James V. An inquiry into Plato's treatment of wealth.
    Boston, 1955.   M123
Miller, Mary Cecilia. The Elegiae in Maecenatem with introduc-
    tion, text, translation and commentary. Pennsylvania, 1942.
    Printed: Philadelphia, 1941. 176 p.   M124
Miller, Mary William, Sister. Rufini Presbyteri Liber de fide:
    a critical text and translation with introduction and com-
    mentary. Catholic, 1964. Printed: Catholic University of
    America, Patristic studies, XCVI (1964). 204 p.   M125
Miller, Wray. An analysis of the New Testament vocabulary.
    Pittsburgh, 1944.   M126
Miller, Wray. Diminutives in the New Testament. Southern
    Baptist, 1954.   M127
Milo, Ronald Dmitri. Aristotle on practical knowledge and weak-
    ness of will. Washington, 1963.   M128
Milroy, William McCracken. The participle in the Vulgate New
    Testament. Johns Hopkins, 1891.   M129
Minar, Edwin LeRoy, jr. Early Pythagorean politics in practice
    and theory. Wisconsin, 1940. Abstract: Summaries of doc-
    toral dissertations, IV (1940), 254–6.   M130
Minton, William Warren. A study of invocational formulae in
    early Greek oral poetry. Columbia, 1959. Abstract: Dis-
    sertation abstracts, XX, 4102.   M131
Misener, Geneva. The particle γάρ in Greek. Chicago, 1905.
    Printed: The meaning of γάρ. Baltimore, The Lord Balti-
    more press, 1904. 75 p.   M132
Mitchel, Fordyce W. An investigation of the chronological sys-
    tems used by Herodotus. Yale, 1954.   M133
Mitchell, Lynn Boal. The moods with quod and quia clauses in
    early and classical Latin. Cornell, 1906.   M134
Mittelstadt, Michael Charles. Longus and the Greek love ro-
    mance. Stanford, 1964.   M135
Mitten, David Gordon. Terracotta figurines from the Isthmian
    sanctuary of Poseidon. Harvard, 1962.   M136
Mix, Irving Russell. Marcus Atilius Regulus: exemplum his-
    toricum. Pittsburgh, 1961. Abstract: Dissertation ab-
    stracts, XXII, 863.   M137

Moe, Phyllis Gainfort. Titus and Vespasian: a study of two
    manuscripts. New York, 1963.   M138

Moehring, Horst Rudolf. Novelistic elements in the writings of
    Flavius Josephus. Chicago, 1958.   M139

Moeller, Walter Otto. The woolen industry at Pompeii. Mary-
    land, 1963.   M140

Moellering, Howard Armin. Plutarch's De superstitione in the
    context of his theological writings. Columbia, 1962. Ab-
    stract: Dissertation abstracts, XXIII, 1690.   M141

Moffatt, Elizabeth Claire. Ideas of knowledge in Sophocles'
    Oedipus Coloneus. Yale, 1964.   M142

Mohler, Samuel Loomis. The cestus. Pennsylvania, 1926.
    Printed: Philadelphia, 1926. 79 p.   M143

Molineux, Maria Ada. The ablative as used by Plautus. Boston,
    1882. Not available in Boston University Library.   M144

Molyneux, Agnes De Sales, Sister. The manuscript tradition of
    the Commentariolum petitionis of Q. Cicero. Cincinnati,
    1934.   M145

Monks, George R. The office of count of the privy purse in the
    late Roman empire. Michigan, 1938.   M146

Montgomery, Thomas Andrew. A linguistic study of the book of
    Matthew in manuscript I.I.6 of the Escorial Library. Wis-
    consin, 1956. Abstract: Dissertation abstracts, XVI, 118.
    M147

Montgomery, Walter Alexander. Dio Chrysostom as a Homeric
    critic. Johns Hopkins, 1899. Printed: Baltimore, J.
    Murphy co., 1901. 33 p.   M148

Mood, James Raider. Some peculiar usages of the Latin verb
    venire. Johns Hopkins, 1904. Printed: Some figurative
    usages of venire and ire. Baltimore, J. H. Furst co., 1907.
    47 p.   M149

Moody, Joseph N. The martyr cult and Prudentius. Fordham,
    1934.   M150

Moon, Albian Anthony. De natura boni [Aurelii Augustini]: a
    translation with an introduction and commentary. Catholic,
    1955. Printed: Catholic University of America, Patristic
    studies, LXXXVIII (1955). 281 p.   M151

Mooney, Robert Newman. Character portrayal and distortion in
    Ammianus Marcellinus. Michigan, 1955. Abstract: Disser-
    tation abstracts, XV, 575.   M152

Mooney, William West. The house-door on the ancient stage.
    Princeton, 1913. Printed: Baltimore, Williams & Wilkins
    co., 1914. 105 p.   M153

Moore, Frank Gardner. De societatis quam vocant initiis, sive
    quomodo scriptores antiqui, praesertim Plato, Aristoteles,
    Lucretius, societatis origines habuerint. Yale, 1890. M154
Moore, Helen Lanneau. The Greek words in Plautus and Ter-
    ence. North Carolina, 1955. Abstract: Research in pro-
    gress, 1955, p. 44-6.   M155
Moore, John Leverett. Servius on the tropes and figures of
    Vergil. Johns Hopkins, 1891. Printed: American journal
    of philology, XII (1891), 94-111.   M156
Moore, Louis Baxter. The stage in Sophocles' plays. Pennsyl-
    vania, 1896.   M157
Moore, Margaret Glover. The Roman colony of Salonae. Michi-
    gan, 1945.   M158
Moorhead, Paul Grady. The comments on the content and form
    of the comic plot in the Commentum Terentii ascribed to
    Donatus. Chicago, 1924. Abstract: Abstracts of theses,
    Humanistic ser., II (1926), 319-25.   M159
Moran, Mary Evaristus, Sister. The consolations of death in
    ancient Greek literature. Catholic, 1917. Printed: Wash-
    ington, D.C., National capital press, inc., 1917. 85 p. M160
Morgan, Morris Hicky. De ignis eliciendi modis apud antiquos
    commentatio. Harvard, 1887. Printed: Harvard studies in
    classical philology, I (1890), 13-64.   M161
Morin, Paul John. The cult of dea Syria in the Greek world.
    Ohio State, 1960. Abstract: Dissertation abstracts, XXI,
    882.   M162
Morris, Kay Don. A comparative study of Marcus Annaeus
    Lucanus and Seneca the philosopher. Ohio State, 1960.
    M163
Morris, Walton. The syntax of the dative case in Aristophanes.
    Johns Hopkins, 1960.   M164
Moscrip, Virginia. Literary patronage in Rome, 240-90 B.C.
    Chicago, 1929. Abstract: Abstracts of theses, Humanistic
    ser., VII (1930), 433-7.   M165
Moseley, Nicholas. Characters and epithets: a study in Vergil's
    Aeneid. Yale, 1925. Printed: New Haven, Yale University
    press, 1926. p. 104, liv.   M166
Moser, Arthur Hurst. Index verborum Eutropianus. New York,
    1931.   M166a
Moss, Beverly Turpin. Sextus Aurelius Victor — Liber de
    Caesaribus: a translation and commentary with introduction
    and notes. North Carolina, 1944. Abstract: Research in
    progress, 1942/45, p. 59.   M167

Moss, James Herbert. Indirect discourse in Antiphon, Andocides, Lysias, and Xenophon's Anabasis. Virginia, 1900.   M168

Motto, Anna Lydia. The extent and range of the ideas in Seneca's philosophy. North Carolina, 1953. Abstract: Research in progress, 1953, p. 40-1.   M169

Mountain, William John. A critical edition of Saint Augustine's De trinitate, book VIII. St. Louis, 1960.   M170

Mourelatos, Alexander. Phoebus Dionysius. The philosophy of Parmenides. Yale, 1964.   M171

Müller, Liguori George. [S. Aurelii Augustini] De haeresibus; a translation with an introduction and commentary. Catholic, 1956. Printed: Catholic University of America, Patristic studies, XC (1956). 229 p.   M172

Mueller, Mary Magdeleine, Sister. The vocabulary of Pope St. Leo the Great. Catholic, 1942. Printed: Catholic University of America, Patristic studies, LXVII (1943). 269 p.   M173

Muldowney, Mary Sarah, Sister. Word-order in the works of St. Augustine. Catholic, 1931. Printed: Catholic University of America, Patristic studies, LII (1937). 155 p.   M174

Mulvey, Thomas John. The seven books of Arnobius' Adversus nationes. New York, 1908.   M175

Murley, Joseph Clyde. The cults of Cisalpine Gaul as seen in the inscriptions. Chicago, 1920. Printed: Menasha, Wis., George Banta publ. co., 1922. 112 p.   M176

Murphy, Charles Theophilus. Quae ratio inter fabulas satyricas et comoediam antiquam intercedat. Harvard, 1935. Abstract: Summaries of theses, 1935, p. 4-7.   M177

Murphy, Francis Xavier. Rufinus of Aquileia (345-411), his life and works. Catholic, 1944. Printed: Catholic University of America, Studies in mediaeval history, new ser., VI (1945). 248 p.   M178

Murphy, Gerard James. The reign of the Emperor L. Septimius Severus from the evidence of the inscriptions. Pennsylvania, 1946.   M179

Murphy, John Paul. Barberini Latin manuscripts 67-76. Fordham, 1963. Abstract: Dissertation abstracts, XXIV, 4182. M180

Murphy, Mable Gant. Nature allusions in the works of Clement of Alexandria. Catholic, 1942. Printed: Catholic University of America, Patristic studies, LXV (1941). 124 p.   M181

Murphy, Paul Robert. De lingua antiqua Illyrica. Harvard, 1942. Abstract: Summaries of theses, 1942, p. 7-10.   M182

Murray, Augustus Taber. On parody and paratragoedia in
Aristophanes, with especial reference to his scenes and
situations. Johns Hopkins, 1890. Printed: Berlin, Mayer
& Müller, 1891. 50 p.   M183

Murray, Robert Duff, jr. The theme of Io in Aeschylus' Suppli-
ants. Princeton, 1949. Abstract: Dissertation abstracts,
XV, 406.   M184

Murray, Robert Joseph. The use of conditional sentences in
Saint John Chrysostom's homilies on the Gospel of Saint
John. Ohio State, 1960.   M185

Murray, Steuben Butler. Hellenistic architecture in Syria.
Princeton, 1912. Printed: Princeton, Princeton University
press, 1917. 54 p.   M186

Muscarella, Grace Freed. A Latin translation of the Pseudo-
Aristotle De Mundo by Argyropoulos: text and analysis.
Bryn Mawr, 1958. Abstract: Dissertation abstracts, XIX,
2606.   M187

Muss-Arnolt, William. The oracles in Herodotus. Johns Hopkins, 1888.   M188

Mustard, Wilfred Pirt. The etymologies in the Servian commentary to Vergil. Johns Hopkins, 1891. Printed: Colorado
College student annual publication, III (1892). 37 p.   M189

Myers, Abraham Linford. The use of the adjective as a substantive in Horace. Pennsylvania, 1919. Printed: Lancaster,
Pa., Press of the New era printing co., 1919. 61 p.   M190

N

Nadell, Jill Barbara. Alexander and the Romans. Pennsylvania,
1959.   N1

Naoumides, Mark. Greek lexicography in the papyri. Illinois,
1961. Abstract: Dissertation abstracts, XXII, 3651.   N2

Nash, Ronald H. St. Augustine's theory of knowledge. Syracuse,
1964.   N3

Needler, Mary Craig. The relation of the Eudemian to the Nicomachean ethics of Aristotle. Chicago, 1927. Abstract: Abstracts of theses, Humanistic ser., V (1928), 389-95.   N4

Nehrkorn, Helga. Die Darstellung und Funktion der Nebencharak-
tere in Lucans Bellum civile. Johns Hopkins, 1960.   N5

Nelson, Dotson McGinnis, jr. The articular and anarthrous pred-
icate nominative in the Greek New Testament. Southern
Baptist, 1945.   N7   (N6 omitted)

Nemiah, Royal Case. The life and works of Publius Rutilius
Rufus. Yale, 1916. N8

Nethercut, William Robert. Propertius and Augustus. Columbia,
1963. Abstract: Dissertation abstracts, XXIV, 3736. N9

Nettles, Kenneth James. A study of hilasmos and its cognates in
the New Testament. Southern Baptist, 1953. N10

Neudling, Chester L. The personalities of the Catullian circle.
Iowa, 1949. N11

Neuerburg, Norman. The architecture of fountains and nymphaea
in ancient Italy. New York, 1960. N12

Neumann, Harry Morris. On Plato's Euthyphro and its relation
to the Theaetetus and the Sophist. Johns Hopkins, 1962. N13

Neville, Kenneth Percival Rutherford. The case-construction
after the comparative in Latin. Cornell, 1901. Printed:
Cornell studies in classical philology, XV (1901). 86 p. N14

Newby, Jessie Dimpley. A numismatic commentary on the Res
gestae of Augustus, with four plates. Iowa, 1938. Printed:
Iowa studies in classical philology, VI (1938). 117 p. N15

Newton, Francis Lanneau. Studies in verbal repetition in Virgil.
North Carolina, 1954. Abstract: Research in progress,
1953/54, p. 42-3. N16

Newton, Homer Curtis. The epigraphical evidence for the reigns
of Vespasian and Titus. Cornell studies in classical philology, XVI (1901). 140 p. N17

Newton, Walter Russell. The interjections in Terence. Syracuse,
1899. Printed: Andover, Mass., Andover press, 1899. 81 p.
N18

Nibley, Hugh. The Roman games as a survival of an archaic
year-cult. California, 1939. N19

Nichols, Edward Wilber. The semantic variability and semantic
equivalents of -osus and -lentus. Yale, 1913. Printed: The
semantic variability and semantic equivalents of -oso and
-lento. Lancaster, Pa., Press of the New era printing co.,
1914. 42 p. N20

Nicolassen, George Frederick. The articular infinitive in Xenophon. Johns Hopkins, 1882. Results appear in B. L. Gildersleeve, Notes from the Greek seminary, American journal of
philology, III (1882), 198. N21

Niedzielski, Zygmunt. The Athenian family from Aeschylus to
Aristotle. Chicago, 1956. N22

Nims, Frederick Boyden. Cicero's law-court cases. North
Carolina, 1945. Abstract: Research in progress, 1942/45,
p. 60. N23

Noble, Alma N. Indices verborum omnium quae in Sexti Aurelii
     Victoris Libro de Caesaribus et incerti auctoris epitoma de
     Caesaribus reperiuntur. Ohio State, 1938.   N24
Nofer, Herman Frederick, jr. A collation of the Praxapostolos
     Gregory 049 in Romans. Dallas Theological, 1960.   N25
Norlin, George. Cosmogenical theories of the Greeks. Chicago,
     1900.   N26
North, Helen F. The concept of sophrosyne in Greek literature
     from Homer to Aristotle. Cornell, 1946.   N27
Norton, Frederick Owen. A lexicographical and historical study
     of διαθήκη from the earliest times to the end of the classi-
     cal period. Chicago, 1907. Printed: Chicago, Universi-
     ty of Chicago press, 1908. 71 p.   N28
Noss, Henry Heiney Boyer. The mystery of native copper in the
     ancient world. Princeton, 1960.   N29
Nugent, M. Rosamond, Sister. The literary treatment of virgin-
     ity in the first four centuries of Greek Christian literature.
     Catholic, 1942.   N30
Nutting, Herbert Chester. The uses of the independent subjunc-
     tive in Cicero's orations. Yale, 1897.   N31
Nybakken, Oscar Richard. An analytical study of Horace's
     ideas. Iowa, 1938. Abstract: Programs announcing candi-
     dates for higher degrees, 1937. 4 p.   N32
Nye, Irene. Sentence connection, illustrated chiefly from Livy.
     Yale, 1911. Printed: Weimar, R. Wagner und Sohn, 1912.
     141 p.   N33
Nyenhuis, Jacob Eugene. Homer and Euripides: A study in
     characterization. Stanford, 1963. Abstract: Dissertation
     abstracts, XXV, 460.   N34
Nyswaner, Roy W. The use of the Praecidanea of Dousa in
     seventeenth-century commentaries on Petronius. Pittsburgh,
     1937.   N35

                                    O

Oates, John Francis P. Yale Inv. 237 and problems of status in
     Ptolemaic Egypt. Yale, 1960.   O1
O'Brien, Mary Ambrose, Sister. "Mysticism" in the works of
     Cicero. Fordham, 1961. Abstract: Dissertation abstracts,
     XXIII, 228.   O2
O'Brien, Michael J. Virtue, knowledge, and the θυμοειδής,
     a study in Platonic ethics. Princeton, 1956. Abstract: Dis-
     sertation abstracts, XVIII, 226.   O3

O'Connell, Edmund B. The Quinctian gens. Pittsburgh, 1935.
Abstract: The Graduate school abstracts of theses, 1936,
p. 39–44.   O4

O'Connor, Charles James. The graecostasis of the Roman forum
and its vicinity. Wisconsin, 1904. Printed: Wisconsin University, Bulletin, no. 94, Philology and literature ser., III,
no. 2 (1904), 159–203.   O5

O'Connor, John Bartholomew. Chapters in the history of actors
and acting in ancient Greece, together with a prosopographia
histrionum graecorum. Princeton, 1908. Printed: Chicago,
University of Chicago press, 1908. 258 p.   O6

O'Connor, Margaret Brown. Religion in the plays of Sophocles.
Chicago, 1919. Printed: Menasha, Wis., George Banta publ.
co., 1923. 151 p.   O7

Odenkirchen, Carl J. The consonantism of the later Latin inscriptions: a contribution to the "vulgar Latin" question.
North Carolina, 1952.   O8

Odom, William Lee. A study of Plutarch: the position of Greek
women in the first century after Christ. Virginia, 1961. Abstract: Dissertation abstracts, XXII, 1617.   O9

Oertel, Hanns. De cottidiani sermonis in Q. Horatii Flacci
sermonibus vestigiis. Yale, 1890.   O10

Ogden, Charles Jones. The construction of the final and consecu-
tive infinitive in early Greek poetry. Columbia, 1909. Printed: De infinitivi finalis vel consecutivi constructione apud
priscos poetas graecos. New York, Columbia University
press, 1909. 65 p.   O11

Ogle, Marbury Bladen. Folk-lore and religious uses of the me-
dicinal herbs in Marcus Porcius Cato's De agricultura.
Johns Hopkins, 1907.   O12

Ogoroskin, Lillian. The effect of Roman imperial policy from
Augustus to Diocletian on the landowners of the Arsinoite
nome of Egypt. Michigan, 1946.   O13

Ojeman, Mary Renelle, Sister. Sancti Augustini De civitate Dei
liber primus: a sense-line arrangement, English translation
and rhetorical study. St. Louis, 1960.   O14

Olcott, George N. Studies in the word formation of the Latin inscriptions, substantives and adjectives, with special reference to the Latin sermo vulgaris. Columbia, 1898. Printed:
Rome, Sallustian typography, 1898. 267 p.   O15

Oldfather, Charles Henry. The Greek literary texts from Greco-
Roman Egypt: a study in the history of civilization. Wisconsin, 1922. Printed: Wisconsin University, Studies in the
social sciences and history, IX (1923). 104 p.   O16

O'Neil, Charles J. The structure and foundation of prudence in
    Aristotle. Toronto, 1939.   O17
O'Neill, Agnes, see Thomas Aquinas, Sister.
O'Neill, Eugene G., jr. Metrical studies in the distribution of
    individual words in Homer and Aratus. Yale, 1936.   O18
O'Neill, John Gerald. Ancient Corinth. Chicago, 1929. Ab-
    stract: Abstracts of theses, Humanistic ser., VII (1930),
    423-6.   O19
Oost, Stewart I. Roman policy in Epirus and Acarnania in the
    age of the Roman conquest of Greece. Chicago, 1951.   O20
O'Reilly, Mary Vianney, Sister. [Sancti Augustini] De excidio
    urbis Romae sermo; a critical text and translation with
    introduction and commentary. Catholic, 1955. Printed:
    Catholic University of America, Patristic studies, LXXXIX
    (1955). 95 p.   O21
Organ, Troy Wilson. An index to Aristotle. Iowa, 1942.   O22
Oscarson, Palme Joel Peterson. The satirical element in
    Lucan's Pharsalia. Yale, 1924. Printed: New Haven, Yale
    University press, 1924.   O23
Osmun, George Feit. Dialogue in Menander, Michigan, 1953.
    Abstract: Dissertation abstracts, XIII, 384.   O24
Ostwald, Martin. The unwritten laws and the ancestral constitu-
    tion of ancient Athens. Columbia, 1952. Abstract: Disser-
    tation abstracts, XIII, 87.   O25
Oswald, Michael Matthias F. The use of the prepositions in Apol-
    lonius Rhodius, compared with their use in Homer. Catholic,
    1904. Printed: Notre Dame, Ind., Notre Dame University
    press, 1904. 208 p.   O26
Otis, Brooks. De Lactantii qui dicitur narrationibus Ovidianis.
    Harvard, 1935. Abstract: Summaries of theses, 1935, pp.
    7-10.   O27
Otis, Margaret. The place and influence of Stesichorus, based
    upon a consideration of the original sources. Cornell, 1906.
    O28
O'Toole, Christopher John. The philosophical theory of creation
    in the writings of St. Augustine. Catholic, 1944. Printed:
    Catholic University of America, Philosophical ser., LXXXI
    (1944). 110 p.   O29
Otten, Robert Theodore. Metron, messos and kairos: a semasi-
    ological study. Michigan, 1957. Abstract: Dissertation ab-
    stracts, XVIII, 1419.   O30
Ould, Frances McAlpine Hopkins. The agoranomos in Ptolemaic
    and Roman Egypt. Wisconsin, 1937. Abstract: Summaries
    of doctoral dissertations, II (1937), 289-91.   O31

Overbeck, John Clarence, III. A study of early Helladic architecture. Cincinnati, 1963. Abstract: Dissertation abstracts, XXIV, 5350.   O32

Owen, Eivion. De ratione civili Aeschylea. Harvard, 1932. Abstract: Summaries of theses, 1932, p. 9–11.   O33

Owen, William Bishop. The customs and laws of naturalization at Athens. Chicago, 1901.   O34

Owen, William Howard, jr. Teiresias, a study in dramatic tradition and innovation. Princeton, 1963. Abstract: Dissertation abstracts, XXV, 461.   O35

P

Pacheco, Armando C. Plato's conception of love. Notre Dame, 1946.   P1

Pack, Frank. The methodology of Origen as a textual critic in arriving at the text of the New Testament. Southern California, 1948.   P2

Pack, Roger A. Studies in Libanius and Antiochene society. Michigan, 1934.   P3

Packer, Mary N. Porter. Cicero's presentation of Epicurean ethics; a study based primarily on De finibus I and II. Columbia, 1938. Printed: New York, Columbia University press, 1938. 127 p.   P4

Palmer, Elizabeth Hatch. The adnominal genitive in Thucydides. Yale, 1905.   P5

Palmer, Hazel. Italo-Corinthian pottery. Johns Hopkins, 1944.   P6

Palmer, Robert Everett Allen, II. Attitudes of Livy toward the incumbents of the chief Roman magistracies. Johns Hopkins, 1956.   P7

Palmer, Walter Hobart. The use of anaphora in the amplification of a general truth, illustrated chiefly from silver Latin. Yale, 1914. Printed: Lancaster, Pa., Press of the New era printing co., 1915. 82 p.   P8

Paluszak, Anthony Blase. The subjunctive in the letters of St. Augustine. Catholic, 1935. Printed: Catholic University of America, Patristic studies, XLVI (1935). 350 p.   P9

Pando, José Carlos. The life and times of Synesius of Cyrene as revealed in his works. Catholic, 1940. Printed: Catholic University of America, Patristic studies, LXIII (1940). 186 p.   P10

Panetta, William Crockard. The androgynous Heracles and
transvestism. Pittsburgh, 1942. Abstract: The Graduate
school abstracts of theses, 1943. p. 339-44.   P11

Panyik, Andrew. A critical and comparative study of the old
Latin texts of the book of Ezekiel and the minor prophets.
Princeton, 1938. Abstract: Dissertation abstracts, XII,
628.   P12

Pappano, Albert E. A critical text of the Casina of Plautus,
with introduction, analysis of the lyric meters, and metrical commentary. Washington, St. Louis, 1937.   P13

Park, Marion Edwards. The plebs in Cicero's day, a study of
their provenance and of their employment. Bryn Mawr,
1918. Printed: Cambridge, Mass., The Cosmos press,
1921. 90 p.   P14

Parker, Douglass Stott. Epicurean imagery in Lucretius' De
rerum natura. Princeton, 1952. Abstract: Dissertation
abstracts, XV, 576.   P15

Parker, Enid Rifner. The training of heirs in the Julio-Claudian
family. Duke, 1942.   P16

Parks, John Howard (i.e., Parks, Edilbert Patrick, Brother).
The Roman rhetorical schools as a preparation for the
courts under the early empire. Johns Hopkins, 1945. Printed: Johns Hopkins University, Studies in historical and political science, ser. LXIII, no. 2 (1945, i.e., 1946). 122 p.
P17

Parks, William Henry. Variations from Attic usage in St. Paul's
earlier epistles (Romans, I-II Corinthians, Galatians, I-II
Thessalonians). Yale, 1888.   P18

Parry, Adam Milman. Λόγος and ἔργον in Thucydides. Harvard, 1957.   P19

Parry, Hugh. The choral odes of Euripides: problems of structure and dramatic relevance. California, Berkeley, 1963.
Abstract: Dissertation abstracts, XXIV, 4182.   P20

Parsons, Arthur Wellesley. Klepsydra and the paved court of
Pythion. Johns Hopkins, 1942.   P21

Parsons, Wilfrid, Sister. A study of the vocabulary and rhetoric
of the letters of Saint Augustine. Catholic, 1923. Printed:
Catholic University of America, Patristic studies, III (1923).
281 p.   P22

Pascal, Cecil Bennett. The cults of Cisalpine Gaul. Harvard,
1956.   P23

Paschal, George Washington. A study of Quintus of Smyrna.

Chicago, 1900. Printed: Chicago, University of Chicago press, 1904. 82 p.   P24

Paschall, Dorothy May. The vocabulary of mental aberration in Roman comedy. Chicago, 1935. Printed: Linguistic society of America, Language dissertation, XXVII (1939). 88 p. P25

Patrick, George Thomas White. The fragments of the work of Heraclitus of Ephesus on nature. Johns Hopkins, 1888. Printed: A further study of Heraclitus, American journal of psychology, I (1888), 557-690.   P26

Patsavos, Christos Christou. A comparison of the Hellenic leagues of Philip II and Demetrius I of Macedonia. Michigan, 1957. Abstract: Dissertation abstracts, XVIII, 1403.   P27

Patterson, Marcia Lewis. Roman magistrates during the second Punic war. Bryn Mawr, 1941.   P28

Pavlovskis, Zoja. The influence of Statius upon Latin literature before the tenth century. Cornell, 1962.   P29

Peabody, Charles. De saturnio versu. Harvard, 1893.   P30

Peabody, Harlan Berkley. Hesiod's Works and days: an exemplar of the ancient Greek oral style. Harvard, 1961.   P31

Peachy, Frederic. The Homeric story of the Cyclops. Harvard, 1948.   P32

Peaks, Mary Bradford. The general, civil, and military administration of Noricum and Raetia. Chicago, 1905. Printed: Chicago University, Studies in classical philology, IV (1907), 161-230.   P33

Pearce, Nancy Rebecca. The political career of Aulus Gabinius. California, Berkeley, 1957.   P34

Pearl, Mary J. Bronzes of Herculaneum and Pompeii. Michigan, 1937.   P35

Pearl, Orsamus M. Fragments of tax rolls from Karanis. Michigan, 1938.   P36

Pearson, Lionel I. C. The tradition of the Atthis. Yale, 1939. P37

Pease, Arthur Stanley. De Sancti Hieronymi commentariolis tractatibusque in Psalmos quaestiones variae. Harvard, 1905.   P38

Pease, Samuel James. The technique of battle descriptions in the Greek historians. Chicago, 1932. Abstract: Abstracts of theses, Humanistic ser., IX (1934), 371-4.   P39

Peebles, Bernard Mann. De Sulpici Severi operum Martinianorum textus priscis fontibus. Harvard, 1940. Abstract: Summaries of theses, 1940 (1942), p. 8-11.   P40

Pendergast, Joseph Sylvester. The philosophy of history of
    Pompeius Trogus. Illinois, 1961.   P41
Penick, Daniel Allen. Herodotos in the Greek renascence. Johns
    Hopkins, 1898. Printed: Baltimore, John Murphy co., 1902.
    41 p.   P42
Peppler, Charles William. Comic terminations in Aristophanes
    and the comic fragments. Part I: Diminutives, character
    names, patronymics. Johns Hopkins, 1898. Printed: Balti-
    more, John Murphy co., 1902. 53 p.   P43
Peradotto, John Joseph. Time and pattern of change in Aeschylus'
    Oresteia. Northwestern, 1963. Abstract: Dissertation ab-
    stracts, XXIV, 3737.   P44
Percy, Garnet D. On the text of Lucan's De bello civili. Cali-
    fornia, 1935.   P45
Perkins, Elizabeth Mary. The expression of customary action
    or state in early Latin. Bryn Mawr, 1904.   P46
Perkinson, William Howard. Observations on the interrogative
    sentences in Plautus and Terence. Virginia, 1888.   P47
Perlzweig, Judith M. The epic and lyric tradition in Sappho and
    Alcaeus. Yale, 1948.   P48
Perrin, Bernadotte. The Elektra of Sophocles and the Choephoroi
    of Æschylus compared. Yale, 1873.   P49
Perry, Ben Edwin. The Metamorphoses ascribed to Lucius of
    Patrae, its content, nature, and authorship. Princeton, 1919.
    Printed: Lancaster, Pa., Press of the New era printing co.,
    1920.   74 p.   P49a
Perry, Charles Donald. The friends and acquaintances of Horace.
    Northwestern, 1947. Abstract: Summaries of doctoral dis-
    sertations, XV (1947), 5–9.   P50
Peters, Francis Edward. Aristoteles Arabus, the oriental trans-
    lations and commentaries on the Aristotelian corpus. Prince-
    ton, 1962.   P51
Petersen, Walter. Studies in Greek diminutives. Part I. Neuter
    substantives in -ιο-, except diminutives and hypocoristica.
    Yale, 1908. Printed: The Greek diminutive suffix -ισκος,
    -ισκη, Connecticut academy of arts and sciences, Trans-
    actions, XVIII (1914), 139–207.   P52
Peterson, Roy Merle. De vaticiniis apud poetas Graecos. Har-
    vard, 1912. Abstract: Harvard studies in classical philol-
    ogy, XXIII (1912), 170–1.   P53
Pharr, Clyde. Hellanicus and the Ionian logography. Printed:
    Weimar, R. Wagner Sohn, 1915.   P54

Phillips, Edward Emerson. On the historic worth of Aeschines'
   oration on the embassy. Harvard, 1880.   P55
Phillips, Henry. De vocis ἁμαρτία vi et usu apud scriptores
   Graecos usque ad annum CCC ante Christian natum. Har-
   vard, 1933. Abstract: Summaries of theses, 1933, p. 9–11.
   P56
Phinney, Edward Sterl, jr. Apollonius Rhodius. California,
   Berkeley, 1963. Abstract: Dissertation abstracts, XXIV,
   5394.   P57
Phoutrides, Aristides Evangelus. The chorus of Euripides.
   Harvard, 1915. Printed: Harvard studies in classical phi-
   lology, XXVIII (1916), 77–170.   P58
Pickel, Frank G. A study of the statement of generality in Livy's
   Ab urbe condita (I–X, XXI–XXX). Chicago, 1950.   P59
Pickhardt, Ernest W. S. De Aeschyli imaginibus. Columbia,
   1904.   P60
Pierce, Elizabeth Denny. A Roman man of letters, Gaius
   Asinius Pollio. Columbia, 1922. Printed: New York, 1922.
   81 p.   P61
Piper, William Taggard. De ratione nominum Romanorum
   praesertim de numero praenominum prisco. Harvard, 1883.
   P62
Pippin, Anne N. Moiragenes and Damis in Philostratus' Life of
   Apollonius. California, Berkeley, 1954.   P63
Pitcher, Seymour Maitland. The Anthus of Agathon. Iowa, 1937.
   Printed: American journal of philology, LX (1930), 145–69.
   P64
Pitman, Annie M. The treatment of nature in the poetry of the
   Roman empire during the Augustan age. Wisconsin, 1903.
   P65
Plass, Paul Christian. Plato's symbolism. Wisconsin, 1959.
   Abstract: Dissertation abstracts, XX, 1019.   P66
Podlecki, Anthony Joseph. The political background of Aeschy-
   lean tragedy. Toronto, 1964.   P67
Poduska, Donald Miles. Synonymous verbs of motion in Plautus.
   Ohio State, 1963. Abstract: Dissertation abstracts, XXIV,
   4685.   P68
Pohlsander, Hans Achim. Metrical studies in the lyrics of
   Sophocles. Michigan, 1962. Abstract: Dissertation ab-
   stracts, XXII (1962), 4347.   P69
Pollitt, Jerry Jordan. The critical terminology of the visual arts
   in ancient Greece. Columbia, 1963. Abstract: Dissertation
   abstracts, XXIV, 3679.   P70

Pope, Helen Müller Bley. Non-Athenians in Attic inscriptions. Columbia, 1935. Printed: New York, Cosmos Greek-American printing co., 1935. 231 p.   P71

Porges, Sarah Berman. A lease of an olive grove from the archive of Aurelius Isidorus (P. COL., INV. No. 65). Columbia, 1961.   P72

Porter, David Hugh. Book IV of Horace's Odes: an interpretive study. Princeton, 1962. Abstract: Dissertation abstracts, XXIV, 290.   P73

Porter, Howard Newton. The Hesiodic hexameter. Yale, 1942. P74

Poss, Richard H. The articular and anarthrous constructions in the Epistle of James. Southwestern Baptist, 1949.   P75

Poteat, Hubert McNeill. Repetition in Latin poetry, with special reference to the metrical treatment of repeated words. Columbia, 1912. Printed: New York, Princeton University press, 1912. 79 p.   P76

Poultney, James Wilson. The syntax of the genitive case in Aristophanes. Johns Hopkins, 1934. Printed: Baltimore, The Johns Hopkins press, 1936. 237 p.   P77

Powell, Benjamin. Erichthonius and the three daughters of Cecrops. Cornell, 1905. Printed: Cornell studies in classical philology, XVII (1906). 86 p.   P78

Powell, Margaret W. Adulteration in the early Roman empire. Indiana, 1939.   P79

Powers, Oscar S. Studies in the commercial vocabulary of early Latin. Chicago, 1941.   P80

Prakken, Donald Wilson. Studies in Greek genealogical chronology. Columbia, 1943. Printed: Lancaster, Pa., Lancaster press, 1943. 113 p.   P81

Pratt, Norman T., jr. Foreshadowing and suspense in the tragedies of Seneca and in his Greek predecessors. Princeton, 1935.   P82

Pray, Ruth Willis. The Neo-Platonic element in aesthetics. Chicago, 1925. Abstract: Abstracts of theses, Humanistic ser., III (1927), 27–32.   P83

Prendergast, Agnes Cecile, Sister. The Latinity of the De vita contemplativa of Julianus Pomerius. Catholic, 1938. Printed: Catholic University of America, Patristic studies, LV (1938). 185 p.   P84

Prescott, Henry Washington. De Daphnide commentatio. Harvard, 1901. Printed: Harvard studies in classical philology, XII (1901), 121–40.   P85

Prescott, Winston Townsend. The rule of the Gordians. Cornell, 1926. P86

Preston, Keith. Studies in the diction of the sermo amatorius in Roman comedy. Chicago, 1914. Printed: Menasha, Wis., George Banta publ. co., 1916. P87

Preus, Jacob A. O. Saint Jerome's translation terminology. Minnesota, 1951. P88

Price, Clifton. Commands and prohibitions in Horace. Yale, 1899. P89

Price, Helen. C. Suetonii Tranquilli De vita Caesarum liber VIII, Divus Titus; an edition with parallel passages and notes. Pennsylvania, 1915. Printed: Menasha, Wis., George Banta publ. co., 1919. 85 p. P90

Price, Robert George. Plato's Cratylus and contemporary analysis. Yale, 1963. P91

Pritchett, William Kendrick. The five Attic tribes after Kleisthenes. Johns Hopkins, 1942. P92

Proussis, Costas M. The subordinate characters in ancient Greek tragedy. Chicago, 1951. P93

Purinton, Carl Everett. Translation Greek in the Wisdom of Solomon. Yale, 1927. Printed: Journal of Biblical literature, XLVII (1928), 276–304. P94

Pusey, Nathan Marsh. Νόμοι Τῶν 'Aθηναίων. Harvard, 1937. P95

R

Rabie, Pieter Jacobus. Evidence of foreigners in the trades and professions of ancient Italy (based on the inscriptions). Michigan, 1943. R1

Rabinowitz, Wilson G. Aristotle's Protrepticus and the sources of its reconstruction: an analysis of the testimonia and of the first five fragments. California, Berkeley, 1955. R2

Radford, Robert Somerville. On Latin strong tenses and modes. A treatise on temporal and modal significance in the Latin indirect discourse. Virginia, 1891. Printed: Charlottesville, The Charlottesville Jeffersonian, 1891. 60 p. R3

Radford, Robert Somerville. Personification and the use of abstract subjects in the Attic orators and Thukydides. Johns Hopkins, 1895. Printed: Baltimore, 1901. 49 p. R4

Radin, Max. The legislation of the Greeks and Romans on corporations. Columbia, 1910. Printed: New Haven, The Tuttle, Morehouse and Taylor press, 1910. 147 p. R5

Radius, William Thomas. The discussion of St. Gregentius
    Archbishop of Taphar with the Jew Herban. Michigan, 1939.
    Abstract: Microfilm abstracts, V, 76-7.   R6
Ragland, George. The genitive case in Euripides. Johns Hop-
    kins, 1921.   R7
Raines, John M. Literary criticism in the writings of the poets
    of old Greek comedy. Cornell, 1935.   R8
Rainey, McKendree Llewellyn. The case-regimen of the verbs
    of hearing in classical Greek from Homer to Demosthenes.
    Johns Hopkins, 1904.   R9
Ralph, John Danby. Ephesis in Athenian litigation. Chicago,
    1936. Printed: Chicago, Private edition, distributed by the
    University of Chicago Libraries, 1941. 64 p.   R10
Ramage, Edwin Stephen. Urbanitas, rusticitas, peregrinitas:
    the Roman view of proper Latin. Cincinnati, 1957. Ab-
    stract: Dissertation abstracts, XVII, 2262.   R11
Rambo, Eleanor Ferguson. Lions in Greek art. Bryn Mawr,
    1918. Printed: Concord, N.H., 1920. 56 p.   R12
Ramsay, Hazel Grace. The Scriptores historiae Augustae: a
    critical study of the reliability as a source of the Vita Alex-
    andri Severi. Wisconsin, 1933. Printed: Government relief
    during the Roman empire, Classical journal, XXXI (1936),
    479-88.   R13
Ramsay, William. Diplomacy and propaganda of the Peloponne-
    sian war. Chicago, 1928. Abstract: Abstracts of theses,
    Humanistic ser., VI (1929), 305-10.   R14
Randolph, Charles Brewster. De mandragora. Harvard, 1905.
    Printed: The mandragora of the ancients in folk-lore and
    medicine, American academy of arts and sciences, Proceed-
    ings, XL 81905), 487-537.   R15
Rankin, Edwin Moore. Quas partes ei qui Μάγειροι vocantur
    in vita cotidiana Graecorum egerint quaeritur. Harvard,
    1903. Printed: The role of the Μάγειροι in the life of the
    ancient Greeks, as depicted in Greek literature and inscrip-
    tions. Chicago, University of Chicago press, 1902. 92 p.
    R16
Rapp, Albert. Studies in Greek verbal humor. Illinois, 1934.
    Abstract: Urbana, 1934. 8 p.   R17
Rau, Catherine Dunn. Plato's views on art. California, Berke-
    ley, 1945.   R18
Raubitschek, Isabelle K. Ionicizing-Doric architecture; a sty-
    listic study of Greek Doric architecture. Columbia, 1950.
    R19

Rayment, Charles Sanford. The unifying element in Lucan's
    Pharsalia. Michigan, 1941.   R20
Raymond, Alfred E. The literary structure of ritual passages
    in Sophocles. Chicago, 1949.   R21
Reagan, James Thomas. The material substrate in the Platonic
    dialogues. St. Louis, 1960.   R22
Reagan, Joseph Nicholas. Κήρυγμα Πέτρου, the oldest Christian
    apology. Chicago, 1921.   R23
Reckford, Kenneth Joseph. Horace, Augustan and Epicurean.
    Harvard, 1957.   R24
Reed, Ivy Kellerman. On the syntax of some prepositions in the
    Greek dialects. Chicago, 1904. Printed: Lancaster, Pa.,
    Press of the New era printing co., 1904. 79 p.   R25
Reents, Arthur Herman. The personal property and sources of
    income of M. Tullius Cicero. Nebraska, 1941.   R26
Rees, Kelley. The so-called rule of three actors in the classical
    Greek drama. Chicago, 1907. Printed: Chicago, University
    of Chicago press, 1908. 86 p.   R27
Reesor, Margaret E. The political theory of the Old and Middle
    Stoa. Bryn Mawr, 1951. Printed: New York, J. J. Augustin,
    1951. 60 p.   R28
Reeves, Charles H. Studies in the technical terminology of the
    Poetics of Aristotle. Cincinnati, 1947.   R29
Reiche, Harald A. T. A history of the concepts θεοπρεπής and
    ἱεροπρεπής. Harvard, 1955.   R30
Reichle, Lewis. De ab de ex praepositionum in inscriptionibus
    usu. Harvard, 1902.   R31
Reid, Charles W. A comparative study of the participial systems
    of the Sanskrit, Greek, Latin, and Teutonic languages. Bos-
    ton, 1887. Not available in Boston University Library. R32
Reider, Joseph. Prolegomena to a Greek-Hebrew & Hebrew-
    Greek index to Aquila. Dropsie, 1913. Printed: Jewish
    quarterly review, new ser., IV (1914), 321–56, 577–620; VII
    (1917), 287–366.   R33
Reilly, Katharine Campbell. Studies in the philosophical termi-
    nology of Lucretius and Cicero. Columbia, 1909. Printed:
    New York, Columbia University press, 1909.   R34
Reinhold, Meyer. Marcus Agrippa, a biography. Columbia, 1934.
    Printed: Geneva, N.Y., The W. F. Humphrey press, 1933.
    203 p.   R35
Reumann, John Henry Paul. The use of oikonomia and related
    terms in Greek sources to about A.D. 100, as a background
    for patristic applications. Pennsylvania, 1957. Abstract:
    Dissertation abstracts, XVII, 3007.   R36

Rexine, John Efstratios. The unity of authorship in Hesiod's
    Theogony and Works and days. Harvard, 1964.   R37
Rice, A. H. The Roman senate. Boston, 1905.   R38
Richards, John Francis Chatterton. De dialecto Milesia. Har-
    vard, 1934. Abstract: Summaries of theses, 1934, p. 6-10.
    R39
Richardson, Laurence, jr. Pompeii: the Casa dei Dioscure and
    its painters. Yale, 1952.   R40
Richardson, Louise Holman. De genere dicendi et casum usu
    Propertiano. Boston, 1891. Not available in Boston Uni-
    versity Library.   R41
Richardson, Rufus Byam. Marcus Aurelius. Yale, 1878.   R42
Ricketson, Robert F. Ablative after διά. Southwestern Baptist,
    1944.   R43
Ridington, William Robbins. The Minoan-Mycenaean background
    of Greek athletics. Pennsylvania, 1935. Printed: Philadel-
    phia, 1935. 94 p.   R44
Riedel, Ernest Henry. Verb-forms in Terence. Cornell, 1909.
    R45
Riggan, George A. The idea of original sin in the thought of
    Aurelius Augustine. Yale, 1949.   R46
Riley, Bruce T. Plutarch's treatment of the Isis-Osiris cult in
    his De Iside et Osiride. Boston, 1940.   R47
Ringwood, Irene Cecilie. Agonistic features of local Greek fes-
    tivals chiefly from inscriptional evidence. Part 1: Non-At-
    tic mainland and adjacent islands, except Euboea. Columbia,
    1927. Printed: Poughkeepsie, N.Y., 1927. 109 p.   R48
Rini, Anthony. Petronius in Italy from the thirteenth century to
    the present time. Columbia, 1937. Printed: New York,
    Cappabianca press, 1937. 181 p.   R49
Ritchie, Mary Helen. A study of conditional and temporal clauses
    in Pliny the Younger. Bryn Mawr, 1899. Printed: Philadel-
    phia, Avil printing co., 1902.   R50
Rivenburg, Marjorie Josephine. Fashionable life in Rome as
    portrayed by Seneca. Pennsylvania, 1938. Printed: Phila-
    delphia, 1939. 130 p.   R51
Robbins, Cleta Olmstead. Ionic chiton clad maidens of the fifth
    century. Bryn Mawr, 1942.   R52
Robbins, David O. Paradigmatism in the philosophy of Plato.
    Princeton, 1939.   R53
Robbins, Edwin Winslow. Theories of characterization in com-
    mentaries on Terence before 1600. Illinois, 1948. Abstract:
    Urbana, Ill., 1948. 8 p.   R54

Robbins, Frank Egleston. The hexaemeral literature; a study of
the Greek and Latin commentaries on Genesis. Chicago,
1911. Printed: Chicago, University of Chicago press, 1912.
104 p.   R55

Roberts, Arthur Wellington. De homicidiis apud Graecos. Harvard, 1883.   R56

Roberts, J. W. The use of conditional sentences in the Greek
New Testament as compared with Homeric, classical, and
Hellenistic uses. Texas, 1955.   R57

Roberts, Martha Lizzie. Status of woman in Roman law. Boston,
1896. Not available in Boston University Library.   R58

Robertson, Hartley Grant. The administration of justice in the
Athenian empire. Chicago, 1921. Abstract: Abstracts of
theses, Humanistic ser., I (1925), 283–90.   R59

Robertson, John Cunningham. The Gorgianic figures in early
Greek prose. Johns Hopkins, 1892. Printed: Baltimore,
The Friedenwald co., 1893. 41 p.   R60

Robinson, C. A. The figures and tropes in Isaeus. Princeton,
1901.   R61

Robinson, David Moore. Ancient Sinope, an historical account
with a prosopographia sinopensis and an appendix of inscriptions. Chicago, 1904. Printed: American journal of philology, XXVII (1905), 125–53, American journal of archaeology,
2d ser., IX (1905), 245–79, 294–333.   R62

Robinson, Dwight Nelson. Quibus temporibus religiones ab
oriente ortae et Romae et in provinciis romanis floruerint
desierintque quaeritur. Harvard, 1911. Abstract: Harvard
studies in classical philology, XXII (1911), 181–3.   R63

Robinson, Edward A. The date of Cicero's De legibus. Harvard,
1950.   R64

Robinson, Henry Schroder. Early Roman pottery from the Agora
excavations. Princeton, 1952. Abstract: Dissertation abstracts, XII, 3.   R65

Robinson, James Johnson. The Annals of Quintus Ennius. A pa-
per treating particularly of the verse. Yale, 1888.   R66

Robinson, Laura. Freedom of speech in the Roman republic.
Johns Hopkins, 1938. Printed: Baltimore, 1940. 93 p. R67

Robinson, Rodney Potter. De fragmenti Suetoniani De grammaticis et rhetoribus codicum nexu et fide. Illinois, 1920.
Printed: Illinois University, Studies in language and literature, VI, no. 4 (1920). 195 p.   R68

Robison, Henry Barton. Syntax of the participle in the apostolic
     fathers in the editio minor of Gebhardt-Harnack-Zahn. Chi-
     cago, 1907. Printed: Chicago University, Department of
     Biblical and patristic Greek, Historical and linguistic studies
     in literature related to the New Testament, 2d ser., Linguis-
     tic and exegetical studies, II, pt. 5 (1913). 46 p.   R69
Rodemann, Georg Richard. De Sibylla et Bacide. Harvard, 1889.
     R70
Roe, Nathaniel W. The final and self-sufficient good: an exami-
     nation of the foundation of Aristotelian ethical theory. Har-
     vard, 1953.   R71
Roebuck, Carl Angus. A history of Messenia from 369 to 146 B.C.
     Chicago, 1941. Printed: Chicago, Private edition, distributed
     by the University of Chicago Libraries, 1941. 128 p.   R72
Rogers, Cleon Louis, jr. A study of the Greek words for righ-
     teousness. Dallas Theological, 1962.   R73
Rogers, James Dennison. Language of Aeschylus compared with
     the language of the Attic inscriptions prior to 456 B.C.
     Columbia, 1894. Printed: New York, The Knickerbocker
     press, 1894. 58 p.   R74
Rogers, Virgil M. The old Greek version of Chronicles. Prince-
     ton, 1954.   R75
Rolfe, John Carew. The tragedy of Rhesus. Cornell, 1885.
     Printed: Harvard studies in classical philology, IV (1893),
     61-97.   R76
Rosborough, Ruskin Raymond. An epigraphic commentary on
     Suetonius's Life of Gaius Caligula. Pennsylvania, 1920. 46 p.
     R77
Rose, Grace L. Plato's interpretation of Heraclitus in the
     Cratylus. Johns Hopkins, 1939.   R78
Rose, Jesse L. The durative and aoristic tenses in Thucydides.
     Duke, 1938.   R79
Rosenblum, Manuel. The Gorgianic figures in the Greek and
     Latin rhetoricians. Cornell, 1934. Abstract: Ithaca,
     N. Y. (?), 1934. 7 p.   R80
Rosenmeyer, Thomas G. The isle of Critias. Harvard, 1950.
     R81
Rosenzweig, Irene. Ritual and cults of pre-Roman Iguvium, with
     an appendix giving the text of the Iguvine tablets. Bryn Mawr,
     1937 (?). Printed: London, Toronto [etc.], Christophers,
     1937. 152 p. (Studies and documents edited by Kirsopp Lake
     and Silvia Lake.)   R82

Ross, Cyril. An analysis of Greek Testament difficulties. Dallas Theological, 1952.   R83

Ross, Helen N. M. Terra-cotta figurines of Macedonia and Thrace. Johns Hopkins, 1939.   R84

Ross, James Thomas. The conception of σωτηρία in the New Testament. Chicago, 1947. Printed: Chicago, 1947., 304 p. R85

Roth, Joseph Moses. Greek papyri lights on Jewish history. New York, 1923. Printed: New York, 1924. 58 p.   R86

Rowe, Galen Otto. The adynaton and the statement of perpetuity in Greek and Latin poetry. Vanderbilt, 1963. Abstract: Dissertation abstracts, XXIV, 5394.   R87

Rowland, Robert Joseph. Roman grain legislation, 133–50 B.C. Pennsylvania, 1964.   R88

Rowland, William Tingle. On the position in the clause of ne and ut in certain documents of colloquial Latin. Columbia, 1918. Printed: New York, Columbia University press, 1918. 44 p. R89

Ruckh, Grace Bernice. The influence of Theocritus in antiquity. Cornell, 1943.   R90

Ruegg, Dominic, Brother. Sancti Aurelii Augustini De utilitate ieiunii; a text with a translation, introduction, and commentary. Catholic, 1951. Printed: Catholic University of America, Patristic studies, LXXXV (1951). 133 p.   R91

Rupprecht, Arthur Albert, jr. A study of slavery in the late Roman republic from the works of Cicero. Pennsylvania, 1960. R92

Russell, Frank Hamblin. The development of allegory in the classic pastoral. Chicago, 1923.   R93

Russell, Harris Livingston. The appropriate name in the Metamorphoses of Apuleius. 150 p. Illinois, 1943. Abstract: Urbana, 1942. 6 p.   R94

Russell, Joseph W. Scipio Maffei and Latin palaeography. Fordham, 1957.   R95

Russo, Joseph Anthony. Word localization and the formulaic nature of the Homeric hexameter: a study of Homeric language. Yale, 1962.   R96

Rutenber, Culbert Gerow. The doctrine of the imitation of God in Plato. Pennsylvania, 1945. Printed: Philadelphia, 1946. 115 p.   R97

Ruth, Thomas De Coursey. The problem of Claudius, some aspects of a character study. Johns Hopkins, 1916. Printed: Baltimore, The Lord Baltimore press, 1924. 138 p.   R98

Rutledge, Harry Carraci. Herodes Atticus: world citizen, A.D.
    101–177. Ohio State, 1960. R99
Ryan, Eileen Patricia. The verse adaptations of Avianus. Part
    1: The Astensis and its derivatives. Illinois, 1940. Ab-
    stract: Urbana, 1940. 5 p. R100
Ryan, George J. The relationship of the manuscripts of Athana-
    sius' De incarnatione. Michigan, 1934. R101

S

Sadler, J. D. A linguistic study of Excidium Troiae. Texas,
    1951. S1
Saffold, William Berney. The construction with iubeo, a portion
    of a dissertation treating of the construction with verbs of
    commanding. Johns Hopkins, 1898. Printed: Baltimore,
    J. Murphy co., 1902. 45 p. S2
Sage, Evan Taylor. The pseudo-Ciceronian Consolatio. Chicago,
    1909. Printed: Chicago, University of Chicago press, 1910.
    64 p. S3
St. Margaret, Mary, Sister. Dracontii satisfactio, with introduc-
    tion, text, translation, and commentary. Pennsylvania, 1935.
    Printed: Philadelphia, 1936. 115 p. S4
Saint-Stanislas de Jésus, Sister. L'art oratoire en Grèce (V–VI
    siècles). Montréal, 1943. S5
Sale, William Merritt, III. Aphrodite in early Greek epic poetry.
    Cornell, 1958. Abstract: Dissertation abstracts, XIX, 1371.
    S6
Salyer, William Clark. Marica, goddess of the Auruncians.
    Pittsburgh, 1939. Abstract: The Graduate school abstracts
    of theses, 1940, p. 311–6. S7
Samuel, Alan Edouard. Ptolemaic chronology: Soter, Philadel-
    phus, and Euergetes. Yale, 1959. S8
San Giovanni, Edoardo. De versu heroico Statiano ad Vergili-
    anum relato dissertatio. New York, 1908. Printed: New
    York University, Series of Graduate school studies, no. 1
    (1914). 29 p. S9
Sanders, Henry Nevill. The Cynegeticus of Xenophon. Johns
    Hopkins, 1903. Printed: Baltimore, The Friedenwald co.,
    1913. 32 p. S10
Sanford, John Augustine. The stage in the Attic theatre of the
    5th century, B.C. Minnesota, 1895. Printed: Minneapolis,
    University press of Minnesota, 1895. S11
Sapone, Gilbert Jude, Brother. Inscriptions illustrative of Ro-

man private life. Pittsburgh, 1953. Abstract: The Graduate
school abstracts of theses, 1944, p. 18–21.   S12
Sarikakis, Theodore Christos. The hoplite general in Athens.
Princeton, 1951. Abstract: Dissertation abstracts, XIII,
543.   S13
Satre, Lowell J. The technique of dual entrance in classical
drama. Iowa, 1949.   S14
Saunders, Catharine. Costume in Roman comedy. Columbiá,
1909. Printed: New York, Columbia University press, 1909.
145 p.   S15
Savage, Charles Albert. The Athenian family: A sociological
and legal study, based chiefly on the works of the Attic ora-
tors. Johns Hopkins, 1903. Printed: Baltimore, The Lord
Baltimore press, 1907. 137 p.   S16
Savage, Susan May. The cults of Trastevere. Bryn Mawr, 1940.
S17
Sawhill, John Alexander. The use of athletic metaphors in the
Biblical homilies of St. John Chrysostom. Princeton, 1926.
Printed: Princeton, Princeton University press, 1928,
116 p.   S18
Saylor, Charles Henry. A comparative scheme of the moods and
tenses in Cicero's translations from the Greek. Johns Hop-
kins, 1907. Printed: Baltimore, J. H. Furst co., 1911. 62 p.
S19
Scanlan, Mary E., Sister. Interest as found in Livy and his
methods of arousing it. Boston College, 1935.   S20
Schaeffer, Rudolf F. An English-Latin-Greek derivative lexicon.
Columbia, 1951.   S21
Scharlemann, Martin H. The influence of the social changes in
Athens on the development of Greek tragedy. Washington,
St. Louis, 1938.   S22
Schendler, Ann Elizabeth Jones. An Aristotelian theory of com-
edy. Michigan, 1955. Abstract: Dissertation abstracts, XV,
1392.   S23
Scherer, Bernard T. The Senecan notion of obligation and its
influence on Tertullian's prescription of heresy. Pittsburgh,
1960.   S24
Schieman, M. Bernard, Sister. The rare and late verbs in St.
Augustine's De civitate Dei: a morphological and semasiological study. Catholic, 1938. Printed: Catholic University
of America, Patristic studies, LIII (1938). 85 p.   S25
Schlaifer, Robert Osher. The Athenian state and religion. Harvard, 1940.   S26

Schlatter, Fredric William. Salamis and Plataea in the tradi-
    tion of the Attic orators. Princeton, 1960. Abstract: Dis-
    sertation abstracts, XXII, 252.   S27

Schlesinger, Alfred Cary. The gods in Greek tragedy, a study
    of ritual survivals in fifth-century drama. Princeton, 1924.
    Printed: Athens, P. D. Sakellarios, 1927. 142 p.   S28

Schlettler, Robert George. Cicero's oratorical career. Penn-
    sylvania, 1961. Abstract: Dissertation abstracts, XXII,
    1166.   S29

Schlicher, John Jacob. The origin of rhythmical verse in late
    Latin. Chicago, 1900. Printed: Chicago, 1900. 91 p.   S30

Schlunk, Robin R. The Homeric scholia and the Aeneid: a con-
    tribution to the comparative study of Homer and Vergil.
    Cincinnati, 1964.   S31

Schmidt, Austin Guildford. The effect of objective presentation
    on the learning and retention of a Latin vocabulary. Michi-
    gan, 1923. Printed: Chicago, Loyola University press,
    1923. 192 p.   S32

Schmidt, Firmin M. The resurrection of the body according to
    Tertullian: an analysis of De carne Christi and De carnis
    resurrectione. Catholic, 1951.   S33

Schneider, John Simeon. The scope and content of and some
    reflections upon the papyri for the period of Diocletian as
    found in the Oxyrhynchus collection. Wisconsin, 1931.
    Printed: The extent of literacy in Oxyrhynchus and its en-
    virons during the late third century A.D., Classical journal,
    XXVIII (1933), 670-4.   S34

Schnur, Harry C. The age of Petronius Arbiter. New York,
    1957. Abstract: Dissertation abstracts, XVII, 2263.   S35

Schoder, Raymond Victor. The classical canons of literary
    character portrayal: a critical synthesis. St. Louis, 1944.
    S36

Schoenheim, Ursula. A study of the major themes of Roman
    satire. Cornell, 1958. Abstract: Dissertation abstracts,
    XIX, 3298.   S37

Scholz, Richard Frederick. Municipal and feudal tendencies in
    Roman imperial administration, with special references to
    the edict of Caracalla. Wisconsin, 1911. Abstract: Ab-
    stracts of theses, I (1917), 83-108.   S38

Schoonover, Draper Tolman. A study of Cn. Domitius Corbulo
    as found in the Annals of Tacitus. Chicago, 1908. Printed:
    Chicago, University of Chicago press, 1909. 55 p.   S39

Schuler, Carl U. The provincial assembly of the Macedonians.
    Wisconsin, 1953.   S40

Schullian, Dorothy May. External stimuli to literary production
in Rome, 90 B.C. to 27 B.C. Chicago, 1932. Printed: Chicago, Private edition, distributed by the University of Chicago Libraries, 1932. 119 p.   S41

Schuman, Verns B. Tax rolls from Karanis. Michigan, 1937.
S42

Schweigert, Eugene W. Studies in select new documents from
the Athenian Agora. Cincinnati, 1940. Printed: Greek inscriptions, Hesperia, IX (1940), 309–57.   S43

Scott, George. The preposition in Horace. Yale, 1890.   S44

Scott, John Adams. A comparative study of Hesiod and Pindar.
Johns Hopkins, 1897. Printed: Chicago, University of Chicago press, 1898. 49 p.   S45

Scott, Kenneth. The identification of Augustus with Romulus-
Quirinus. Wisconsin, 1925. Printed: American philological
association, Transactions, LVI (1925), 82–105.   S46

Scott, Russell True, jr. Religion and philosophy in the history
of Tacitus. Yale, 1964.   S47

Scott, William Clyde. The oral nature of the Homeric simile.
Princeton, 1963.   S48

Scramuzza, Vincent Mary. The Emperor Claudius. Harvard,
1929. Printed: Cambridge, Mass., Harvard University
press, 1940. 328 p. (Harvard historical studies, XLIV).
S49

Scranton, Robert Lorentz. The chronology of Greek walls. Chicago, 1939. Printed: Chicago, 1941. 29 p.   S50

Seaman, William Millard. The appropriate name in Plautus.
Illinois, 1939. Abstract: Urbana, 1941. 7 p.   S51

Sears, Otis Burgess. On Latin conditional sentences of unreality
in indirect discourse proper. Virginia, 1902. Printed:
Charlottesville (?), 1902.   S52

Sears, Vaudrey W. The use of the future tense in the New Testament. Southern Baptist, 1950.   S53

Seaver, James E. The Jews in the Roman Empire from Constantine to Theodosius II. Cornell, 1947.   S54

Seay, Dorothy R. Tests of authorship in the Corpus tibullianum.
Chicago, 1945.   S55

Segal, Charles Paul. Reason, emotion, and society in the sophists
and Democritus. Harvard, 1961.   S56

Seidenadel, Charles William. Quid de musicae universae eiusque
aliquot partium singularum potestate ἦθος aut πάθος et
exprimendi et efficiendi veterum graecorum scriptores, im-
primis Plato nec non Aristoteles iudicarint. Chicago, 1897.
S57

Seittelman, Elizabeth E. A study of the dramaturgical functions
    of the prayers in the comedies of Aristophanes. Fordham,
    1952.   S58
Sell, Lewis Lazarus. De Catulli carmine sexagesimo quarto
    quaestiones diversae. Columbia, 1918. Printed: New York,
    W. D. Gray, 1918. 110 p.   S59
Semple, William Tunstall. Authenticity and sources of the
    Origo gentis romanae. Princeton, 1910. Printed: Cincin-
    nati University, University studies, ser. 2, VI, no. 2 (1910).
    47 p.   S60
Senftner, A. On the problem of Cicero's De inventione and the
    Rhetorica ad Herennium. New York, 1904.   S61
Senger, Joachim Henry. Aristophanes' use of the preposition.
    California, 1888.   S62
Settle, James Norwood. The publication of Cicero's orations.
    North Carolina, 1962. Abstract: Research in progress,
    1961–62, p. 33.   S63
Setton, Kenneth Meyer. Christian attitude toward the emperor
    in the fourth century, especially as shown in addresses to
    the emperor. Columbia, 1941.   S64
Shaeffer, Rudolf Franz. An English-Latin derivative lexicon.
    Columbia, 1951. Abstract: Microfilm abstracts, XI, 672–
    4.   S65
Shaffer, William Frederick. The administration of the Roman
    province of Galatia from 25 B.C. to A.D. 72. Princeton,
    1946. Abstract: Dissertation abstracts, XII, 257.   S66
Shannon, Charles H. Repetition in Aeschylus. Wisconsin,
    1897.   S67
Shapiro, Leo. A dictionary of some normative terms in Aristot-
    le's rhetoric. Northwestern, 1947. Abstract: Summaries
    of doctoral dissertations, XV (1947), 73–82.   S68
Sharrard, George M. A history of the dative with intransitive
    compound verbs for the pre-Augustan period. Cornell,
    1908.   S69
Shaw, Chandler. A study of Perugia in pre-historic and Etruscan
    times. North Carolina, 1935. Abstract: Research in prog-
    ress, 1934/35, p. 49–50.   S70
Shear, Theodore Leslie. The influence of Plato on St. Basil.
    Johns Hopkins, 1904. Printed: Baltimore, J. H. Furst co.,
    1906. 60 p.   S71
Shechter, Stanley Jacob. The Hellenistic aition in Virgil's
    Georgics. Harvard, 1964.   S72

Sheerin, Joseph Edward. Studies in the interpretation of Hera-
  clitus' Proem. California, Berkeley, 1957.   S73
Sheldon, Edward Louis. Publius Cornelius Dolabella. New York,
  1937. Printed: New York, Published under the auspices of
  the Graduate school of New York University, 1939. 27 p.
  S74
Shelley, Henry Vogel. A study of piety in the Greek tragic chorus.
  Pennsylvania, 1919.   S75
Sheridan, James. Horace's Ars poetica and its relation to previ-
  ous works on literary criticism. Toronto, 1944.   S76
Sherlock, Richard Bartholomew. The syntax of the nominal
  forms of the verb, exclusive of the participle, in St. Hilary.
  Catholic, 1948. Printed: Catholic University of America,
  Patristic studies, LXXVI (1947). 365 p.   S77
Sherman, Charles Lawton. Quo modo ingenia moresque perso-
  narum descripserit Aeschylus. Harvard, 1928. Abstract:
  Summaries of theses, 1928 (1931), p. 5–7.   S78
Shero, Lucius Rogers. The satirist's apologia. Wisconsin, 1919.
  Printed: Wisconsin University, Studies in language and lit-
  erature, XV (1922), 148–67.   S79
Shields, Emily Ledyard. The cults of Lesbos. Johns Hopkins,
  1915. Printed: Menasha, Wis., George Banta publ. co.,
  1917. 100 p.   S80
Shipley, Frederick William. A palaeographical study of an un-
  used MS of Livy, Cod. regin. 762. Chicago, 1901. Printed:
  Certain sources of corruption in Latin manuscripts; A study
  based upon two manuscripts of Livy: Codex puteanus (fifth
  century), and its copy, Codex reginensis 762 (ninth century).
  Classical journal, I (1906), 237. American journal of archae-
  ology, 2d ser., VIII (1903), 1–25, 157–97, 405–28.   S81
Shisler, Famee Lorene. The technique of the portrayal of emo-
  tion in Greek tragedy. Michigan, 1942.   S82
Shoe, Lucy T. Profiles of Greek architectural mouldings. Bryn
  Mawr, 1935.   S83
Short, Henry Alford. On the development and use of ὡς final.
  Johns Hopkins, 1885. Results appear in B. L. Gildersleeve,
  On the final sentence in Greek, American journal of philol-
  ogy, IV (1883), 416–44.   S84
Showerman, Grant. The great mother of the gods. Wisconsin,
  1901. Printed: Wisconsin University, Bulletin, no. 43,
  Philology and literature ser., I, no. 3 (1901), 221–333.   S85
Shriver, John R. Documents from the Persian wars. Cincin-
  nati, 1964.   S86

Shute, Clarence W. The psychology of Aristotle; an analysis of
    the living being. Columbia, 1941. Printed: Columbia
    studies in philosophy, I (1941). 148 p.   S87
Sibley, Henry Orrin. Mythical elements in Roman literature.
    Syracuse, 1893. (Cf. also dissertation by S. T. Dial, Syra-
    cuse, 1894.)   S88
Siefert, George J., jr. Meter and case in the Latin elegiac
    pentameter. Pennsylvania, 1948.   S89
Sihler, Ernest Gottlieb. Plato's use of metaphor and comparison.
    Johns Hopkins, 1878.   S90
Silverman, Irving S. Augustus and his opponents. Washington,
    St. Louis, 1946.   S91
Simonds, Roger Tyrrell. The naturalistic philosophy in classical
    Roman law. Yale, 1957.   S92
Simonds, Thomas Stanley. The themes treated by the elder
    Seneca. Johns Hopkins, 1896. Printed: Baltimore, The
    Friedenwald co., 1899. 100 p.   S93
Simpson, Adelaide Douglas. M. Minvcii Felicis Octavivs, prole-
    gomena, text and critical notes. Columbia, 1938. Printed:
    New York, 1938. 110 p.   S94
Simpson, Stephen Michael. Chariot and bow and arrow metaphors
    for poetry in Pindar's Epinician odes. Yale, 1964.   S95
Sinaiko, Herman L. Dialogue and dialectic in Plato. Chicago,
    1961.   S96
Sinclair, Donald E. The value and practical use of New Testa-
    ment Greek in Bible translation works. Dallas Theological,
    1955.   S97
Singer, Mary Rebecca White. Octavia Minor, sister of Augustus:
    an historical and biographical study. Duke, 1945.   S98
Sinnigen, William Gurnee. The officium of the urban prefecture
    during the later Roman empire. Michigan, 1954. Abstract:
    Dissertation abstracts, XIV, 1203.   S99
Skalet, Charles Hannord. Sicyon, an archaeological and histori-
    cal study with a prosopographia Sicyonia. Johns Hopkins,
    1923. Printed: Chapters in the history of ancient Sicyon.
    Baltimore, The Johns Hopkins press, 1928. 62 p.   S100
Skerrett, Harriet Margretta Thompson. C. Suetonii Tranquilli
    De vita Caesarum liber VIII Divus Vespasianus: Suetonius's
    life of Vespasian with notes and parallel passages. Pennsyl-
    vania, 1915. Printed: Philadelphia, 1924. 121 p.   S101
Slaten, Arthur Wakefield. Qualitative nouns in the Pauline Epis-
    tles and their translation in the revised version. Chicago,

1913. Printed: Chicago, University of Chicago press, 1918.
70 p.   S102

Slaughter, Moses Stephen. The substantives of Terence. Johns
Hopkins, 1891. Printed: Boston, Press of Rockwell and
Churchill, 1891. 57 p.   S103

Sledd, Andrew. Sentence connection in the letters of Pliny. Yale,
1903.   S104

Small, Stuart Gerard Paul. The epigrams of Marcus Argentarius:
introduction, revised text and commentary. Cincinnati, 1942.
S105

Smertenko, Clara Elizabeth Millerd. On the interpretation of
Empedocles. Chicago, 1901. Printed: Chicago, University of Chicago press, 1908. 94 p.   S106

Smetana, Alexander. The best form of government according to
Aristotle, Cicero, St. Thomas, and Locke. Catholic, 1951.
S107

Smiley, Charles Newton. Latinitas and ἑλληνισμός : the influ-
ence of the stoic theory of style as shown in the writings of
Dionysius, Quintilian, Pliny the Younger, Tacitus, Fronto,
Aulus Gellius and Sextus Empiricus. Wisconsin, 1906.
Printed: Wisconsin University, Bulletin, no. 143, Philology
and literature ser., III (1906), 205–72.   S108

Smith, Charles Sidney. Metaphor and comparison in Epistulae
ad Lucilium of L. Annaeus Seneca. Johns Hopkins, 1906.
Printed: Baltimore, J. H. Furst co., 1910. 192 p.   S109

Smith, David Eugene. Polygnotos ethnographos — Polygnotos,
the painter of character. Syracuse, 1887.   S110

Smith, Edith Marion. Naukratis, a chapter in the history of the
hellenization of Egypt. Bryn Mawr, 1924. Printed: Vienna,
1926. 88 p.   S111

Smith, Edwin Oscar. The character of Oedipus in the Oedipus
Rex of Sophocles. Stanford, 1926. Abstract: Abstract of
dissertations for degree of doctor of philosophy, I (1924–
1926), 87–90.   S112

Smith, Kendell Kerfoot. Quid peregrini prioribus saeculis
Athenis habitantes ad artes attulerint. Harvard, 1909. S113

Smith, Kirby Flower. Archaisms of Terence mentioned in the
commentary of Donatus. Johns Hopkins, 1889.   S114

Smith, Leslie F. The genuineness of the ninth and third letters
of Isocrates. Columbia, 1940. Printed: Lancaster, Pa.,
1940. 44 p.   S115

Smith, Lilian S. On the adnominal genitive in Tacitus. Cornell,
1905.   S116

Smith, Mattie Frances. The technique of solution in Roman
    comedy. Chicago, 1940. Printed: Chicago, Private edition,
    distributed by the University of Chicago Libraries, 1940.
    136 p.   S117
Smith, Minnie Jameson. Fear of eastern influences in Roman
    life as expressed in Latin literature of the republic. North
    Carolina, 1932. Abstract: Research in progress, 1931–32,
    p. 20.   S118
Smith, Peter Lawson. Ausonius' verse techniques. Yale, 1958.
    S119
Smith, Ralph D. The idea of God in the philosophy of Aristotle.
    American, 1934.   S120
Smith, Richard Carlisle, jr. Hellenistic attitudes toward war.
    Illinois, 1961. Abstract: Dissertation abstracts, XXII, 3622.
    S121
Smith, Wesley D. Dramatic structure and technique in Euripides'
    Suppliants. Harvard, 1955.   S122
Smithson, Evelyn Lord. A study of the find-groups of submycene-
    an, protogeometric and earliest date from the excavations
    of the Athenian Agora, 1931–55. Bryn Mawr, 1956.   S123
Smothers, Edgar R. The twofold tradition of Saint John Chrysos-
    tom's Homilies on Acts. Michigan, 1937.   S124
Smutny, Robert Jaroslav. The text history of the epigrams of
    Theocritus. California, Berkeley, 1953. Printed: California
    University, Publications in classical philology, XV, no. 2
    (1955), 29–94.   S125
Snowden, Frank Martin, jr. De servis libertisque Pompeianis.
    Harvard, 1944. Abstract: Summaries of theses, 1943–45,
    p. 7–10.   S126
Snyder, Walter F. Chronological studies in the history of the Ro-
    man emperors. Yale, 1936.   S127
Sochatoff, A. Fred. The commentary in the MSS. d, k, m, of
    Petronius. Pittsburgh, 1934.   S128
Soffray, Marius, Brother. Étude sur la syntaxe de Saint Jean
    Chrysostome. Montréal, 1934. Printed: Recherches sur la
    syntaxe de saint Jean Chrysostome d'après les "Homélies
    sur les statues." Paris, Société d'édition "Les belles let-
    tres," 1939. 261 p.   S129
Soho, Aristogeiton Marcus. Did the lion exist in Greece within
    historic times? Johns Hopkins, 1898.   S130
Soles, Myrtle. Studies in colloquial language in the poems of
    Catullus. Michigan, 1954. Abstract: Dissertation abstracts,
    XIV, 669.   S131

Soulé, Henry D. B. The cults of Plataea and the Daedala. Cali-
    fornia, 1941.   S132
Southern, Paul. The New Testament use of the preposition κατά
    with special reference to its distributive aspects. Southern
    Baptist, 1949.   S133
Spence, Emily Marie. Studies in the topography and history of
    the Argolid in the fifth century B.C. Bryn Mawr, 1962. S134
Spencer, Floyd Albert. The influence of Isocrates in antiquity.
    Chicago, 1924. Abstract: Abstracts of theses, Humanistic
    ser., II (1926), 287–92.   S135
Sperling, Jerome. Troy I. Cincinnati, 1937.   S136
Spiegel, Daniel. Aristotle's biology and the paradoxographers.
    Cornell, 1951.   S137
Spieker, Edward Henry. On the so-called genitive absolute and
    its use especially in the Attic orators. Johns Hopkins, 1882.
    Printed: American journal of philology, IV (1885), 310–43.
    S138
Spitzer, Adele Ruth. The unity of Plato's theory of art. Yale,
    1962.   S139
Spring, Evelyn. A study of exposition in Greek tragedy. Rad-
    cliffe, 1915. Printed: Harvard studies in classical philol-
    ogy, XXVIII (1917), 135–224.   S140
Springer, Lawrence A. Temple treasures, a study based on Livy.
    Pennsylvania, 1949. Printed: Philadelphia, 1949. 74 p.
    S141
Stagakis, George John. Institutional aspects of the hetairos rela-
    tion. Wisconsin, 1963.   S142
Stahl, William H. The moon in early medicine. New York, 1934.
    S143
Stanley, Alice Davies. Lucius Aemilius Paulus. Bryn Mawr,
    1954. Abstract: Dissertation abstracts, XV, 397.   S144
Stanley, Dennis Keith, jr. Cosmos and demiurge in Roman poet-
    ic tradition. Johns Hopkins, 1961.   S145
Stannard, Jesse Willmert. The psychology of passions in the
    Old Stoa. Illinois, 1958.   S146
Stansfield, Martha. The use of personal names in Roman satire.
    Chicago, 1932. Abstract: Abstracts of theses, Humanistic
    ser., IX (1934), 393–400.   S147
Starr, Chester G., jr. The Roman imperial navy to the age of
    Diocletian. Cornell, 1938.   S148
Stearn, Clement Hodgson. Aristophanes and his audience. To-
    ronto, 1940.   S149
Stecchini, Livio C. Origin of money in Greece. Harvard, 1946.
    S150

Steele, Robert Benson. Chiasmus in Sallust, Caesar, Tacitus
    and Justinus. Johns Hopkins, 1890. Printed: Northfield,
    Minn., Press of Independent publ. co., 1891. 61 p.   S151
Stein, James Aloysius, Sister. Encomium of Saint Gregory,
    bishop of Nyssa, on his brother Saint Basil, archbishop of
    Cappadocian Caesarea; a commentary, with a revised text,
    introduction, and translation. Catholic, 1928. Printed:
    Catholic University of America, Patristic studies, XVII
    (1928). 166 p.   S152
Steiner, Grundy. The Urbana manuscript of selections from the
    Vergilian appendix. Illinois, 1940. Abstract: Urbana, 1940.
    8 p.   S153
Steinlauf, Nathan Trattner. The coins of Gallienus and his fami-
    ly in the Wulfing collection of Washington University, with a
    commentary. Washington, St. Louis, 1941.   S154
Stella, Curtis. Rhetorical patterns in the history of Ammianus
    Marcellinus. Princeton, 1936.   S155
Stephans, Dorothy. Critias: his life and literary remains. Cin-
    cinnati, 1939.   S156
Stephens, Wade Carroll. The function of religious philosophical
    ideas in Ovid's Metamorphoses. Princeton, 1957. Abstract:
    Dissertation abstracts, XVIII, 227.   S157
Stephenson, Andrew. Public lands and agrarian laws of the Ro-
    man republic. Johns Hopkins, 1890. Printed: Johns Hopkins
    University studies in historical and political science, 9th ser.,
    VII-VIII (1891). 101 p.   S158
Stephenson, Rufus Town. Some aspects of the dramatic art of
    Aeschylus. Stanford, 1909. Printed: Stanford, Stanford Uni-
    versity press, 1913. 73 p.   S159
Stevens, Edward Boucher, II. Commonplace and theory of counsel
    and deliberation from Homer to Aristotle. Chicago, 1930.
    Abstract: Abstract of theses, Humanistic ser., VIII (1932),
    327-33.   S160
Stewart, Douglas James. Nature and purpose: a study of Greek
    teleological theories. Cornell, 1963. Abstract: Disserta-
    tion abstracts, XXIV, 4183.   S161
Stewart, Manson Alexander. Word-study in Latin abstract sub-
    stantives. Michigan, 1908. Printed: Michigan University,
    Studies, Humanistic ser., III, pt. 2 (1910), 113-78.   S162
Stirewalt, Martin Luther. The letter in Greek literature. Duke,
    1945.   S163
Stocker, Arthur Frederick. De novo codicum Servianorum
    genere. Harvard, 1939. Abstract: Summaries of theses,
    1939, p. 3-6.   S164

Stockin, Frank Gordon, jr. Sequence of thought and motivation in the Metamorphoses of Apuleius. Illinois, 1954. Abstract: Dissertation abstracts, XIV, 824. S165

Stokes, Ella Harrison. The conception of a kingdom of ends in Augustine, Aquinas, and Leibniz. Chicago, 1910. Printed: Chicago, University of Chicago press, 1912. 129 p. S166

Stone, Isabelle. The life of Simonides of Ceos, from the sources. Cornell, 1908. S167

Stone, Robert Conrad. The language of Codex Bezae d. Illinois, 1936. Abstract: Urbana, 1936. 6 p. S168

Stout, Selatie Edgar. The governors of Moesia. Princeton, 1910. Printed: Princeton, 1911. 97 p. S169

Stow, Harry Lloyd. The violation of the dramatic illusion in the comedies of Aristophanes. Chicago, 1936. Printed: Chicago, Private edition, distributed by the University of Chicago Libraries, 1936. 76 p. S170

Straw, Sylvester Byron. The testimonia regarding Euripides. Illinois, 1941. Abstract: Urbana, 1941. 8 p. S171

Straw, William R. Aion and aionios, a word study of their most important occurrences. Dallas Theological, 1952. S172

Street, James Howell, jr. Agricultural technology in classical Attica. North Carolina, 1952. S173

Strickler, Robert Parvin. Tenses of the Homeric imperative. Johns Hopkins, 1919. S174

Strout, Donald Everett. The latent Greek element in the technical vocabulary of Donatus. Illinois, 1933. Abstract: Urbana, 1933. 15 p. S175

Stuart, D. R. The attitude of Dio Cassius toward epigraphic sources. Michigan, 1904 (?). Printed: Michigan University, Studies, Humanistic ser., I (1904), 101−47. S176

Stuart, Meriwether. The portraiture of Claudius; preliminary studies. Columbia, 1938. Printed: New York, 1938. 93 p. S177

Stuckey, Harold J. The conception of purity in Plato. California, 1935. S178

Sturgis, James Wellings. The second person singular of the Latin future indicative as an imperative. Michigan, 1910. Printed: Oklahoma University, Bulletin, new ser., no. 109, University studies ser., no. VI (1916). 51 p. S179

Sturtevant, Edgar Howard. Contraction in the case forms of the Latin ĭo- and ĭā stems, and of deus, is, and idem. Chicago, 1902. Printed: Chicago, Scott, Foresman and co., 1902. 35 p. S180

Suffern, Richard Munn. The treatment of evidence in extant
    Greek tragedy. Johns Hopkins, 1941.   S181
Suhr, Elmer George. Sculptured portraits of Greek statesmen.
    Johns Hopkins, 1926. Printed: Johns Hopkins University,
    Studies in archaeology, XIII (1931). 189 p.   S182
Suits, Thomas Allan. Structure of the Propertian elegy, Books
    I–III. Yale, 1958.   S183
Sullivan, Francis A. Ideas of after-life in the Latin verse in-
    scriptions. Johns Hopkins, 1936.   S184
Sullivan, John Joseph. Deification in Cicero. Pittsburgh, 1941.
    S185
Sullivan, Margaret Mary, Sister. Roman tradition and Greek in-
    fluence: moral and cultural attitudes of some prominent Ro-
    mans of the second century B.C. Columbia, 1954. Abstract:
    Dissertation abstracts, XIV, 1712.   S186
Sullivan, Patrick A. Cicero's philosophical plan. Fordham,
    1951.   S187
Sullivan, Wilbur Mark. The logic of the Περί ἑρμηνείας, as-
    cribed to Apuleius of Madaura. Stanford, 1964.   S188
Sullwold, George John, jr. Lucretius' imagery, a poetic reading
    of the De rerum natura. Washington, Seattle, 1957. Ab-
    stract: Dissertation abstracts, XVIII, 1419.   S189
Surbled, Lillian Green. The figures of speech in the works of
    Horace. Pittsburgh, 1945.   S190
Suskin, Albert Irving. The arrangement of material in Livy,
    books 31–45. North Carolina, 1937. Abstract: Research in
    progress, 1936/37, p. 25–6.   S191
Sutherland, Donald. The Senecan temper in Lucan. Princeton,
    1939. Abstract: Dissertation abstracts, XII, 257.   S192
Sutherland, Priscilla Warren. The use of Quintilian in the medi-
    eval florilegia. North Carolina, 1950. Abstract: Research
    in progress, 1950, p. 35–6.   S193
Sutphen, Morris Crater. A study of the diction and phraseology
    of Lucius Annaeus Seneca, with special reference to the
    sermo cotidianus. Johns Hopkins, 1899.   S194
Swain, Joseph Ward. The hellenic origins of Christian asceticism.
    Columbia, 1916. Printed: New York, 1916. 147 p.   S195
Swan, F. T. The adjectives used as substantives by Lucretius.
    Michigan, 1903. Printed: The use of the adjective as a sub-
    stantive in the De rerum natura of Lucretius. Michigan Uni-
    versity, Studies, Humanistic ser., III, pt. 2 (1910), 179–214.
    S196
Swanson, Donald Carl. The Greek and Sanskrit written accent.
    Princeton, 1941. Abstract: Dissertation abstracts, XII, 182.
    S197

Swanson, Roy Arthur. Pudor as a criterion in Latin literature.
    Illinois, 1954. Abstract: Dissertation abstracts, XV, 118.
    S198
Swartz, Mifflin Wyatt. The personal characteristics and the
    dramatic use of the old in the dramas of Euripides. Vir-
    ginia, 1910. Printed: Nashville, Tenn., Publishing house of
    the M. E. Church, South, 1911. 115 p.   S199
Swearingen, George Crawford. A study in the manuscripts of
    Horace. Chicago, 1902.   S200
Sweet, Louis Matthews. Roman emperor worship. New York,
    1919. Printed: Boston, R. G. Badger, 1919. 153 p.   S201
Sweet, Waldo Earle. Demetrius Poliorcetes: a study in literary
    sources. Princeton, 1943.   S202
Swindler, Mary Hamilton. Cretan elements in the cults and
    ritual of Apollo. Bryn Mawr, 1913. Printed: Bryn Mawr
    College monographs, Monograph ser., XIII (1913). 77 p.
    S203
Sykes, Richard Dodgson. The doctrine of substance in the logical
    works of Aristotle. Princeton, 1960.   S204

T

Tait, Jane Isabella Marion. Philodemus' influence on the Latin
    poets. Bryn Mawr, 1939. Printed: Bryn Mawr, 1941. 118 p.
    T1
Tamblyn, William Ferguson. The establishment of Roman power
    in Great Britain. Columbia, 1899. Printed: Hamilton, Ont.,
    McPherson & Drope, 1899. 105 p.   T2
Taran, Leonardo. Parmenides. A text with translation, com-
    mentary, and critical essays. Princeton, 1962.   T3
Tarbell, Frank Bigelow. Notes on the First Philippic of Demos-
    thenes. Yale, 1879. Printed: The Philippics of Demosthenes,
    New York, Ginn and co., 1880, xxxviii, 100 p.   T4
Tavenner, Eugene. Studies in magic from Latin literature. Co-
    lumbia, 1916. Printed: New York, Columbia University
    press, 1916. 155 p.   T5
Taylor, Charles H. Studies in the relation between the Roman
    cadaster and the Frankish polyptych: a study of the tax-as-
    sessment in the later Roman Empire. Harvard, 1927.   T6
Taylor, George Erwin. The apocryphal correspondence of St.
    Paul with the church at Corinth. Chicago, 1962.   T7
Taylor, John H. Sancti Aureli Augustini De genesi ad litteram
    liber duodecimus: with introduction, translation, and com-
    mentary. St. Louis, 1948.   T8

Taylor, John Prentice. The mythology of Vergil's Aeneid ac-
    cording to Servius. New York, 1917. Printed: New York,
    1918. 62 p.   T9

Taylor, Lily Ross. The cults of Ostia. Bryn Mawr, 1912. Print-
    ed: Bryn Mawr College monographs, Monograph ser., XI
    (1912). 98 p.   T10

Teall, John Leland. The wheat economy of the Byzantine Empire,
    325-1025. Yale, 1956.   T11

Tenney, Merrill Chapin. The quotations from Luke in Tertullian
    as related to the texts of the second and third centuries.
    Harvard, 1944. Abstract: Summaries of theses, 1943/45,
    p. 5-7.   T12

Terrell, Glanville. De apodosi enuntiati irrealis condicionalis
    in oratione obliqua Latina. Harvard, 1900. Printed: Amer-
    ican journal of philology, XXV (1904), 59-73.   T13

Tew, Susan Dinsmore. Notes on the vocabulary of Aeschylus.
    Yale, 1895.   T14

Thackray, Edgar. A comparative study of sense perception in
    Greek philosophy. Harvard, 1907.   T15

Thelemann, Frances Adeline. An examination of early classical
    Latin manuscripts with reference to evidence of the use of
    cursive script and ancient notae in their archetypes. Chica-
    go, 1930. Abstract: Abstracts of theses, Humanistic ser.,
    VIII (1932), 355-9.   T16

Thibault, John Crowell. A critical analysis of the hypotheses
    concerning Ovid's Error. Illinois, 1961. Abstract: Disser-
    tation abstracts, XXI, 3773.   T17

Thomas, James David. The Greek Text of Tobit. Chicago, 1958.
    T18

Thomas Aquinas, Sister (secular name, Agnes O'Neill). The pre-
    Socratic use of ψυχή as a term for the principle of motion.
    Catholic, 1915. Printed: Washington, D.C., National capital
    press, inc., 1915. 51 p.   T19

Thomas, Ruth Edith. The sacred meal in the older Roman reli-
    gion. Chicago, 1935. Printed: Chicago, Private edition,
    distributed by the University of Chicago Libraries, 1937.
    59 p.   T20

Thompson, Alexander Mackenzie. De ratione quae inter scholi-
    astam in Statii Thebaida et Hyginum mythographum inter-
    cedat. Harvard, 1907.   T21

Thompson, Clara Louise. Taedium vitae in Latin sepulchral in-
    scriptions. Pennsylvania, 1911. Printed: Lancaster, Pa.,
    Press of the New era printing co., 1912. 53 p.   T22

Thompson, Effie Freeman. Μετανοέω and μεταμέλει in Greek literature to 100 A.D., including discussion of their cognates and of their Hebrew equivalents. Chicago, 1907. Printed: Chicago University, Department of Biblical and patristic Greek, Historical and linguistic studies in literature related to the New Testament, 2d ser., Linguistic and exegetical studies, I, pt. 5 (1908). 29 p. T23

Thompson, George Clarence. The Periclean tradition. Yale, 1888. T24

Thompson, George Raynor. Theophrastus on plant flavors and odors. Princeton, 1941. Abstract: Dissertation abstracts, XII, 72. T25

Thompson, Guy VanGorder. The Draconian constitution. Yale, 1894. T26

Thompson, Lynette. Lucan's Bellum civile and the tragedies of Seneca. Chicago, 1957. T27

Thompson, Mary Lee. Programmatic painting in Pompeii; the meaningful combination of mythological pictures in room decoration. New York, 1960. T28

Thompson, Maud. The property rights of women in ancient Greece. Yale, 1906. T29

Thompson, Wesley Eugene. The Athenian gold and bronze coinage of the Dekeleian War. Princeton, 1963. Abstract: Dissertation abstracts, XXIV, 3705. T30

Thompson, Wilmot Haines. The use of prepositions in the Greek dialect inscriptions. Yale, 1906. T31

Thomson, William Gregory. An evaluation of a technique for improving reading comprehension in Latin. Michigan, 1961. T32

Thorne, John. Syntax and style of Macrobius. Johns Hopkins, 1896. T33

Throop, George Reeves. A new manuscript of Cicero's De senectute. Cornell, 1905. Printed: Classical philology, III (1908), 258–301. T34

Thurlington, Bayly. Dioscorides of the Palatine anthology. Johns Hopkins, 1949. T35

Thweatt, William H. A historical survey and exegetical study of hupomeno and hupomone in the New Testament. Southern Baptist, 1954. T36

Tibbetts, Mary Ann. The myths in the Odyssey. Cornell, 1942. T37

Tibbetts, William Frank. The indicative indirect question in Latin. Chicago, 1901. T38

Tierney, Helen M. Corinthian power politics. Chicago, 1958.
     T39

Tilroe, Welcome A. The Ilias latina: a study of the Iliad, includ-
     ing translation, commentary, and concordance. Southern
     California, 1939. Abstract: Abstracts of dissertations, 1939,
     p. 37–42.   T40

Titchener, John Bradford. The manuscript tradition of Plutarch's
     Aetia graeca and Aetia romana. Illinois, 1923. Printed: Il-
     linois University, Studies in language and literature, IX, no.
     2 (1924). 68 p.   T41

Titchener, Margaret Seymour. The guardianship of women in
     Egypt during the Ptolemaic and Roman eras. Wisconsin,
     1920. Printed: Wisconsin University, Studies in language
     and literature, XV (1922), 20–8.   T42

Tobin, Mildred Dolores, Sister. Orientii Commonitorium: a
     commentary with an introduction and translation. Catholic,
     1945. Printed: Catholic University of America, Patristic
     studies, LXXIV (1945). 143 p.   T43

Todd, Richard Allen. Popular violence and internal security in
     hellenistic Alexandria. California, Berkeley, 1963. Ab-
     stract: Dissertation abstracts, XXIV, 4156.   T44

Toland, John Martin. De vocalium mutatione illa apud Graecos
     antiquos quae hodie sandhi dicitur. Harvard, 1935. Ab-
     stract: Summaries of theses, 1935, p. 10–14.   T45

Toliver, Hazel May. The theater as a force in Roman society.
     Iowa, 1945. Abstract: Programs announcing candidates for
     higher degrees, 1945. 4 p.   T46

Tolles, Delight. The banquet-libations of the Greeks. Bryn
     Mawr, 1940.   T47

Tolman, Herbert Cushing. De gerundio latino atque modo in-
     finitivo sanscrito. Yale, 1890.   T48

Tongue, William R. An epigraphic commentary on Suetonius's
     life of Nero. Pennsylvania, 1936.   T49

Tonks, O. S. Brygos. Harvard, 1903. Printed: Brygos—his
     characteristics, American academy of arts and sciences,
     Memoirs, XVII (new ser., XIII, 1904), 65–117.   T50

Torrance, Catherine. The names of the warriors in Vergil's
     Aeneid vii–xii: his sources and his methods. Chicago,
     1927. Abstract: Abstracts of theses, Humanistic ser., V
     (1928), 405–8.   T51

Townsend, Emily Dickinson. Bacchylides and lyric style. Bryn
     Mawr, 1956. Abstract: Dissertation abstracts, XVI, 2452.
     T52

Townsend, Prescott Winson. The administration of Gordian III. Yale, 1926. Printed: Yale classical studies, IV (1934), 59–132. T53

Tracy, Hermann Lloyd. The theory and philosophy of punishment in Greek literature. Chicago, 1924. Abstract: Abstracts of theses, Humanistic ser., II (1926), 293–9. T54

Tracy, Theodore James. Physiological theory and the doctrine of the mean in Plato and Aristotle. Princeton, 1962. Abstract: Dissertation abstracts, XXIV, 291. T55

Trahey, James Joseph. De sermone Ennodiano Hieronymi sermone in comparationem adhibito. Catholic, 1905. Printed: Notre Dame, Ind., University press, 1904. 200 p. T56

Trahman, Carl Richard. The Latin language and literature in the Greek world. Cincinnati, 1942. T57

Trapp, Richard La Prentice. The development of the Aias legend from Homer to Sophocles. California, Berkeley, 1959. T58

Traub, Henry W. Death and fame in silver Latin literature. North Carolina, 1954. Abstract: Research in progress, 1953/54, p. 43–4. T59

Traupman, John Charles. The life and reign of Commodus. Princeton, 1956. Abstract: Dissertation abstracts, XVII, 606. T60

Travis, Albert Hartman. De Servii carminum Vergilianorum interpretis dicendi rationibus. Harvard, 1940. Abstract: Harvard University, Summaries of theses, 1940, p. 11–12. T61

Trever, Albert Augustus. A history of Greek economic thought. Chicago, 1913. Printed: Chicago, University of Chicago press, 1916. 162 p. T62

Trimble, Helen Bell. Juvenal and the Roman emperors, the evidence in his satires compared with that in the extant works of contemporary historians. Pennsylvania, 1912. Printed: Lancaster, Pa., Press of the New era printing co., 1912. 82 p. T63

Trotter, Julius C., jr. The use of the perfect tenses in the Pauline epistles. Southern Baptist, 1951. T64

Trouard, Mary Alexaidia, Sister. Cicero's attitude toward the Greeks. Chicago, 1942. Printed: Chicago, 1942. 104 p. T65

Truesdale, James Nardin. A comic prosopographia graeca. Duke, 1936. Printed: Menasha, Wis., The Collegiate press, George Banta publ. co., 1940. 76 p. T66

Tucker, Norval. A catalogue of Etruscan and Roman art and
    architecture in the three dimensional slide collection in the
    State University of Iowa. Iowa, 1959.   T67
Tukey, Ralph Hermon. The syntax of Isaeus: I. The syntax of
    the cases. Yale, 1906.   T68
Turnbull, Lucy Curtis. Some aspects of Greek geometric
    bronzes. Radcliffe, 1960.   T69
Turner, James Hilton. Studies in the history of Roman public
    baths. Cincinnati, 1944.   T70
Turner, James Lee. The use of οὖν in the Pauline epistles.
    Southern Baptist, 1945.   T71
Tuthill, L. H. The exempla in Ad Herennium and in Cicero's De
    inventione. New York, 1907.   T72
Tuttle, Preston Heath. Comedy as a reprojection of childhood
    experience: a study of the process by which emotional con-
    tent determines dramatic form. Illinois, 1963. Abstract:
    Dissertation abstracts, XXIV, 4316.   T73

U

Ueberhorst, L. K., and Ullman, B. L.: Entered after Urdahl.
Upson, Frieda Schauroth. The kernos in ancient cult. Radcliffe,
    1942.   U1
Upson, Hollis Ritchie. Mediaeval lives of Virgil. Harvard, 1940.
    Abstract: Summaries of theses, 1940, p. 13-4.   U2
Urch, Erwin J. The evolution of the inquisitorial procedure in
    Roman law. St. Louis, 1930.   U3
Urdahl, Lloyd Bernard. Foreigners in Athens: a study of the
    grave monuments. Chicago, 1959.   U4
Ullman, Berthold Louis. The identification of the manuscrpts of
    Catullus cited in Statius' edition of 1566. Chicago, 1909.
    Printed: Chicago, Press of the H. G. Adair printing co.,
    1908. 64 p.   U5
Ueberhorst, Louis K. An investigation into the sources of the
    commentary on the Acts of the apostles in manuscript no.
    146. Michigan, 1936.   U6

V

Vail, James M. The dramatic use of death ritual in Euripides.
    Chicago, 1949.   V1
Vallillee, Gerald. The plague in Lucretius and later Latin poets.
    Chicago, 1961.   V2
Van Buren, Albert William. Studies in Roman archaeology.
    Yale, 1915. Printed: The Ara Pacis Augustae, Journal of

Roman studies, III (1913), 134-41; The temples of Castor and of Concord in the Roman Forum, Classical review, XX (1906), 77-84, 184; A medallion of Antoninus Pius, Journal of Roman studies, I (1911), 187-95; and A transcription of the palimpsest of Cicero's De republica, American school in Rome, Supplementary papers, 1908, p. 84-262.   V3

Van Buskirk, Elizabeth G. Seneca's use of the historical exemplum. Cornell, 1938.   V4

Van Deman, Esther Boise. The cult of vesta publica and the vestal virgins. Chicago, 1898.   V5

Van Deventer, Harry Brown. Subordinate verb clauses in Gaius. Yale, 1907.   V6

Van Hoesen, Henry Bartlett. Roman cursive writing. Princeton, 1912. Printed: American philological Association, Transactions, XLIV (1913). 268 p.   V7

Van Hook, Larue. The metaphorical terminology of Greek rhetoric and literary criticism. Chicago, 1905. Printed: Chicago, University of Chicago press, 1905. 51 p.   V8

Van Nostrand, John James. The reorganization of Spain by Augustus. California, Berkeley, 1915. Printed: California University, Publications in history, IV, no. 2 (1916), 83-154. V9

Van Sickle, Edwin Clifton. The coregency and the succession in the early Roman Empire. Chicago, 1928. Abstract: Abstracts of theses, Humanistic ser., VI (1929), 235-9.   V10

Vannoy, Charles Amzi. Studies on the Athena Parthenos of Pheidias. Iowa, 1914. Printed: Iowa University, Humanistic studies, I, no. 5 (1917). 57 p.   V11

Vardaman, George Truett. An analysis of some factors relating to the dialectic of Plato, Aristotle, and Cicero. Northwestern, 1952. Abstract: Summaries of doctoral dissertations, XX (1952), 173-7.   V12

Vaschalde, A. A. Three letters of Philoxenus. Catholic, 1900. V13

Vaughan, Agnes Carr. Madness in Greek thought and custom. Michigan, 1917. Printed: Baltimore, J. H. Furst co., 1919. 74 p.   V14

Vaughan, Alden Gibson. Latin adjectives with partitive meaning in republican literature. Pennsylvania, 1942. Printed: Linguistic society of America, Language dissertation, XXXVI (1942). 70 p.   V15

Vazakas, Alexander Aristides. The Greek of Acts I:I-15:35. Chicago, 1928. Abstract: Abstracts of theses, Humanistic ser., VI (1929), 407-13.   V16

Vlachos, Nicholas Panagis. The subject of Sophocles' Antigone.
Pennsylvania, 1901. Printed: Philadelphia, International
printing co., 1901. 52 p.   V17

Vogel, Arthur A. The Aristotelian theory of explanation and
some recent criticisms. Harvard, 1952.   V18

Vogel, Grace Sybil. The major manuscripts of Cicero's De
senectute. Chicago, 1936.   Printed: Chicago, Private edition, distributed by the University of Chicago Libraries,
1939. 82 p.   V19

Voogd, Henry. A critical and comparative study of the old Latin
of the first book of Samuel. Princeton Theological, 1947.
V20

Votaw, Clyde Weber. The use of the infinitive in Biblical Greek.
Chicago, 1896. Printed: Chicago, Published by the author,
1896. 59 p.   V21

W

Waagé, Frederick Oswin, III. The Hellenistic and Roman tableware of north Syria. Princeton, 1943.   W1

Wachholder, Ben Zion. Nicolaus of Damascus. California, Los
Angeles, 1960.   W2

Wagener, Anthony Pelzer. Popular associations of right and left
in Roman literature. Johns Hopkins, 1910. Printed: Baltimore, J. H. Furst co., 1912. 58 p.   W3

Wagner, Monica, Sister. Rufinus, the translator: a study of his
theory and his practice as illustrated in his version of the
Apologetica of St. Gregory Nazianzen. Catholic, 1945. Printed: Catholic University of America, Patristic studies,
LXXIII (1943). 100 p.   W4

Waisglass, Abraham Asron Isaac. An historical study of Cyrene
from the fall of the Battiad monarchy to the close of the
fourth century B.C. Columbia, 1954. Abstract: Dissertation abstracts, XV, 256.   W5

Walden, John William Henry. De participiis praesentium usu
Ammianeo. Harvard, 1891.   W6

Walker, Alice Leslie. The pottery of the necropolis of Locrian
Halae. California, 1917.   W7

Walker, Arthur Tappan. The sequence of tenses in Latin. Chicago, 1898.   W8

Walker, Israel. Kynouria; its history in the light of existing remains. Columbia, 1936. Printed: Williamsport, Pa., The
Bayard press, 1936. 66 p.   W9

Walker, Louisa Viola. Latin in current periodicals and news-
papers. Wisconsin, 1923. Printed: Iowa City, Ia., 1926.
54 p.   W10

Wallace, Malcolm V. T. The epic technique of Silius Italicus.
Harvard, 1955.   W11

Wallace, William P. The history of Eretria to 198 B.C. Johns
Hopkins, 1936.   W12

Walsh, James Jerome. Aristotle's conception of ἀκρασία.
Columbia, 1960.   W13

Walton, Alice. The cult of Asklepios. Cornell, 1892. Printed:
Cornell studies in classical philology, III (1894). 136 p.
W14

Walton, Francis Redding. De dis syriis apud Graecos cultis.
Harvard, 1938. Abstract: Summaries of theses, 1938, p. 9–
10.   W15

Wannemacher, William L. The development of imperial civil
officia during the principate. Michigan, 1940.   W16

Ward, Ralph L. The relative chronology of the phonetic changes
in primitive Greek. Yale, 1935.   W17

Ware, Elmer W. A study in the tense of the Book of Revelation.
Southern Baptist, 1954.   W18

Warren, Arletta L. L. Annaeus Seneca quid de summo bono
censuerit. Michigan, 1898.   W19

Warren, Edward Willard. The concept of consciousness in the
philosophy of Plotinus. Johns Hopkins, 1961.   W20

Warren, Winifred. A study of conjunctional temporal clauses in
Thukydides. Bryn Mawr, 1898. Printed: Berlin, Gebrüder
Unger, 1897. 76 p.   W21

Waters, William Everett. Studies on the forms of words in
Petronius, together with an introduction on his identity. Yale,
1887. Results appear in Waters' edition of Cena Trimalchionis. Boston, B. H. Sanborn and co., 1902. 143 p.   W22

Watkins, Roy Edward. A history of paragraph divisions in
Horace's Epistles. Iowa, 1941. Printed: Iowa studies in
classical philology, X (1940). 134 p.   W23

Watson, John Calvin. De scaenarum titulis imaginibusque per-
sonarum Terentianis in codicibus pictis. Harvard, 1902.
Printed: Harvard studies in classical philology, XIV (1902),
55–172.   W24

Watson, William Lee. A stylistic commentary on Cicero In
Vatinium. Texas, 1964.   W25

Watts, Winifred F. Dares—a hitherto unpublished manuscript.
Southern California, 1937.   W26

Waugh, R. B. The philosophical system of Parmenides. Cornell,
    1907.   W27

Way, Evelyn Lee. Seneca as a source for Tacitus, Suetonius, and
    Dio. North Carolina, 1941. Abstract: Research in progress,
    1940/41, p. 30.   W28

Webb, Robert Henning. Quomodo restituendus sit liber unde orti
    sunt codices Terentiani C P O. Harvard, 1909.   W29

Webster, Edwin White. Virtus and libertas: the ideals and
    spirit of the Roman senatorial aristocracy from the Punic
    wars through the time of Augustus. Chicago, 1934. Printed:
    Chicago, Private edition, distributed by the University of Chi-
    cago Libraries, 1936. 84-108 p.   W30

Weeple, Thomas. Lucilius: an introduction to the Satires, and a
    commentary on the first book. Harvard, 1964.   W31

Weinberg, Saul S. The prehistoric house of the mainland of
    Greece. Johns Hopkins, 1936.   W32

Weiskotten, Herbert Theberath. Sancti Augustini vita scripta a
    Possidio episcopo, edited with revised text, introduction,
    notes, and an English version. Princeton, 1918. Printed:
    Princeton, Princeton University press, 1919. 174 p.   W33

Weissinger, Reinhard Theodore. A study of act divisions in
    classical drama. Iowa, 1940. Printed: Iowa studies in
    classical philology, IX (1940). 141 p.   W34

Weiswurm, Alcuin A. The nature of human knowledge according
    to St. Gregory of Nyssa. Catholic, 1953.   W35

Welch, John Joseph. Latin initial syllables: an historical phono-
    logical study. Pennsylvania, 1962. Abstract: Dissertation
    abstracts, XXIII, 1691.   W36

Wellein, Lawrence Theodore. Time past and the hero: a sug-
    gested criterion for Sophoclean tragedy as exemplified by
    Ajax, Trachiniae and Electra. Washington, Seattle, 1959.
    Abstract: Dissertation abstracts, XX, 1020.   W37

Weller, Charles Heald. The pre-Periclean propylon of the Acrop-
    olis at Athens. Yale, 1904. Printed: American journal of
    archaeology, 2d ser., VIII (1904), 35-70.   W38

Welles, Mary C. The appropriation and latent criticism of Herod-
    otus in Thucydides. Yale, 1904.   W39

Weltin, Edward George. Origen and the Roman empire. Illinois,
    1946. Abstract: Urbana, 1946. 7 p.   W40

Wender, Dorothea Schmidt. The last scenes of the Odyssey: a
    defense. Harvard, 1964.   W41

Wente, Walter Hermann. Aristotle's discrimination of synoyms.
    Chicago, 1932. Printed: Chicago, Private edition, distrib-

uted by the University of Chicago Libraries, 1935. p. 44, 98–119, 183–4.   W42

West, Allen Brown. The history of the Chalcidic league. Wisconsin, 1912. Printed: Wisconsin University, Bulletin, no. 969, History ser., IV, no. 2 (1918). 176 p.   W43

West, Charles M. The nature of the Aristotelian intellect. Laval, 1951.   W44

West, Mildred G. Pegasus in classical literature and art. Johns Hopkins, 1937.   W45

Westervelt, Peter. Pindar's poetic craft and purpose. Harvard, 1961.   W46

Westgate, Reginald Isaac Wilfred. De casibus indogermanicis, praecipue sociativo, in lingua Graeca ab Homero usque ad Thucydidem, summotis. Harvard, 1935. Abstract: Summaries of theses, 1935, p. 14–7.   W47

Westington, Mars McClelland. Atrocities in Roman warfare to 133 B.C. Chicago, 1938. Printed: Chicago, Private edition, distributed by the University of Chicago Libraries, 1938. 139 p.   W48

Weston, Arthur Harold. Latin satirical writing subsequent to Juvenal. Yale, 1911. Printed: Lancaster, Pa., Press of the New era printing co., 1915. 165 p.   W49

Weter, Winifred Elberta. Encouragement of literary production in Greece from Homer to Alexander. Chicago, 1933. Printed: Chicago, Private edition, distributed by the University of Chicago Libraries, 1936. 113 p.   W50

Wetmore, Monroe Nichols. The plan and scope of a Vergil lexicon, with specimen articles. Yale, 1904. Printed: New Haven, Ryder publishing house, 1904. 128 p.   W51

Wevers, Richard Franklin. Isaeus: chronology, prosopography and social history. Wisconsin, 1962. Abstract: Dissertation abstracts, XXII, 3651.   W52

Whallon, William Wheeler. Distinctive epithets in Homer. Yale, 1957.   W53

Wheeler, Arthur Leslie. The use of the imperfect indicative in Plautus and Terence. Yale, 1893. Printed: The uses of the imperfect indicative in Plautus and Terence, American philological association, Transactions, XXX (1899), 14–23; The imperfect indicative in early Latin, American journal of philology, XXIV (1903), 163–91; and The syntax of the imperfect indicative in early Latin, Classical philology, I (1906), 357–90.   W54

Wheeler, Francis M. An analysis of method and purpose in the
  Cyropaedia of Xenophon. Chicago, 1962.   W55
Wheeler, James Rignall. De comparationibus et translationibus
  quas e mari et re navali mutuati sunt Aeschylus et Sopho-
  cles. Harvard, 1885.   W56
Wheeler, Nathaniel. Problem of mythology. Syracuse, 1883.
  W57
Wheelock, Frederick Melvin. De Probi commentariorum
  Vergilianorum textu recensendo. Harvard, 1933. Abstract:
  Summaries of theses, 1933, p. 11-4.   W58
Whitaker, Frederic Earle. The legal fiction of adoption in an-
  cient Greece. Brown, 1899.   W59
White, Andrew Curtis. De A. Persi Flacci genere dicendi.
  Cornell, 1885.   W60
White, Donald. Ἁγνὴ θεά a study of Sicilian Demeter. Prince-
  ton, 1963.   W61
White, Dorrance Stinchfield. The mechanism and instrumentali-
  ties of Roman international intercourse under the empire.
  Chicago, 1932. Abstract: Abstracts of theses, Humanistic
  ser., IX (1934), 401-7.   W62
White, Glenn F. The meaning and use of ἀπολύτρωσις and its
  cognates in the New Testament. Southern Baptist, 1948.
  W63
White, John Williams. On the Homeric uses of the subjunctive
  and optative moods. Harvard, 1877.   W64
White, Ronald Erwin. Some techniques of development in Proper-
  tius and their bearing on poem division. North Carolina,
  1958. Abstract: Dissertation abstracts, XIX, 2607.   W65
White-Stevens, Lillian Jaffin. The myths of Homer's Iliad.
  Cornell, 1944.   W66
Whitehead, Philip Barrows. The conversion of pagan buildings
  in the city of Rome into Christian churches. Yale, 1914.
  Printed: Nuovo bulletino di archeologia christiana, XIX
  (1913), 143-65; American journal of archaeology, 2d ser.,
  XXXI (1927), 1-18.   W67
Whitman, Cedric H. The religious humanism of Sophocles.
  Harvard, 1947.   W68
Whiton, James Morris. Ars longa, brevis vita. Yale, 1861.
  W69
Wiebenson, Dora Louise. Stuart and Revett's Antiquities of
  Athens: the influence of archaeological publications on the
  neo-classical concept of hellenism. New York, 1964.   W70
Wiegand, Edna. Notes on the eighth book of the Commentary of

Servius on Vergil's Aeneid. Columbia, 1936. Printed:
Menasha, Wis., 1936. 133 p.   W71

Wiencke, Matthew I. Greek household religion. Johns Hopkins,
1947.   W72

Wiesen, David Stanley. St. Jerome as a satirist. Harvard, 1961.
W73

Wiggin, Roy E. A study of the Glasgow glosses. Harvard, 1948.
W74

Wightman, Alfred Reynolds. De dum, donec, quoad coniunctionum
usu apud Ciceronem, Caesarem, Tacitum, Plinium Minorem,
Suetonium. Harvard, 1909.   W75

Wigodsky, Michael Mashe. Imitations of early Latin poetry in
Vergil's Aeneid. Princeton, 1963.   W76

Wilcox, Alexander Martin. Aristotle's criticism of Plato's Republic. Yale, 1880.   W77

Wilcox, Stanley. The destructive hypothetical syllogism in Greek
logic and in Attic oratory. Yale, 1938. Printed: New Haven,
1939 (?).   W78

Wilde, Robert. The treatment of the Jews in the Greek Christian
writers of the first three centuries. Catholic, 1949. Printed:
Catholic University of America, Patristic studies, LXXXI
(1949). 239 p.   W79

Wildes, Adele Madeleine. Coordinations in ancient Greek and Roman temple plans. Johns Hopkins, 1925.   W80

Wilhelms, John William. The language of Cicero's De legibus.
Minnesota, 1942.   W81

Wilkerson, Jerome Francis. The concept of friendship in the
Nicomachean ethics of Aristotle. Catholic, 1963. Abstract:
Dissertation abstracts, XXIV, 2084.   W82

Wilkinson, Beryl Marie. The names of children in Roman imperial epitaphs: A study of social conditions in the lower
classes. Bryn Mawr, 1961. Abstract: Dissertation abstracts, XXII, 2768.   W83

Willard, E. P., jr. Seneca as a source for information on the
early Roman caesars. North Carolina, 1929. Abstract: Research in progress, 1928/29, p. 23-4.   W84

Willets, Robert H. The causes, culmination, and consequences of
the destruction of Jerusalem in 70 A.D. Southern Baptist,
1949.   W85

Williams, Caroline Louise Ransom. Studies in ancient furniture:
couches and beds of the Greeks, Etruscans and Romans.
Chicago, 1905. Printed: Chicago, University of Chicago
press, 1905. 128 p., XXIX pl.   W86

Williams, Charles Bray. The participle in the book of Acts.
  Chicago, 1909. Printed: Chicago, University of Chicago
  press, 1909. 80 p.   W87
Williams, John Carter. Patterns and variations of rhythm in
  Hesiod's Works and days. Yale, 1962.   W88
Williams, Lois V. The Venus cult; a study based upon study of
  the writings of Suetonius and Tacitus. Johns Hopkins, 1946.
  W89
Williams, Mary G. De Julia Domna. Michigan, 1897.   W90
Williams, Phyllis Lourene. A numismatic approach to the sculp-
  ture of southern Italy and Sicily in the classical period.
  New York, 1943.   W91
Willis, Gwendolen Brown. The ancient gods in Greek romance.
  Bryn Mawr, 1905.   W92
Willis, William Hailey. Compound words in Aeschylus. Yale,
  1940.   W93
Wills, Garry. The architectonics of strife: a study in the dynam-
  ics of Aeschulus' Oresteia. Yale, 1961.   W94
Wilner, Ortha Leslie. The technique of character protrayal in
  Roman comedy. Chicago, 1929. Abstract: Abstracts of
  theses, Humanistic ser., VII (1930), 451-4.   W95
Wilson, Harry Langford. The metaphor in the epic poems of
  Publius Papinius Statius. Printed: Baltimore, J. Murphy
  and co., 1898. 30 p.   W96
Wilson, Lillian May. A study of the Roman toga. Johns Hopkins,
  1924. Printed: The Johns Hopkins University studies in
  archaeology, I (1924). 132 p.   W97
Wilson, Tom Bullock. Frederick J. E. Woodbridge, interpreter
  of Greek philosophy. Arkansas, 1964.   W98
Wilt, Henry Toomey. Religio: a semantic study of the pre-
  Christian use of the terms religio and religiosus. Columbia,
  1954. Abstract: Dissertation abstracts, XIV, 1713.   W99
Wing, Herbert. The financial relations of Athens to her allies in
  the Vth century. Wisconsin, 1915. Printed: Tribute assess-
  ments in the Athenian empire. American historical associa-
  tion, Annual report, 1916 (1919), I, 287-97.   W100
Wingo, Elvis Otha. Latin punctuation in the classical age. Illi-
  nois, 1963. Abstract: Dissertation abstracts, XXIV, 5395.
  W101
Winston, David. Iambulus: a literary study in Greek utopianism.
  Columbia, 1956. Abstracts: Dissertation abstracts, XVI,
  2154.   W102
Wirth, Frederick E. Amplified ornamentation in Cicero's orations. Chicago, 1947.   W103

Witke, Edward Charles. Latin satire: the classical genre and
　　its medieval developments. Harvard, 1962.　W104

Wittman, Robert Joseph. Classics, art and archeology — com-
　　mentary. Cicero In Verrem, IV. Tufts, 1959.　W105

Wolcott, John Dorsey. New words in Thucydides. Yale, 1898.
　　Printed: American philological association, Transactions,
　　XXIX (1898), 104-57.　W106

Wolfe, Ethyle R. The papyrus texts in the New York university
　　library. New York, 1950.　W107

Wolfe, Ruby Luella. Studia corinthia and a prosopographia
　　corinthia. Johns Hopkins, 1936.　W108

Wolff, Emily A. Aeschylus' Danaid Tetralogy: A study. Colum-
　　bia, 1957. Abstract: Dissertation abstracts, XVII, 1757.
　　W109

Wolverton, Robert Earl. Laudatores temporis acti: knowledge
　　of the Roman republic as found in the silver age authors of
　　the first century A.D. North Carolina, 1954. Abstract: Re-
　　search in progress, 1953/54, p. 44-5.　W110

Womble, Cecil Hilburn. The relation of the pseudo-Proban com-
　　mentary on Vergil to the scholia of the Servian Corpus.
　　Johns Hopkins, 1958.　W111

Wood, Frederic Marcus, jr. Some imperial virtues of Domitian.
　　Duke, 1942.　W112

Wood, Myrtle E. The use of the psychological terms ψυχή, σῶμα,
　　σάρξ and πνεῦμα, in the New Testament. Southwestern Bap-
　　tist, 1953.　W113

Woodard, Thomas Marion. Elektra by Sophocles: the dialectical
　　design. Harvard, 1962.　W114

Woodbury, Leonard Ernest. Quomodo risu ridiculoque Graeci usi
　　sint. Harvard, 1944. Abstract: Summaries of theses, 1943/
　　45, p. 10-4.　W115

Woodhead, William Dudley. Etymologizing in Greek literature
　　from Homer to Philo Judaeus. Chicago, 1920. Printed:
　　Toronto, University of Toronto press, 1928. 101 p.　W116

Woodman, Willis Patten. De arte piscandi apud antiquos Graecos.
　　Harvard, 1902.　W117

Woodruff, Loura Bayne. Reminiscences of Ennius in Silius Itali-
　　cus. Michigan, 1906.　W118

Woods, Virginia N. Types of rulers in the plays of Aeschylus.
　　Chicago, 1941.　W119

Woodworth, Dorothea Clinton. The Holkham Hall codex of Pliny's
　　Letters. Chicago, 1924. Abstract: Abstracts of theses, Hu-
　　manistic ser., II (1926), 327-30.　W120

Woolsey, Robert B. Pompeius Trogus' History of Alexander the
      Great. Yale, 1950.   W121
Workman, Allen J. An inquiry into sources of aesthetic in pre-
      Socratic philosophy. Southern California, 1951.   W122
Workman, John Rowe. The evolution and meaning of ἀγαθός in
      the philosophy of Plato. Princeton, 1944.   W123
Wright, Frederick Warren. Studies in Menander. Princeton,
      1910. Printed: Baltimore, Williams and Wilkins co., 1911.
      109 p.   W124
Wright, Henry Burt. A historical and critical study of the liter-
      ary evidence for the battle of Plataea. Yale, 1903. Printed:
      The campaign of Plataea (September, 479 B.C.). New Haven,
      The Tuttle, Morehouse and Taylor co., 1904. 148 p.   W125
Wright, Henry Parks. The letters of Pliny the Younger. Yale,
      1876.   W126
Wright, Horace Wetherill. The sacra Idulia in Ovid's Fasti; a
      study of Ovid's credibility in regard to the place and the
      victim of this sacrifice. Pennsylvania, 1917. Printed: New-
      ark, N.J., The Essex press, 1917. 54 p.   W127
Wright, Wilmer Cave France. The Emperor Julian's relation to
      the new sophistic and neo-platonism: with a study of his
      style. Chicago, 1895.   W128
Wyatt, William Frank, jr. Metrical lengthening in Homer. Har-
      vard, 1962.   W129
Wyckoff, Elizabeth. Pindar's handling of ethical problems raised
      by traditional mythology. Bryn Mawr, 1941. Abstract: Mi-
      crofilm abstracts, VI, 89.   W130

                                    Y

Yallaly, Jules G. Sancti Aureli Augustini De consensu evange-
      listarum, liber primus; with introduction, translation, and
      commentary. St. Louis, 1952.   Y1
Yanitelli, George A. The islands of the blest in classical liter-
      ature and legend. Fordham, 1943.   Y2
Yanofsky, Thelma J. Early Boeotian figurines of terracotta.
      Johns Hopkins, 1939.   Y3
Yavis, Constantine George. Greek altars. Johns Hopkins, 1942.
      Y4
Yoder, Edward. The position of possessive and demonstrative
      adjectives in the Noctes atticae of Aulus Gellius. Pennsyl-
      vania, 1928. Printed: Linguistic society of America, Lan-
      guage dissertation, II (1928). 103 p.   Y5

Yoder, J. Otis. New Testament synonyms in the Septuagint.
    Northern Baptist, 1954.   Y6
York, Harry Clinton. The Latin versions of First Esdras. Yale,
    1908.   Y7
Youman, Alfred Eliot. Achilles and the Iliad. Yale, 1959.   Y8
Young, Clarence Hoffman. Erchia; a deme of Attica. Columbia,
    1891. Printed: New York, Young, 1891. 67 p.   Y9
Young, David Charles. Studies in Pindaric criticism. Iowa,
    1963. Abstract: Dissertation abstracts, XXIV, 4686.   Y10
Young, John Howard. Sunium: an historical survey of an Attic
    deme. Johns Hopkins, 1942.   Y11
Young, Joseph James. Studies on the style of the De vocatione
    ominum gentium ascribed to Prosper of Aquitaine. Catholic,
    1952. Printed: Catholic University of America, Patristic
    studies, LXXXVII (1952). 192 p.   Y12
Young, Norma Dorothy. Index verborum Silianus. Iowa, 1939.
    Printed: Iowa studies in classical philology, VIII (1939).
    262 p.   Y13
Young, Rodney Stuart. Late geometric graves and a seventh
    century well in the Athenian Agora. Princeton, 1939. Print-
    ed: The American excavations in Athenian Agora, Hesperia,
    Supplement II (1939). 250 p.   Y14

Z

Zamiara, Alphonse Mary. Homeric man's sense of dependence
    on the gods in the light of Christian principles. St. Louis,
    1936. Abstract: Microfilm abstracts, II, 58–9.   Z1
Zarker, John William. Studies in the Carmina latina epigraphica.
    Princeton, 1958. Abstract: Dissertation abstracts, XIX,
    2342.   Z2
Zebian, Georg Joseph. The use of the ablative of quality and ab-
    lative of respect in Latin literature. Johns Hopkins, 1959.
    Z3
Zeinz, Joseph H. Recent critical work in the prose writings of
    Seneca. Ohio State, 1965.   Z3a
Zervopoulos, Gerassimos. The gospels-text of Athanasius.
    Boston, 1955.   Z4
Zickgraf, Palmer Louis. Aspects of tax exemption under the Ro-
    man Empire. Illinois, 1939. Abstract: Urbana, 1939. 3 p.
    Z5
Zimmerman, Charles Hamline. The independent subjunctive in
    Tacitus. Yale, 1897.   Z6

Ziolkowski, John Edmund. Thucydides and the tradition of funeral speeches at Athens. North Carolina, 1963. Abstract: Dissertation abstracts, XXIV, 3329.   Z7

Zucker, Lois Miles. S. Ambrosii De Tobia; a commentary, with an introduction and translation. Catholic, 1933. Printed: Catholic University of America, Patristic studies, XXXV (1933). 210 p.   Z8

Zweig, Arnulf. Theories of real definition: a study of the views of Aristotle, C. I. Lewis, and Wittgenstein. Stanford, 1960. Z9

A

*Greek words are given exactly as they were found in the bibliographical source, but it is suspected that some have been transliterated from the original titles. Some headings not apparent in the title have been taken from subject entries on Library of Congress printed cards. On the other hand, some subjects that may be important have not been given due to the fact that such subjects are not apparent from the title and that no abstract or even printed catalogue cards are available.

Apologists, Latin Christian, C20
apostolic fathers, R69
Apotheosis of the Roman emperors (The), H6
appellate procedure, Greek, R9
Appendix Vergiliana, B174, H89
Appian's exposition of the Roman republican constitution, L73
Appollonius Rhodius; his figures, syntax, and vocabulary, G55
Appropriate name in the Bucolics of Vergil (The), C23
Appropriate name in Petronius (The), G50
Appropriate name in Plautus (The), S51
Appropriate name of the Metamorphoses of Apuleius (The), R94
Appropriation and latent criticism of Herodotus in Thucydides
      (The), W39
Apuleius as a source for the social history of his time, L76
Apuleius Madaurensis, F21, G46, L18, L76, M12, M37, P49a,
      R94, S165, S188
Aquila of Pontus, R33
Aquinas, Saint Thomas, H103, S107, S166
Aratus of Soli, B56, G27; metrics and rhythmics, O18
Archaic sculpture in Boeotia, G64
Archaism in Aulus Gellius (Studies in), F48
Archaism in Euripides (A study of), M73
Archaisms of Terence mentioned in the commentary of Donatus,
      S114
Archilochus, H45
Architectonics of strife: a study in the dynamics of Aeschylus'
      Oresteia (The), W94
Architectural terracottas in the Greek archaic period, E26
Architecture: archaic Greek, E26; Cyprus, F5; Doric, R19;
      early Helladic, O23; Etruscan, T67; Hellenistic, B163, M186;
      Italian, N12, W80; Mithraic, C125; Roman, F5, O5, T67, V3,
      W80
Architecture of fountains and nymphaea in ancient Italy (The), N12
Archival material in Livy 218–167 B.C., C120
Archives of the temple of Socnobrasis at Bacchias (The), H137
archons, Athenian, F17
Arena-bath area at Curium in Cyprus: a study of Roman and
      early Christian architecture (The), F5
Ares, G47
Argentarius, Marcus, S105
Argonautic expedition as literary theme, H57
Argos: history, K26, S134
Argument from probability in early Attic oratory (The), K80

B

Burgo Sancti Sepulchri, Dionysius de, B78
burial customs, C127, G92
Byzantine Empire: administrative organization, L65; economic
      history, 325-1025 A.D., T11
βωμός in classical Greek literature (A study of the Greek), M78

C

C. Suetonii Tranquilli De vita Caesarum liber VIII, Divus Titus; an
      edition with parallel passages and notes, P90
C. Suetonii Tranquilli De vita Caesarum liber VIII, Divus Vespa-
      sianus: Suetonius's life of Vespasian with notes and parallel
      passages, S101
C. Suetonii Tranquilli vita Domitiani; Suetonius's life of Domitian,
      with notes and parallel passages, G17
cadaster, Roman, T6
Caesar, Julius, A66, C87a, G20, S151; De bello gallico, A23, C5,
      Greek version, C76; language, W75; manuscripts, C76
Caius Trabatius Testa. Jurisconsulte correspondant de Cicéron,
      ami de César et d'Auguste, G109
calendar: Athenian, M28; Roman, H126
Caligula, M96, R77
Calpurnius, Piso Caesoninus, Lucius, see Piso Caesoninus, Lu-
      cius Calpurnius
Calpurnius, Piso, Lucius, see Piso, Lucius Calpurnius
Campana Supellex: the pottery deposit at Minturnae, L3
Capital punishment in ancient Athens, B26
Cappadocia, G94
Caracalla, G97, M35, S38
Carmina latina epigraphica (Studies in the), Z2
carvings, wood and iron, from Gordion, K71
caryatid mirrors, Greek, C94
case, see Greek language and Latin language
Case-construction after the comparative in Latin (The), N14
Case construction of words of time (A study of the), B168
Case construction on similis and its compounds, J46
Case forms, with and without prepositions, used by Plautus and
      Terence to express time, K5
Case-regimen of the verbs of hearing in classical Greek from
      Homer to Demosthenes (The), R9
Case rivalry: being an investigation regarding the use of the
      genitive and accusative in Latin with verbs of remembering
      and forgetting (A study in), B5
Case usage in Petronius' satires, H149

Character Presentation in Tacitus, A6
characters and characteristics in literature, R54
Characters and epithets: a study in Vergil's Aeneid, M166
Characters in Cicero's dialogues emphasizing the principles of
      character selection (A study of the), A71
Chariot and bow and arrow metaphors for poetry in Pindar's
      Epinician odes, S95
charities: Rome, D40, R13
Charity among the Romans, D40
Chiasmus in Sallust, Caesar Tacitus and Justinus, S151
Chiasmus in the New Testament, L81
Child-life, adolescence and marriage in Greek new comedy and
      in the comedies of Plautus, a study of the relations repre-
      sented as existing between parents and their children, L24
Chimaera (The), C2
China: relations with Rome, L47
Chitons, B27, R52
Choral odes of Euripides: problems of structure and dramatic
      relevance (The), P20
Choral odes of Seneca: theme and development (The), B96
Choregia in Athens and at Ikaria (The), B185
Chorus, B137, P58. See also Greek drama
Chorus in the dialogue portions of Sophocles (The use of the),
      B137
Chorus of Euripides (The), P58
Christian Latin poetry, early history and criticism, H81
Christian literature (early Greek authors), W79
Christian utilization of pagan educational facilities, L30
Christmas customs, classical origins of, J30
Chronological studies in the history of the Roman emperors,
      S127
Chronology of Greek middle comedy (The), G41
Chronology of Greek walls (The), S50
Chronology of Horace's satires and epistles, A69
Chronology of Pindar's Persian War and Sicilian odes (The), B72
Chronology of the extant plays of Euripides (The), M53
Chronology of the plays of Plautus (A), B186
Chrysippus, G61
Chrysostomus, Dio, see Dio Chrysostomus
Chrysostomus, Joannes, Saint: Commentary on Galatians, H85;
      Commentary on John, H35; De sacerdotio, M1; Homilies on
      Acts, S124; Homilies on Ephesians, H85; Homilies on Gene-
      sis, M81; Homilies on Saint John, M185; language, D52, S18;
      Quod nemo laeditur nisi a seipso, C13; syntax, S129

D

De Daphnide commentatio, P85
De decretis atticus quae e memoria scriptorum veterum tradita
     sunt, G72
De deis dacicis, J42
De dialecto Milesia, R39
De dis syriis apud Graecos cultis, W15
De dum, donec, quoad coniunctionum usu apud Ciceronem, Caesa-
     rem, Tacitum, Plinium Minorem, Suetonium, W75
De enuntiatorum temporalium apud Herodotum usu atque ratione
     commentatio, B135
De epithetis compositis apud epicos latinos, A59
De Euripidis Antiopa, B2
De exsecrationibus laminis plumbeis insculptis, B46
De fragmenti Suetoniani De grammaticis et rhetoribus codicum
     nexu et fide, R68
De frenis apud antiquos, B19
De genere dicendi et casum usu Propertiano, R41
De gente Attica Eumolpidarum, M33
De gerundio latino atque modo infinitivo sanscrito, T48
De graecis verbis apud Plautum inventis, B123
De graecorum theoris et theoriis, B88
De homicidiis apud Graecos, R56
De ignis eliciendi modis apud antiquos commentatio, M161
De insignibus in clipeis Graecis descriptis, C51
De Julia Domna, W90
De Lactantii qui dicitur narrationibus Ovidianis, O27
De libertinorum statu apud Romanos antiquos, C26
De libris aliquot Suetonianis, F36
De licentiis metricis quae in canticis Sophocleis reperiuntur,
     M49
De lingua antiqua Illyrica, M182
De mandragora, R15
De metaphonis Latina, B39
De novo codicum Servianorum genere, S164
De natura deorum quid senserint antiqui Graeci, C101
De numeris lyricis Graecis qui in carminibus quibusdam nuper
     repertis audiuntur, A75
De nympharum cultu quaestiones selectae, B21
De operibus Boethii quaestiones variae, M38
De oraculis ad res Graecas publicas pertinentibus, K58
De Ovidii Metamorphoseon aliquot codicibus, B179
De participiis praesentium usu Ammianeo, W6
De Plauti diphthongi ei usu quaestiones, A41

E

G

Greek drama (The), M58
Greek drama: techniques, W34
Greek drama (comedy), B14, B60, B87, C104, C131, D62, D94,
    G41, G89, H11, L24, M58, M179, P43, R8, S11, S14, S23;
    see also names of individual writers
Greek drama (satyr plays), G53, M179
Greek drama (tragedy), B6, B185, B215, D61, D93, E21, F4,
    K74, M41, M58, M114, R27, S22, S82, S181; actors, R27;
    characters, P93; chorus, S75; history and criticism, S28;
    language, J40; narrative speech, K65; technique, A1, B137,
    B159, C1, C17, C107, D55, F34, H106, H114, O35, P82,
    S11, S14, S28, S122, S140; see also names of individual
    tragedians
Greek economic thought, T62
Greek epic, A37, B25, B36, B76, B192, C16, C28, C90, C100,
    E25, F24, F56, F29
Greek epigrammatists at Rome in the first century B.C., H32
Greek epigrams, H173
Greek foreshadowings of modern metaphysical and epistemolog-
    ical thought, K82
Greek genealogical chronology (Studies in), P81
Greek historians: figures of speech, K36
Greek household religion, W72
Greek idea of limitation; an interpretation of Greek ethos and of
    Plato's philosophy in relation to it (The), F22
Greek influence on Roman tradition in the second century B.C.,
    S186
Greek language: accent, S197; adjective, M2; adverb, S84; al-
    phabet, F64; article, F66, L36, S102; aspect, L31; case,
    B59, B168, C104, E16, F42, G51, K37, M66, M164, P5,
    P77, R7, R9, R43, S116, S139, T68, W47; compound words,
    D53, H22; dialects, R25, T31, T45, Ionian, A33, Boeotian,
    C57, Milesian, R39; diminutives, P52; figures of speech,
    B7, B75, F57, G55, K21, K36, P60, R61, S18, S90, S95;
    history, W17; infinitive, A25, N21, V21; legal terms, B107,
    F16; loan words, L84; loan words in Latin, B123, D30,
    K20, M155; metrics and rhythmics, C91, L83, M49, O18,
    P69, P74, W88, W129, in prose, B13, B41, G43; mood, A26,
    D52, F30, H91, L31, S174, W64; morphology, G113; N. T.,
    A49, B98, B107, B152, C84, C111, C121, C139, D72, D73,
    E2, E39, F16, G6, G42, G73, H9, H50, H61, K28, L12,
    L80, L81, L82, M39, M126, M127, M129, M147, N7, N10,
    P18, P75, R57, R83, R85, S53, S97, S133, T64, T71, V16,

V21, W18, W63, W87, W113, Y6; nouns, S102; participle,
A20, A64, B112, C38, L59, R32, R69, W87; particles, D58,
F20, G1, G30, J37, L80, M120, M129, M132, R69; phonol-
ogy, M115, W17; prepositions, B98, H7, M29, O26, R25,
S62, S133, T31; rhetoric, B7, H54, V8; semantics, M11,
N10, N28, O30, P56, R9, R30, R73, R85, S57, T223; Septu-
agint, V16; style, A50, J40, L68, S108, see also entries on
various aspects of the language of individual authors; suf-
fixes and prefixes, M2, P52; synonyms, W42; syntax, B82,
B178, C57, C59, F66, G6, G55, M7, M164, M185, P77,
R25, R69, S129, T68, W21; tense, C78, L31, L82, R79, S53,
S174, T64, W18; verb, B3, C111, H132, L6, R9; vocabularies,
glossaries, etc., R35, N2, P70, R33, S21; vowels, A72,
C124, D14, T45; word formation, C18; word order, C97,
M117

Greek letters, E47, G48, S163
Greek lexicography in the papyri, N2
Greek literary texts from Greco-Roman Egypt; a study in the
    history of civilization (The), O16
Greek literature: bibiliography, O16; history and criticism,
    B177, C31, H10, H11, K8, L41, M15, M65, N27, N30, O16,
    P53, R8, T54, W50, W115, see also names of specific au-
    thors and genres; study and teaching, H100
Greek love-names (A study of the), F35
Greek music, see music, Greece
Greek names of Roman priests, military officers, legislative
    bodies, and magistrates (The), D30
Greek novel, M134, W92
Greek of Acts I:1−15:35 (The), V16
Greek of the Gospel of Mark (The), D72
Greek oratory, B7, B43, B97, B164, C78, H78, H130, K80,
    M66, S5, S16, S27, W78; figures of speech, B95; language, D64,
    E9, R4, S138, see also names of orators
Greek papyri lights on Jewish history, R86
Greek participles in the doctrinal Epistles of Paul, G30
Greek philosophy, B158, C29, C92, G89, M90, T19, W78, W98;
    see also entries under names of philosophers and schools of
    philosophy
Greek poetry: bucolic, L14; elegaic, C133; history and criticism,
    A4, A75, C105, D67, K46, K57, K68, P53, R87, S6; word
    order, C97, see also names of individual poets and gemes
Greek priestess (A study of the), H127
Greek religion, see religion, Greece

H

Hellenistic statues of Aphrodite: studies in the history of their stylistic development, B151
Hellenistic aition in Virgil's Georgics (The), S172
Hellenistic and Roman tableware of north Syria (The), W1
Hellenistic architecture in Syria, M186
Hellenistic attitudes toward war, S121
Helleno-semitica: an ethnic and cultural study in west semitic impact on Mycenaean Greece, A68
Hellespont, Athenian activity from 600 to 450 B.C., K47
Heracles, P11; in Greek art, L72
Heraclidae of Euripides: an introduction and commentary (The), B127
Heraklids (The), A34
Heraclitus, K54, P26, R78, S73
Herban, R6
Herculaneum, P35
Hermas, D39
Hermes the "thief": with special reference to the Homeric hymn to Hermes, B170
Herms, mutilation of, A30, K38
Herodes Atticus, D12, R99
Herodes Atticus: world citizen, A.D. 101–177, R99
Herodianus, Aelius, B205
Herodotus, A33, B135, C86, L5, M133, M188, P42, W39; language, L68; syntax, B178, F20; vocabulary, A33, B53
Herodotos in the Greek renascence, P42
Hesiod, B112, G117, P31, P74, R37, S45, W88
Hesiod and his view of man, G117
Hesiodic hexameter (The), P74
Hesiod's Works and days: an exemplar of the ancient Greek oral style, P31
Hesychia in Pindar, B191
Hesychius, B160
hetairos relationship, institutional aspects of, S142
Hexaemeral literature; a study of the Greek and Latin commentaries on Genesis (The), R55
hexameter: Greek, P74; Latin, B29, H46
Hexameters in the Carmina epigraphica of Bücheler (A study of the), H46
Hieronymus quatenus artem criticam noverit, H163
Hieronymus, Eusebius, G33, H98, K25; commentaries on Psalms, P38; Epistulae, H158, L50, W73; language, T56; terminology (translation), P88; Vita Malchi, J6; Vita Pauli, H121, K3; Vita sancti Hilarionis, F62

I

M

M. Tullii Ciceronis pro A. Cluentio Habito, oratio ad judices, G79

Mabillon, Dom Jean, F25, M74

Macedon, R84; history, E13, J5, M32, P27, S40; relations with Athens, M31

Maecenas elegies in the Appendix Vergiliana (A study of the), B174

Macrinus and Diadumenianus, B40

Macrobius, T33; Saturnalia, B68

Madness in Greek thought and custom, V14

Maffei, Scipio, R95

Magic from Latin literature (Studies in), T5

magism, Roman, A57

magistri, Roman, B105a

Major manuscripts of Cicero's De senectute (The), V19

Major themes of Roman satire (A study of the), S37

make-up, theatrical, S15

mandragora, R15

Manticism in Lucan's epic technique (The role of), D51

Manufactures for the state in the later Roman empire, M46

Manuscript tradition of Jerome's Vita sancti Malchi (The), J6

Manuscript tradition of Plutarch's Aetia graeca and Aetia romana (The), R41

Manuscript tradition of St. Jerome's Vita Sancti Hilarionis (The), M48

Manuscript tradition of the Commentariolum petitionis of Q. Cicero (The), M145

Manuscripts of Propertius (The), F13

Manuscripts of the Florilegium of the Letters of Symmachus (A study of the), K75

Marcellinus, Ammianus, see Ammianus Marcellinus

Marcian, I7

Marcus Agrippa, a biography, R35

Marcus Atilius Regulus: exemplum historicum, M137

Marcus Aurelius, R52

Marian party (The), F53

Marica, goddess of the Auruncians, S7

maritime courts at Athens in the fourth century, B.C., C79

Marius, Gaius, M95

market officials, Egyptian, O31

marriage, L24; Rome, B154

marriage, sacred, see Daedala

Martialis, Marcus Valerius, C88, C119; syntax, L71

Μετανοέω and μεταμέλει in Greek Literature to 100 A.D., in-
    cluding discussion on their cognates and of their Hebrew
    equivalents, T23
metaphony, B39
Metaphor and comparison in Epistulae ad Lucilium of L. Ann-
    aeus Seneca, S109
Metaphor and comparison in the dialogues of Plato, B75
Metaphor in the epic poems of Publius Papinius Statius (The),
    W96
Metaphorical terminology of Greek rhetoric and literary criti-
    cism (The), V8
Metaphors and similes of Plato (The), H169
Metaphors in Aeschines the orator, F57
Metaphors of Propertius (Some aspects of the), M77
Metempsychosis in Greece from Pythagoras to Plato (A study of
    the doctrine of), L63
Meter and case in the Latin elegiac pentameter, S89
Meter and diction in Catullus' hendecasyllabics, C141
Method and scientia in St. Augustine: a study of books VIII to XV
    in his De trinitate, H60
Methodology of Origen as a textual critic in arriving at the text
    of the New Testament (The), P2
Metrical lengthening in Homer, W129
Metrical studies in the distribution on individual words in Homer
    and Aratus, O18
Metrical studies in the lyrics of Sophocles, P69
Metrical variants in Plautus (The), H118
Metrical word-types in the Latin hexameter, B29
metrics and rhythmics, see Greek language and Latin language
Metron, messos and kairos: a semasiological study, O30
Michigan University, Library, manuscripts (Greek), M81; papyri,
    P36
middle-class loyalty to the Roman empire, A45
middle comedy, Greek, see Greek drama (comedy)
Middle helladic matt-painted pottery, B187
Milesian dialect, see Greek language—dialects
Milesian Didyma, cults of, F40
Miletus, H159
military architecture: Greece, S50
military camps in Attica, M10
military devices, Roman, M3
Mineral resources of the Roman empire, sources of information,
    and places of deposit, M107

N

naturalization laws at Athens, O34
nature: Aristotelian concept, C137; in Heraclitus of Ephesus,
    P25; in literature, A27, B20, B105, C42, F4, M181, O34;
    in the poetry of the Roman Empire in the Augustan Age, P65;
    in the poetry of the Roman Republic, A27
Nature allusions in the works of Clement of Alexandria, M181
Nature and extent of the lost prose works of the Roman republic
    (The), H115
Nature and purpose: a study of Greek teleological theories,
    S161
Nature and the vocabulary of nature in the works of St. Cyprian,
    B20
Nature and use of the ἵνα clause in the New Testament, C139
Nature of human knowledge according to St. Gregory of Nyssa
    (The), W35
Nature of the Aristotelian intellect (The), W44
Naukydes, discobolos of, M29
Naukratis, a chapter in the history of the Hellenization of Egypt,
    S111
Near East: history, E10a; religion, E10a
Necropolis of Locrian Halae, W7
Negative compounds in Greek (The), H22
Neglected uses of iste, K23
Nekuia, second (The), K77
Nemesius, E22
Neo-Platonic element in aesthetics (The), P83
Neo-Platonism, G9, G115, K60, P83, W128. See also Platonism
    and names of individual Neo-Platonists
"Nereid" monument at Xanthos, restoration of, G59
Nero, J4, T49
New comedy, Greek, see Greek drama (comedy)
New manuscript of Cicero's De senectute (A), T34
New study of the genitive of description and the ablative of de-
    scription (A), C15
New Testament, see Bible and Greek language, N. T.
New Testament synonyms in the Septuagint, Y6
New Testament use of the preposition κατά with special refer-
    ence to its distributive aspects (The), S133
New words in Thucydides, W106
New York University, Library, manuscripts (papyri), W107
Nicholas, Saint, C125
Nicias — his family and the tradition of his great wealth, K59
nicknames, Greek, T66

O

P

R

S

Syria, M186; Roman province, D77, H38, H42
Syrian Decapolis and the Hauran under Roman administration to
    Diocletian (The), B109
Syrian deities in Greece, W15
Syrian immigrants to Rome from 200 B.C. to 230 A.D., M79

                                    T

table, cult, G24
tableware, Hellenistic and Roman, W1
Tabulae Iguvinae, see Iguvium
Tacite et la littérature française, D33
Tacitus, A6, D26, D33, G68, S47, S116, W89; Annales, S39;
    language, H94, S108, S151, W75; manuscripts, A30, A42;
    sources, W28; syntax, C84, L62, M105, Z6
Taedium vitae in Latin sepulchral inscriptions, T22
Tarsus: antiquities, G36
Tatian, H117
Tautometric repetition in the responsive lyrics of Sophocles,
    M13
tax exemption under the Roman Empire, Z5
Tax rolls from Karanis, S42
taxes: Egypt, C37, L9, P36, S42; Rome, G54, T6, Z5
Technical history of the white lecythi (The), M45
technical terminology of the Poetics of Aristotle (Studies in the),
    R29
Technical terms in Cicero's rhetorical works (The), J19
Technical vocabulary of the rhythmic of Aristoxenos (The), A28
Technological study of the unglazed pottery and figurines from
    Seleucia on the Tigris (A), M93
technological theories, Greek, S161
Teiresias, a study in dramatic tradition and innovation, O35
Temple estates of Delos, Rheneia, and Mykonos (The), K34
Temple treasures, a study based on Livy, S141
Temple treasures: a study based on the work of Cicero and the
    Fasti of Ovid, G95
temples: Greece, W80; Italy, S141, W80
temples of Castor and Pollux in the Roman Forum (The), V3
tense, see Greek language and Latin language
Tense of the Book of Revelation (A study in the), W18
Tenses in I John (The use of), C134
Tenses of the Homeric imperative, S174
Terentius Afer, Publius, A22, C75, J31, L7, L27, M75, P47,

U

Varro's Menippean satires, L23
vase painting, Greek, L16, L72. See also pottery
vases (Greek), A40, A46, M45, Y14
Vatican, Biblioteca Apostolica Vaticana, Mss. (Reg. 597), M100
Vatican manuscripts of the Greek letters of Brutus (The), A38
Vatican mythographer (first), E29
Velleius Paterculus, A45, H125
Venetic language, B57
Venus cult; a study based upon study of the writings of Suetonius
     and Tacitus (The), W89
Veracity of Thucydides (Studies in the), C44
verb, see Greek language and Latin language
verb uses in Pliny's Letters (Some), H15
Verb-forms in Terence, R45
Verbal categories in the Greek of the Synoptic Gospels (The),
     C111
Verbal repetition in Virgil (Studies in), N16
Verb of saying in Plautus (A study of), J52
Vergil and Aratus: a study in the art of translation, B56
Vergil, Aratus, and others; the weather-sign as a literary sub-
     ject, G27
Vergil in the works of Prudentius, W63
Vergil's treatment of the Templum in the Aeneid, C53
Vergilius Maro, Publius, G27, G86, H53, M63, W51; Aeneid,
     B76, C53, C61, C85, D8, D48, F10, H134, H167, J8,
     K43, L49, M70, M166, S9, S31, T51, W76; commentaries,
     A12, D79, E24, H2, H134, J41, M156, M189, S164, T9,
     T61, W58, W71, W111; commentaries on Aeneid, M98; in-
     dex verborum, W51; Georgics, B130, B162, G36, S72; Ec-
     logues, A43, B162, C23, H126; language, C61, H8, N16;
     manuscripts, G16, S153; mediaeval interpretation, M54;
     mediaeval lives of, U2; spurious and doubtful works, B174,
     H89, M124, S153
Verres, Gaius, C117
Verse adaptations of Avianus. Part I: The Astensis and its de-
     rivatives (The), R100
Vespasian, H82, M138, N17, S101
Vesta, publica, V5
Vestal virgins, V5
Victor, Sextus Aurelius: Liber de Caesaribus, M167; index ver-
     borum, N24
Village administration in the Roman province of Syria, H38
Violatio sepulcri: an epigraphical study, C127

W

X

INDEX OF GREEK WORDS*

A

ἀγαθός, W123
Ἀγνὴ θεά, W61
αἰών, S172
αἰώνιος, S172
ἀκρασία, W13
ἀλιτήριος, H64
ἀλιτρός, H64
ἁμαρτία, F32, P56
ἀνά, K37
ἀντί, K28
ἀντίθεσις, L68
ἅπαξ λεγόμενα, F43
ἀπολύτρωσις, W63
ἀπὸ κοινοῦ, construction, E28, G98
ἀραῖος, H64
ἀρχή, L39
ἄρχω, L39
ἀσκέω, D84
Ἀτθίς, P37

B

βάπτισμα, C21
βασιλεία, H9
βωμός, M78

Γ

γάρ, M132

Δ

διά, R43
διαθήκη, N28
δικανικός λόγος, L26
δόξα, H50

E

ἐν τῷ, G73
ἐναγής, H64
ἐνέργεια, B99
ἐνθύμιος, H64
ἐντελέχεια, B99
ἐπί, F41, M29
ἔργον, P19

H

ἦθος, S57

Θ

θεία μοῖρα, B79
θεία τύχη, B79
θεοπρεπής, R30
θεωρία, B88
θεωρός, B88
θυμοειδής, O3

I

ἱεροπρεπής, R30
ἱλασμός, N10
ἵνα, C139
-ισκος, -ισκη, P52

*Included in this index are: (1) words in titles of dissertations which have been given in Greek letters by the sources (although it is suspected that some have been re-transliterated from a Romanized form in the originals), and (2) words given in Roman letters by the sources (although it is suspected that many were transliterated from the Greek form in the original). Errors may have arisen through so much transliteration and re-transliteration. In general, only words, suffixes, and phrases which would seem to be useful for linguistic, semantic, or syntactical studies have been included.

INDEX OF LATIN WORDS*

*In general, only suffixes and words which would seem to be useful for linguistic, semantic, or syntactical studies have been included.